The Tangled Roots
of Feminism, Environmentalism,
and Appalachian Literature

Ohio University Press Series in Ethnicity and Gender in Appalachia
Series Editor: LYNDA ANN EWEN

Memphis Tennessee Garrison:
The Remarkable Story of a Black Appalachian Woman,
edited by Ancella R. Bickley and Lynda Ann Ewen
The Tangled Roots of Feminism, Environmentalism,
and Appalachian Literature,
by Elizabeth S. D. Engelhardt

The Tangled Roots of Feminism, Environmentalism, and Appalachian Literature

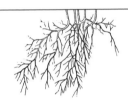

Elizabeth S. D. Engelhardt

Ohio University Press, Athens

Ohio University Press, Athens, Ohio 45701
© 2003 by Ohio University Press

Printed in the United States of America
All rights reserved

Ohio University Press books are printed on acid-free paper ⊗ ™

11 10 09 08 07 06 05 04 03   5 4 3 2 1

The cover image is from a photograph located in the John Charles and Olive Dame Campbell Papers #3800, Southern Historical Collection, Wilson Library, University of North Carolina at Chapel Hill.

Library of Congress Cataloging-in-Publication Data

Engelhardt, Elizabeth Sanders Delwiche, 1969-
The tangled roots of feminism, environmentalism, and Appalachian literature / Elizabeth Sanders Delwiche Engelhardt
    p. cm. — (Ohio University Press series in ethnicity and gender in Appalachia.)
Includes bibliographical references (p.) and index.
ISBN 0-8214-1509-3 (cl. acid-free) — ISBN 0-8214-1510-7 (pbk. acid-free)
1. American literature—Appalachian Region—History and criticism. 2. Murfree, Mary Noailles, 1850-1922—Knowledge—Appalachian Region. 3. Cooke, Grace MacGowan, 1863-1944—Knowledge—Appalachian Region. 4. Smith, Effie Waller, 1879-1960—Knowledge—Appalachian Region. 5. Miles, Emma Bell, 1879-1919—Knowledge—Appalachian Region. 6. American literature—Women authors—History and criticism. 7. Feminism and literature—Appalachian Region. 8. Women and literature—Appalachian Region. 9. Environmentalism—Appalachian Region. 10. Appalachian Region—In literature. 11. Ecofeminism—Appalachian Region. 12. Ecofeminism in literature. I. Title. II. Series.

PS286.A6.E54 2003
810.'974—dc21

2003048692

In memory of Iva Sanders Whitmire

Contents

Illustrations

Series Editor's Preface

The Tangled Roots of Feminism, Environmentalism, and Appalachian Literature is a significant addition to the Ohio University Press Series in Ethnicity and Gender in Appalachia. The first book in this series—*Memphis Tennessee Garrison: The Remarkable Story of a Black Appalachian Woman*—gave voice to a political activist and educator. In this book, Elizabeth Engelhardt offers the voices of women writers, many of whom have not been heard by a wide audience. At the same time, she places these women in an analytical context that explains why their writings are relevant not only to history, but also to our time. She avoids the trap of portraying her subjects in terms of an idealized universal historical woman writer by careful examination of the differing backgrounds, ideologies, and ethnicities of these women. They emerge in this book as honest (although sometimes misguided) women writing the Appalachian reality as they experienced it.

Elizabeth Engelhardt is a scholar with a passion for women's studies and for Appalachia. In this book, she brings scholarly literary criticism to a subject that is important for any woman who has sought to understand the roots of women's writing, the natural world these writers inhabit, and their sense of place. But Engelhardt also brings a compassion to her analysis that reveals her respect for—and admiration of—those women about whom she writes.

This book is more than a literary analysis. It is a contribution to the general fields of Appalachian studies, women's studies, and American culture. It is my hope that the reader will learn something, not only about the subject matter, but also about himself or herself.

Lynda Ann Ewen

Acknowledgments

Thanks first to all the Appalachian women I have met over the course of this project—either in person or through their letters, diaries, and fiction. Their honesty, courage, creativity, and humanity continue to inspire me. Librarians and staff at archives around the region helped me to connect with the historical women in this project, and I am deeply grateful. They include Steve Gowler, Shannon Wilson, and the staff at Berea College, as well as everyone at the Southern Historical Collection of the University of North Carolina–Chapel Hill, the University of North Carolina–Asheville, the Chattanooga–Hamilton County Bicentennial Public Library, and the cheerful staff at libraries I visited in the many research trips I took around the mountains. A special thanks goes to the women's studies librarians at Duke University, from whom I received enthusiastic help as well as a Rare Book, Manuscript, and Special Collections Library Research Grant for Women's Studies at a crucial point in the process.

Frances Smith Foster, Beverly Guy-Sheftall, Beverly Ladd, and Pamela Hall always took seriously their role as mentors—even when what I needed was a light-hearted cup of coffee on a late afternoon or early morning. I am grateful to Gillian Berchowitz and everyone at Ohio University Press; Lynda Ann Ewen; Alden Waitt, copy editor and friend; and the anonymous readers who helped to make this project better. I extend further sincere thanks to my new colleagues at West Virginia University who have made me feel welcome and supported, especially Barbara Howe of the Center for Women's Studies and Dean M. Duane Nellis of the Eberly College of Arts and Sciences. I am grateful to administrative staff at Emory University, Ohio University, and West Virginia University's women's studies programs: Lee Ann Lloyd, Linda Callaway, Deborah Daniels, Cathy Jasper, and Marlene Robinson.

Thanks to all my friends in Atlanta, Morgantown, Hillsborough, and Hendersonville who kept me human through the process; James Engelhardt; Wendy White; Mickey Jo Sorrell; Jennifer Bernhardt Steadman, whose grace and scholarship are unparalleled; Imogene Eaker, more than a godmother; and, finally, my family, most especially Robert and Betty Delwiche—whom I am privileged to know both as my parents and as my friends.

The Tangled Roots
of Feminism, Environmentalism,
and Appalachian Literature

Introduction

When I began writing this book, construction workers were completing six houses crowded onto barely an acre and a half of land next to my apartment. The houses carried astounding price tags because the lot sat in the prestigious Druid Hills neighborhood of Atlanta, Georgia. Until then, the land had been full of pines, vines, some oaks and maples, native plants, and escapees from my neighbor's organic shade garden. It sheltered small animals, served as a play space for neighborhood kids, regulated water runoff, and helped keep my apartment cool enough to live without air conditioning. The real estate speculator's motivation that led to the six homes was not far from Mary Noailles Murfree's devastating 1894 portrait of a developer who coldly "appraised, in the interest of possible summer sojourners, the rare, pure, soft air." She has him conclude: "Such resources—infinitely smaller resources—elsewhere in the world meant a fortune; why not here?"[1] and begin a gigantic resort hotel despite community protest. In Druid Hills, Atlanta, there was no organized protest.

In Gainesville, Georgia, a group of women who used to deliver flowers to the sick and dying in their community now fight to stop the environmental pollution that is causing a frightening number of illnesses and deaths in their town. The power of community runs deep in their story. But the Newtown Florist Club has found that holding individual factories accountable for their roles in the creation of the toxic soup on which the town rests is complicated; their book, *The Newtown Story*, testifies to the crushing effects of racial, class, and environmental injustices in the United States at the beginning of the twenty-first century. When, in 1905, Emma Bell Miles described the "old prophetesses" who hold the "tradition and song, medical and religious learning" of communities and whose "wisdom commands the respect of all," she could have been talking of the 1990s' Newtown Florist Club and why women so often lead these difficult struggles.[2]

In my hometown of Hendersonville, North Carolina, in the Appalachian mountains, strip malls compete with antique stores for the soul of the town.

The mountaintops around the town now sport gigantic houses with what I am sure are beautiful views—unless they, too, can only see other huge homes from up there. And yet, many of the people with whom I started kindergarten care passionately about their mountains. Some work on alternative energy, gardening, teaching, and improving society on the small and large scale—and they are trying to save our hometown from being just one more town in carbon-copy, chain-store America. Back in 1910, Grace MacGowan Cooke wrote about whole communities in the Tennessee mountains—both the "Space—air, earth and sky"[3] and the local and recently arrived humans. She talked about the tensions between competing groups and about the potential for women's organizing to save her fictional town's heart—and it reminds me strongly of Hendersonville in 2002.

Around West Virginia, my present home state, the "rugged, rocky peaks I climb" are linked in time and space to Effie Waller Smith's Kentucky mountains, which she wrote about in 1904. Unfortunately, mountaintop removal, the latest tool of the extractive coal industry, threatens to flatten both states' "majestic, mighty, huge, sublime" peaks.[4] Perhaps Smith's passion can be harnessed to make sure new generations can enjoy the freedom she felt hiking Appalachia. African American Appalachian women like Smith are being remembered and recovered by scholars who realize that Appalachia benefits from celebrating all its residents, not just the ones who fit long-held but little-supported ideas about who Appalachians are.

For the past five years, I have read letters, diaries, novels that were almost forgotten, short stories, essays, and memoirs written by women writers and activists in Appalachia. I have lingered over photographs, postcards, and paintings. My research has taken me on journeys around the region and back through the century. What I have come to believe—and what this book is about—is that Appalachia's women writers and activists from the turn of the past century defined a philosophy of living that can help address social and environmental justice issues at the turn of this century.

Yet the philosophies of Murfree, Miles, Smith, and Cooke did not evolve in a vacuum. Their writings, which form the roots of ecological feminism, are tangled up with other women's writing about Appalachia. Behind Amelie Rives Troubetzkoy's claim that certain groups of mountain people are "a awful wild lot, mostly bad as they make 'em, with no more idea of right an' wrong than a lot o' ground horgs" lies a view of mountain residents as freaks and oddities for a voyeur to enjoy. When Maria Louise Pool's narrator and friend spend an afternoon sketching, sightseeing, and botanizing, Pool celebrates Appalachia as a commodity for tourists to buy. When Daisy

Gertrude Dame wrote a letter home to Massachusetts from Kentucky saying, "The women here are very ignorant, even about washing and ironing," she draws a portrait of herself as a social crusader ready to save "needy" Appalachians. The writings of Murfree, Miles, Smith, and Cooke are surrounded by many such voyeurs, tourists, and social crusaders. Troubetzkoy, Pool, and Dame were, as Miles, Cooke, Murfree, and Smith were, aware of feminism and environmentalism in the United States. What makes one group's writings so different from the other's?[5]

What Is Ecological Feminism?

Miles arguing for women's roles in sustaining Appalachia, Cooke linking water pollution in mill towns with women's health problems, Murfree criticizing undebated development, and Smith celebrating women's physical and intellectual abilities—all imply parallels to today's ecological feminism. These parallels separate Miles, Cooke, Murfree, and Smith from their historical counterparts Troubetzkoy, Pool, and Dame. Historically and in the present day, feminisms are difficult to define absolutely, because almost all juggle the desire to be inclusive with the need to be coherent. As a working definition to begin the discussion, however, ecological feminism is a philosophy, formal or informal, in which:

- Humans are not conceived of as separate from and superior to the world around them (in other words, the nonhuman world).[6] Rather, humans and nonhumans together are part of the total ecology. As a result, ecological feminists generally avoid "us-*versus*-them" thinking. In Patrick D. Murphy's terms, "self-Other" is replaced by "self-another"—meaning that humans and nonhumans are in reciprocal relationships with each other. We affect, but also can benefit from, each other.[7]
- Further, the nonhuman world has agency—at its most basic, the ability to consider and to act. Some Western theorists worry that giving the nonhuman world agency means saying rocks can move and talk. But Native American and Eastern critics such as Leslie Marmon Silko or Gary Snyder point out that what Snyder calls the "watching and listening world"[8] does not have to have exactly the same agency as humans for it to be recognized and valued. With agency possible for all community members, then, ecological feminism includes voices of the whole community in decision making.
- Relatedly, activism and actions in communities must consider long-term

sustainability for the community. In order to do so, ecological feminists must try to identify environmental as well as social injustices. Frequently, identifying injustices involves a critique (although not necessarily a rejection) of capitalism and United States corporate models. Structures of power that use hierarchies (for instance, of gender, race, class, or species) to oppress, damage, and silence community members are also criticized. Ecological feminists work for justice for all community members, recognizing that the least socially empowered may be the most environmentally threatened.

* Ecological feminists recognize the particular effects on and roles for women in activism without erasing differences. In other words, ecological feminisms are not essentialist: women are not necessarily united in sisterhood, nor are they equally oppressed, nor are they the only gender to have a role in enacting justice.

Ecological feminism is closely related to much ecological, environmental, feminist, and environmental feminist activism. Yet, as I use it here, ecological feminism differs from environmental or ecological theorizing when they presume all humans are the same. Ecological feminism argues that race matters, gender matters, class matters, and that all of us have complicated identities. My working definition differs from certain feminist theories that downplay humans' connections to the material world, and it differs from environmental feminism that presumes all women are the same and that middle-class solutions fit all problems. Finally, although many people use "ecological feminism" and "ecofeminism" interchangeably, I do not, because this working definition is closer to the environmental justice movement in its anti-essentialism than it is to some ecofeminism. In other words, the final point of the definition is absolutely crucial.

However, as I examine historical texts from the turn of the previous century, two things are important. First, I do not expect to find writers in absolute agreement with today's interpretations of environmental and social justice. Instead, I find writers who are the *roots* of ecological feminism—writers who express similar philosophies through the filter of their own societies and assumptions. For instance, I argue that Cooke, in her novel, *The Power and the Glory,* is one of these roots despite the fact that she relies on an automobile to outline her vision of social and environmental justice. Cooke could not have anticipated the number of cars that would be in Appalachia (and the world) by the year 2002. She could not have foreseen the environmental threat their use, production, and disposal would be. She could and does criticize mills that pollute water, killing people and animals in their drive for profit. In her social and cultural world, she identifies an environmental threat to the human and nonhuman community and works to end it—thus, I argue, she is one of the roots in Appalachia of ecological feminism.

Second, I do not claim that Appalachia is the only place these roots emerged. Sarah Orne Jewett in New England, Mary Austin in the West, and Willa Cather in the Midwest all write from similar perspectives. Surprising and exciting, however, is the degree to which some women writing about Appalachia agree closely with the tenets of modern ecological feminism. Ecological feminists today and the women who are the roots of the movement in Appalachia could understand each other. If we sat around a table, we could work together as well. In fact, although one side of the conversation has to be on paper, that is how I hope you approach the texts by the women in this book.

Before turning to the texts by women about Appalachia, however, chapter 1 looks at the social, cultural, and intellectual context in which the texts were produced. It begins with the problem of defining Appalachia, examines feminism in the United States and in Appalachia, and discusses the environmental activism of feminists during the era. The chapter introduces many of the women who wrote about Appalachia and their friends; they are women with college educations, friends creating settlement houses across the United States, members of Audubon clubs, and leaders of women's clubs. Some were born in Appalachia, while others arrived later in life; among them are teachers, artists, Progressives, explicit feminists, conservative women, and nature lovers. With the diversity of experiences, the chapter sets up the conversation about how, even among texts explicitly addressing women and nature, the roots could be so tangled.

Because Appalachia was such a popular literary topic at the turn of the last century, the number of Appalachian stories written by women is astounding. In order to make some sense of the different approaches women writers took to Appalachia and Appalachians, I group the stories into the previously mentioned four types: the literature of the voyeur, the tourist, the social crusader, and the literature that forms the roots of ecological feminism.

Chapter 2, "Voyeurs and Tourists: Appalachian Women in Sketches and Stories," explores the first two approaches to storytelling. The literature of the voyeur trades on the idea that Appalachians were freaks and oddities to be viewed by superior outsider readers, hallmarks of us-*versus*-them thinking. It insists on an absolute separation between outsider spectator subjects and Appalachian spectacle objects. Not only does the nonhuman world have no agency, but the Appalachian human characters, who are closely associated with "uncivilized" nature, have no agency either. Thus, neither the Appalachians nor the mountains in which they live are valued in the voyeur's stories. Although the literature of the tourist shares with the literature of the voyeur a belief in a gulf between local Appalachians and outsiders, its authors emphasize the liberation and transformation of the female (outsider and tourist) subject through her travel and interaction with Appalachian human and nonhuman others. The tourist's body enters more into the story than did the voyeur's, which at least slightly erodes the distance between subject and object, us-*versus*-them. In the end, however, the potential for individual transformation overshadows any discussion of Appalachia or Appalachians. Both literatures, for the most part, champion American capitalism, progress, and civilization. Finally, both are essentialist in their claims that one is either American or Appalachian and that American is clearly the superior identity. The literatures of the voyeur and the tourist ultimately support the status quo systems of hierarchy and power that led to Appalachia's environmentally damaging extractive industries and the region's economic and social oppression with which so many women had to struggle throughout the century.

Not all women authors around 1900 wrote as tourists and voyeurs. Chapter 3 explores the literature of the social crusaders. Along with short stories and novels, unpublished materials such as letters, diaries, and photographs are the texts of this literature, which was based on the experiences of scores of women who came to Appalachia to teach, found settlement houses, nurse, and research the "needy" Appalachians. The social crusaders intend to become involved in Appalachian communities; they try to erase the distance between themselves as subjects of their stories and the Appalachian objects they encounter. Ideally, the social crusaders celebrated a social arrangement similar to Murphy's "self-another" thinking, but in practice they supported the same us-*versus*-them arrangements as the literatures of the voyeurs and tourists.

In the social crusaders' literature, more descriptions of Appalachian nature appear, as they hike, sketch, botanize, and explore the world around them over several seasons. Yet, instead of considering the role the nonhuman community plays in the lives of people residing in Appalachia (and giving the nonhuman agency), they use the botany and nature study to categorize not only the plants, animals, and land around them but also the people they encounter. Their practices were especially dangerous for non-white Appalachians. The social crusaders write constantly of the dirt, dust, and fleas they encounter in their new jobs in Appalachia. Rather than identifying the social injustices leading to the dirtiness, the social crusaders use it to justify their own presence in the mountains, judge their successes in the mountain work, and ultimately reinscribe the separateness between themselves and Appalachian people and places. They promote the essentialist idea that their middle-class, white way of being women is the only helpful model. As a result, the social crusaders join the voyeurs and tourists in never escaping status quo views of Appalachians. Ultimately, Appalachians are rendered inferior to the crusaders' American "civilization."

None of these approaches challenged turn-of-the-century structures of power and privilege. Appalachia continued to be logged, mined, and polluted; many of its workers were exploited, abused, and ignored. Yet, a fourth group of writers approached Appalachia with a strong sense of community. Although they were not all born in Appalachia, they wrote stories that included the nonhuman community with a more diverse portrait of human residents. The final two chapters explore the roots of Appalachian ecological feminism.

Chapter 4 begins with a novel by Mary Noailles Murfree, *His Vanished Star,* and ends with a discussion of Effie Waller Smith's poetry. Although Murfree has long been controversial in Appalachian studies, with some people holding her responsible for stereotypes about Appalachians, in this later novel she dismantles both the distance and hierarchy of outsider subjects over Appalachian objects. By bringing animals, meteorology, and geography into the story as autonomous, fully participating "self-another" subjects, her resulting community includes human and nonhuman residents and blurs the distinctions between people who are insiders and people who are outsiders. Murfree strongly criticizes corporate culture and celebrates effective interventions by an Appalachian community against unwanted, unsustainable development and the developers trying to make their fortunes from Appalachia's resources. Departing from the voyeurs, tourists, and social crusaders, Murfree writes early ecological feminist literature.

Joining Murfree is Smith, an African American poet and teacher from Pike County, Kentucky. Smith counters essentialist views of both women and Appalachians at the turn of the century with her fully realized African American Appalachian characters. More importantly, Smith is unapologetic about reciprocal, loving human and nonhuman Appalachian relationships—between women like her and the "majestic, mighty, huge, sublime" peaks they hike.[9] She fully embraces her own mountain identity. Writing poems for other Appalachians, Smith celebrates women's physical capabilities and explicitly champions woman's rights. Smith suggests that whole communities must be consulted when making decisions for the sustainable health of Appalachia. Both authors significantly revise the literatures of the voyeurs, tourists, and social crusaders to become part of the roots of ecological feminism.

Chapter 5 focuses on two women writers from Tennessee who were acquaintances and collaborators, Emma Bell Miles and Grace MacGowan Cooke. In her writing, Miles analyzes mountain gender roles and foretells the damaging effect of industrial and tourist capitalism on Appalachian human and nonhuman communities. She outlines the contribution "old prophetesses" and young women—in other words, all the women in a community—must make in addressing Appalachia's environmental and social justice questions. Cooke specifically outlines women's experiences in the new, environmentally dangerous cotton mills around Chattanooga, Tennessee. She analyzes the structures of power that make the "Space—air, earth, and sky" unavailable to certain community members. Both Cooke and Miles demonstrate a familiarity and sympathy with turn-of-the-century feminism and the confidence to criticize and modify its philosophies to fit Appalachia. They criticize misguided voyeurs, tourists, and social crusaders and build "self-another" relationships between the human and nonhuman community of Appalachia. Both give women agency, responsibility, and support emerging from and answerable to whole communities. Their writings contain the fullest expression of the roots of ecological feminism in Appalachia at this time.[10]

Charted at the turn of the twentieth century, the roots of ecological feminism emerged in Appalachia. Although I am not claiming an original uniqueness for Appalachia, its stark divisions between classes, highly charged and constructed discussions of race, and peopled wilderness *are* particularly illuminating in the early years of the present century. As members of global and local communities face stark divisions between classes, highly charged and constructed discussions of race, and *very* peopled wilderness, the Appalachian model is particularly timely.

The town in which my godmother was born and lived as a child now lies under the waters of Fontana Lake, a project of the Tennessee Valley Authority. Hearing her stories of Bushnell, North Carolina, and the scattering of its people was an important part of my own childhood. My grandmother's tales of playing in the luxurious but empty Toxaway Inn in Toxaway, North

Carolina, while her father served as caretaker after the 1916 floods caused its decline, are similarly embedded in my own life. His lifelong subscription to the Atlanta newspaper, brought in by train to western North Carolina, suggests how wrong the images of a completely isolated Appalachia so present in the voyeurs' accounts were. Social crusader Olive Dame Campbell's photographs remind me of my grandmother's stories of researchers wanting to photograph the beautiful, blond "native" child that she was and her family's nervousness about how they were going to be represented by such people. All of my family's Appalachian female ancestors—whom so much of history has tried to erase, but who remain memorable, intelligent, ambitious and dynamic figures nevertheless—are present in the background of the chapters that follow. They would have had something to say to Atlanta's developers, Hendersonville's homeowners, the Newtown women, and West Virginia's coal operators. The midwives, herb doctors, women farmers, barefoot walkers, storekeepers, mothers, daughters, and aunts remind me of the diversity of Appalachia's life, history, and culture.

In his book about the Appalachian Trail, Ian Marshall writes: "The Appalachians are the only American mountain chain for which we have written accounts of encounters with the land from the earliest days of European settlement to the present. As a result, in the body of literature set in the Appalachians, one can trace our evolving legacy of landscape aesthetics and our changing attitudes toward nature and the wild."[11] I agree, but that is only part of it. Appalachian women's literature, broadly defined, also can reveal changing attitudes toward gender and environmental justice in the United States. Competing philosophies about people and their interactions with nonhuman Appalachia model triumphs and failures for the turn of this century.

CHAPTER ONE

How the Roots Became So Tangled

Appalachia, Feminism, and Environmentalism around 1900

THE PURPOSE of this chapter is to examine how the three main subjects of the book—Appalachia, feminism, and environmentalism—entangled in individual women's lives at the turn of the century. Of the three subjects, Appalachia is on its face the easiest to cover. The women were either from the mountains, living or working in the mountains, or writing about them. However, Appalachia has never been an easy place to discuss. I regularly meet people who want to know where and what Appalachia is—although I often find they are really asking for permission to try out cherished, ingrained ideas about Appalachia on a "real" person from the mountains. Appalachia and stereotypes go hand in hand, it seems, much to the frustration of those of us for whom it is simply home. Books have been written countering, wrestling with, and talking back to the stereotypes about the region.[1]

If you live outside of Alabama, Georgia, Tennessee, North Carolina, Virginia, Kentucky, and West Virginia, and if you think of Appalachia at all, you probably think of the Appalachian Trail. Or you may think of Aaron Copeland's *Appalachian Spring*. You might think of the *Dukes of Hazzard* or the *Beverly Hillbillies* (although the Clampetts were technically from Arkansas's Ozarks instead). You may be a fan of bluegrass, *O Brother, Where*

Art Thou?, and the roots of country music. If you lived through the 1960s, you may remember the War on Poverty, launched from an Appalachian mountain cabin. If you got back to the land, *Mother Earth News* or the *Foxfire* books may have been on your shelf. Once you turn your mind to it, you can probably list people with Appalachian connections: Loretta Lynn, Dolly Parton, Lee Smith, Mother Jones, or even Thomas Wolfe. For the most part, however, you do not have to think about Appalachia much at all.

Many people who are from Appalachia can remember when they first learned they were not simply residents of the United States—they were something called "an Appalachian." Growing up middle class in Hendersonville, I always knew I was from the mountains of North Carolina. From a young age, I sensed that being from the mountains was different than simply being from North Carolina. I knew how far away—physically and spiritually—the state capital was. But I remember distinctly the day I learned that I was Appalachian. In tenth grade I was invited to join a group that offered me career counseling while at Governor's School and leadership conferences at other times during the year. Other North Carolinians were invited because they were African American or Lumbee Indian. I was included because my mother and her mother (and, in truth, several grandmothers before that) were from the western counties of the state. In short, I was Appalachian— and on that basis alone, I was judged to be needy.

Was I? In terms of class, at least, I was not (although my mother's generation was the first in her family consistently to achieve the security of the middle class, we were comfortable). As a European American, with pale skin and red hair, I benefited from the skin-color privilege that falls to white people in the United States. Educationally, I was lucky to attend excellent public schools and to have encouragement to go to college from both my mother's and my father's side of the family. Role models in my father's family had gone beyond undergraduate education, so that was familiar to me as well.

Culturally, however, yes, I may have been needy. I certainly needed to understand (and had to learn quickly) that you can never predict when someone else's prejudices about Appalachians will appear. If you are Appalachian, they argue, you must be lazy, stupid, backward, lawless, or inbred. You have probably never seen an African American or a homosexual. You wear Daisy Duke shorts; you have a moonshine still in the backyard; you talk funny. I needed to develop responses and ways of coping with such attitudes. I had to learn that social class and wealth are relative, that middle class in Appalachia is not middle class to the students at Duke University, where I attended college. I had to learn that my region of the country draws national attention only sporadically, most often for the gain of others—politicians, corporations, authors.

I also learned that I did talk funny, although my mother would have been appalled if my speech had been grammatically incorrect. I found that I truly believe you should go barefoot sometimes, so that you do not forget how the ground feels. I learned that knowing the names of plants and animals connects me both to my ancestors and to the mountains. After seeing some of the rest of the world, I decided that parts of Appalachia are among the most beautiful on earth and ought to be kept that way. And I decided that I was thankful to have come from a part of the country where people are independent enough to stand up and speak out about injustices.

Yet that "part of the country" remains difficult to define. It seems like an obvious, easy question: what is Appalachia? A federal government agency, the Appalachian Regional Commission (ARC), provides an answer. Appalachia is the mountainous counties of thirteen states, Alabama, Georgia, Kentucky, Maryland, Mississippi, New York, North Carolina, Ohio, Pennsylvania, South Carolina, Tennessee, Virginia, and West Virginia.[2] However, the ARC's definition, as well as most other definitions of Appalachia, dissolves on close inspection. The Appalachian Trail begins in north Georgia and extends through Maine; yet not all states on the trail are in the region. Besides sharing a mountain range, Pennsylvania and Alabama share precious little else. Most New Yorkers, even rural ones, do not consider themselves Appalachian. Although many residents of southeastern Ohio do, most South Carolinians do not. Drawing lines labeling one county mountainous and its neighbor merely hilly can inspire fights. In cities such as Cincinnati, Akron, and even Chicago, far outside of Appalachia, long-established communities founded by out-migrants from the mountain regions persuasively argue that they, too, are Appalachian, despite the geographical evidence. In a final irony, unlike any other well-known region of the United States (the Midwest, the Pacific Northwest, the Northeast, the South), Appalachia gets its own federal commission. Quickly, the question of Appalachia becomes more difficult than it seems; physical geography is not enough.

Most definitions draw on a combination of geographical and cultural factors. The Appalachian mountain range is one of the oldest on the planet, and it lends its name to the region; however, while the mountain range (and the Appalachian Trail) extends from Georgia and Alabama to Canada, most people mean the southern half when they say Appalachia, bringing culture into the definition. Which culture, however, can be as difficult to pin down as deciding which counties or states to include. Some people count Appalachia as merely a subset of the South, but others, such as West Virginians, use history to disagree firmly; West Virginia was founded to stay in the Union (with Pennsylvania, New York, and Maine) and to separate itself from Confederate Virginia. Still other people want a personal connection to, a love of, the mountains in order to be Appalachian. But a nature-based definition can alienate the residents of Appalachia's cities, some of whom have long embraced urban lives. Further, dictionaries have suggested that an Appalachian is a white resident of the Appalachian mountains, a definition unlikely to sit well with the generations of African Americans, Native Americans, Jews, Asian Americans, and Hispanic Americans who live in the mountains. In fact, all definitions of Appalachia are partial, debated, and insufficient, which is not to say that Appalachia does not exist. Sources used in the chapters to follow come from North Carolina, Tennessee, West Virginia, Kentucky, Virginia, and Georgia. The idea of Appalachia contained in texts by women at the turn of the twentieth century combines geographical and cultural notions of what the mountains represent.

As with definitions of Appalachia, on close inspection the stories of feminism and environmentalism are more complicated than they once seemed. United States feminism used to be discussed as a primarily white, northeastern movement: out of the hotbed of the Northeast, American feminism spread across the nation. In that deceptive story, racial and class diversity did not enter feminism until the late twentieth century. American environmentalism, the movement to preserve, conserve, and value nature, wilderness, and the nonhuman, was once told as a story of great men—Bartram, Audubon, Emerson, Thoreau, and Muir. Environmentalism's stereotypical story also privileged the Northeast, from which many early environmentalists came, as well as the American West, to which many went. The frequently repeated stories of feminism and environmentalism united only around Rachel Carson's *Silent Spring* in the 1960s.

In recent years, however, feminist and environmental theorists and historians have complicated the two movements' narratives to include multiple voices and issues at any given time from across the country. African American women, diverse Southern women, Latina women, Asian women, working-class women, poor women, Native American women, lesbians, Jewish women, immigrant women, and others worked throughout the century for improved social conditions, family health, suffrage, environmental concerns, and equality. They had political interests, went to college, worked in the Progressive movement, claimed their individual lives, and supported themselves as authors. Although simply participating in any one of these things does not necessarily make one a feminist, it was likely to make one aware of feminism and thus in its legacy. When environmental work includes more than great men's stories, women's roles in the histories of national parks and forests emerge. State and county parks, community gardens, urban green spaces, and local water issues are all legacies of diverse women activists who lived and worked well before the 1960s.

Resisting easy definitions recognizes the connections between Appalachia and the United States around feminism and environmentalism, connections that have existed politically, socially, and intellectually all along. At the risk of understatement, the women who wrote about Appalachia at the turn of the previous century knew the rest of the United States existed (although at times they claim the people they meet do not). They had readers who lived both inside and outside of Appalachia—and some who lived in both places. Simplistic definitions that accept at face value the absolute isolation to which some writers cling obscures the reasons those writers may have had for creating an isolated Appalachia.

Further, resisting stereotypes as well as simplistic definitions allows a larger range of questions to be asked about Appalachia, feminism, and environmentalism. If Appalachia was not backward, then Progressive social movements such as feminism or environmentalism might appear there as in the rest of the United States. But also, if Appalachians were not lazy, then forms of environmentalism and feminism should differ from elsewhere (in other words, Appalachians will not have simply copied models developed in other parts of the country).

In fact, Appalachia and the women writing and working there played an important role in turn-of-the-century feminist movements. They were aware of and connected to turn-of-the-century environmental movements well before Carson in the 1960s. Yet, unlike activists elsewhere, most did not combine environmental and feminist issues in their mountain work and writing. So who were the women who wrote about Appalachia? What shaped their lives and influenced their writing? What was happening nationally in feminism and environmentalism about which they would have been aware?

Political Women

Sarah Barnwell Elliott (1848–1928) was born into a prominent southern tidewater family in the same year the famous Seneca Falls convention put suffrage on the national scene. The coincidence is fitting because as an adult

method:
lit as reflection

Elliott served as president of the Tennessee Equal Suffrage Association during a crucial point in its history: she invited and then hosted in Tennessee the national conference of the National American Woman Suffrage Association. Tennessee's role in the final suffrage campaign emerged from that national meeting in 1914. Two years earlier, Elliott wrote an equal rights manifesto that argued in part: "[W]e cannot get equal pay for equal work unless we get the ballot." Her vision of suffrage went beyond voting rights into issues of economic justice and social equality, even as it was limited elsewhere in her writing by the racism characterizing much of the national suffrage campaign.[3]

Although suffrage was not secured across the country until 1920, the fight for it was ongoing, occupying much national attention and press. Regardless of one's region or race, it was hard to come of age around the turn of the last century without some awareness of political women such as Elliott. Suffrage was not simply a white women's fight, although the racism of some national organizations tried to keep it that way; suffrage clubs founded and run by black women, such as Ida B. Wells-Barnett's Chicago Alpha Suffrage Club, were in place by the 1890s. In the end, an Appalachian state, Tennessee, aided by Elliott's activism, served as the crucial thirty-sixth legislature to approve the vote, bringing the amendment support from the necessary three-quarters of the states. Behind suffrage activism lay a national debate about the abilities, rights, and responsibilities of American women, about which women writing of Appalachia would have known.[4]

In her personal life, Elliott tested her own abilities, rights, and responsibilities. Never married, Elliott balanced family responsibilities (such as caring for an aging mother and adopting her deceased sister's children) with her own education, professional career, and volunteer commitments. She was one of the first female students at Johns Hopkins University and later was awarded an honorary degree from the University of the South, located in Appalachia. Leading magazines of the day—*Harper's*, *Lippincott's*, and *Scribner's*—published her stories, while her novels, biographies, plays, and reviews were financially successful and popular. Elliott traveled extensively (to Europe and the Holy Land) and lived in cities in New York, Texas, and Tennessee. But Tennessee and Tennessee's (white) women remained a priority for her. The female characters Elliott created in her fiction reflect the feminist issues in which she was involved. Elliott did not separate feminism from Appalachia, as witnessed by the stories she set in the mountains.[5]

Elliott was not the only author to combine her political interests with women of Appalachia. Despite her cosmopolitan life in New York and

Europe, Amelie Rives Chanler Troubetzkoy (1863–1945) not only wrote about mountain women, but also worked for the vote for women in Virginia, her native state. From Chattanooga, Tennessee, Emma Bell Miles (1879–1919) wrote newspaper columns supporting suffrage, as well as poems, novels, and stories about her home in Appalachian Tennessee. Her diary reveals ongoing interest in political systems as, within its pages, she debates socialism and labor issues. In the 1890s, Helen Morris Lewis organized one of North Carolina's first suffrage activities from her home in mountainous Asheville. In other words, political women used the pen to develop and explore innovations in the political arena that would bring far-reaching social change to themselves and their communities.[6]

Lingering perceptions about Appalachia at the turn of the twentieth century, however, proposed that the region was out of step with the modern world and hence ignorant of national political debates and political women. Naturalist Margaret W. Morley (1858–1923), in her 1913 work, *The Carolina Mountains,* interrupts her celebration of her own ability to hike twenty miles a day to dismiss the Appalachian women she meets. Morley claims: "The mountain woman has her duties and her privileges. She loves, honors, and obeys, innocent of any knowledge of the suffrage movement."[7] Although Morley may not have met them or wanted to recognize them, many mountain women were quite aware of suffrage and national policies.

Ideas about suffrage and woman's rights were not limited to college towns (like Elliott's Sewanee), urban areas (like Lewis's Asheville and Miles's Chattanooga), or educated women's agendas (like Troubetzkoy's). These issues appear in the letters and papers of women living in more rural communities, such as those of Frances Louisa Goodrich (1856–1944) written from her new home well outside of Asheville, North Carolina. She narrates an 1892 Sunday school election in a rural mountain community during which a local man "said he was a woman's suffrage man they all knew, and that he was in favor of a woman." Whether women should vote had implications throughout society, not only on national levels, but on the intensely local—Sunday school—level as well. The debate did not simply engage token individuals either. An entire mountain community experiments with political feminism in Miss Matt Crim's 1895 story, "The Strike at Mr. Mobley's." Although the story ends on an antifeminist note, Mrs. Mobley says: "Melissy Davis 's been over this mornin', an' we talked a long time 'bout the rights o' women. She 'lows it 's a burnin' shame the way we put up with men folks an' their lazy ways, doin' all the work while they do all the talkin' an' the votin'." In fact, women both living in and producing literature about

Appalachia—including Elliott, Troubetzkoy, Miles, Lewis, "Melissy Davis," and perhaps even the woman elected to run the Sunday school—all belonged to and shaped the political world.[8]

Many political women in Appalachia were middle class, leading scholars David E. Whisnant and Henry D. Shapiro to criticize sharply settlement workers such as Katherine Pettit, May Stone, and Frances Louisa Goodrich and writers such as Mary Noailles Murfree for erasing any mention of labor struggles and the effects of industrialization on Appalachian life. What Whisnant suggests about Lucy Furman's novels could also be said about the novels and diaries of many middle-class political women: "One could read them all and never know that the timber cutters and coal operators even knew where Knott County was." Some of this ignorance (willful or not) came from the middle-class privileges many political women wielded. Yet, working-class women were also politically active during the era. Annelise Orleck describes the period's "industrial feminism," and although she does not talk specifically of Appalachia, some of the most famous labor activists have Appalachian connections—including Mother Jones and the balladeer Ella May Wiggins. Less famous labor movement women took center stage in a strike that closed a rayon plant in mountainous Elizabethton, Tennessee, in 1929; striking women had extensive support from their rural community, but women became the most visible participants in this struggle. As early as 1880 in North Carolina, women and children made up 75 percent of the work force in textile mills; difficult, dangerous work for pay was a feature of many turn-of-the-century Appalachian women's lives. Such difficult jobs and the labor struggles associated with them motivated many women working in mills, as wives of coal miners, and in other industries in the mountains to become political.[9]

Magazines and newspapers with Appalachian audiences connected political women across the region. From publications with national distribution such as Hampton Institute's *Southern Workman* and Berea College's *Berea Quarterly*, to private student publications such as Hampton's *Talks and Thoughts* written by its Native American students for one another, diverse political voices debated across Appalachia. African American presses published newspapers in the Appalachian mountains that supported, advertised, and even criticized community work, education for women and men, and activist authors. For instance, *The Mountain Gleaner* of Asheville, North Carolina, "worked zealously for the betterment of the Afro-American's condition, and likewise took a part in everything looking to the development of North Carolina, particularly the city in which it was published." On the one hand,

news from across the nation was available and of interest to mountain readers. On the other, Appalachian publications spread the word about local
political issues and provided news about local political women.[10]

Progressive Women

Sarah Barnwell Elliott's voting rights manifesto hints at the broader
political conversation about women's roles and abilities behind the suffrage
fight. She claims women "have awakened into political consciousness by
realizing that in trying to do our work for the home we have to follow it
out into the world; that in doing so we have come, and helplessly against
the laws of the city, the state, the county." Elliott's version of suffrage shared
the set of philosophies undergirding much Progressive women's work. Moving the responsibility of women from inside the domestic scene "out into
the world" motivated many women to organize for social change that often
included, but was broader in scope than, simple suffrage.[11]

The earliest text discussed here appeared in 1875, the latest, 1925, roughly
bracketing the Progressive Era in the United States. Across the country, the
Progressive decades were an era of settlement houses, public libraries, adult
literacy projects, anti-child-labor lobbying, tree planting, clean water and
clean cities campaigns, antituberculosis programs, "Lifting as We Climb,"
temperance, and, of course, suffrage. Women founded local clubs with friends
and neighbors, connected their hometown clubs to national organizations,
and used Progressive rhetoric to argue for social change. Included among
the dedicated activists organizing for social change were a corps of feminist
activists and leaders—Jane Addams, Ida B. Wells-Barnett, Alice Paul, Lucy
Stone, Mary Church Terrell, and others.[12]

Katherine Pettit (1868–1936) helped bring the settlement house movement to Appalachia. Settlement houses, which were popping up across the
nation, featured groups of dedicated, usually female teachers who lived in
the communities with their students. Programs offered by settlement houses
balanced classical education with practical, vocational teaching. Often settlement houses were involved in jobs programs, childcare, nursing, and
hygiene. For Appalachia, Pettit and others had to modify the settlement
house model, which was usually an urban phenomenon, to fit the rural,
mountain communities they served.[13]

Much like the settlement houses themselves, Pettit's own activism was
multifaceted, bringing her in line with many Progressive women: in addition

to helping found two settlement schools in Appalachian Kentucky, Pettit established libraries, taught elementary school, facilitated girls' applications to college, and planted trees. Because she guarded her privacy, the early history of Pettit's association with the Kentucky branch of the Federation of Women's Clubs is obscured, yet her life's work was made possible by the Progressive women's clubs to which she belonged. By her twenties, the Lexington, Kentucky-born Pettit had joined the Women's Christian Temperance Union. Her work for temperance in the mountains was coupled with her involvement in the State Federation of Women's Clubs' rural library service. Through her club memberships, she found enough intellectual stimulation, financial support, and fellow Progressive women to create the early "Camp Industrials" and the later permanent Hindman and Pine Mountain Settlement Schools. Although she was twenty years younger than Elliott, Pettit shared with her a comfortable upbringing and the credentials that arose from belonging to a prominent white southern family. When the opportunity came, she left with her associate, May Stone (1867–1946), for a lifetime of work in Kentucky's Appalachia as a Progressive woman.[14]

The Progressive movement gathered participants from across racial, class, and ethnic lines. In Appalachia, black club women organized schools and community centers. The 1900–1901 "Colored Section" in the Asheville, North Carolina, city directory includes Alsie Dole, principal of the Asheville Colored Industrial School. In fact, Asheville's African American women had an industrial school available to them as early as 1885. With its kindergarten and literary organization, the Young Men's Institute, an African American community center partially funded by Vanderbilt money, suggests further work by black Progressive women in North Carolina's largest mountain city. Chattanooga, in eastern Tennessee, and the southern coal fields of West Virginia had similarly dynamic African American communities during this era. When in the 1930s Memphis Tennessee Garrison began her career as a Progressive woman working in clubs and schools, and organizing for the National Association for the Advancement of Colored People, she built on black West Virginia women's Progressive networks from earlier in the century. Deborah Weiner's work has shown that Jewish women in the southern West Virginia coal fields similarly relied on clubs and networks to organize mutual aid and charity societies. Diverse Progressive women across Appalachia, despite working on projects specific to their own communities, shared a commitment to social change and community welfare.[15]

College Women

Many women who worked for political or Progressive causes were first exposed to these ideas in colleges and schools around the United States. University education for women emerged out of the 1860s and 1870s, but a national consensus about what women would do with their educated lives remained elusive. In 1884, Kentucky native May Stone entered Wellesley College, scarcely nine years after it opened. There, Stone gained entrance into the group of socially conscious, educated women looking for careers. Some of her friends went to Chicago to help with Jane Addams's Hull House; other Wellesley students became doctors, lawyers, nurses, and teachers. Stone found her career in "mountain work" in eastern Kentucky, where she joined Pettit to found the Hindman Settlement School. Stone, in fact, remained head of the school until her death. During the decades around 1900, many newly graduated women searched for work that would be both satisfying and financially sustainable. Many landed in Appalachia.[16]

Although Stone taught in settlement schools, many women made careers in the more traditional small public schools in the mountains. Anna D. McBain combined teaching in Appalachia with attending Berea College for further training. As an African American schoolteacher in Appalachian Kentucky, she reports back to the *Berea Quarterly* in 1901 about her "first school in Garrard Co., a very hilly but beautiful section of the country." McBain discusses not only teaching the students who arrived in her schoolhouse but also helping those students continue on to college. Effie Waller Smith (1879–1960), after completing her education at the Kentucky Normal School for Colored Persons, joined her sister and brother as a rural schoolteacher. Smith worked in schools in eastern Tennessee and Kentucky, supporting herself and, later, an adopted daughter on her wages and her writing. The successes of Pettit and Stone's schools, as well as McBain and Smith's experiences, prove that diverse local communities in Appalachia were interested in education, women's expanding roles, and national Progressive ideals.[17]

Colleges specifically for black students thrived alongside ones for white students around the region; for instance, Tennessee had African American schools in Knoxville, Morristown, Bristol, Athens, Cleveland, and Riceville in 1905. Storer College in West Virginia had a full complement of classes, clubs, and even sporting activities for its black female college women. Native Americans joined African Americans as consumers of, participants in, and organizers of schools in Appalachia. Berea College in Appalachia and

Hampton Institute in eastern Virginia recruited mountain students and were notable for their coeducational focus. Berea enrolled African American and European American men and women until the Kentucky Legislature made them stop admitting black students in 1904. Hampton educated African American and Native American men and women from around the United States, including Appalachia. In 1880, eleven Cherokee women enrolled at the Asheville Female College; the North Carolina legislature had approved funds for teacher training, including black and white women, in 1877, and they extended funding to Native American women in 1887. The pool of women only grew as college women joined Progressive and political women in shaping life in Appalachia and the United States.[18]

Modern Women

Women at the turn of the century with connections to Appalachia were never simply political, Progressive, or college women; all led complicated and surprisingly modern lives. Olive Dame Campbell (1882–1954) combined Appalachian life, American life, and individual triumph and struggle. She was the second wife of a scholarly man, maintained close relationships with women and men in the United States and Europe, and established a successful career after her husband's death. She arrived in the Appalachian mountains from Massachusetts in 1907 with her new husband, John Charles Campbell. He had plans to study the mountains with the help of his wife, recognizing that "a woman may often learn many essential facts from the women teachers and from the women of the mountains which would not otherwise be available." The Campbells received funding from the Russell Sage Foundation; their work eventually resulted in *The Southern Highlander and His Homeland,* which she published in 1921 under her husband's name, and which was an early classic in Appalachian studies. In fact, when he died before finishing the manuscript, she organized and completed it, announcing, "It has not been possible . . . to follow exactly the outline suggested [by John]. There are too, doubtless, certain things to which Mr. Campbell would have given an interpretation somewhat different from that presented here; other things perhaps to which he would not have given expression; still others which would have been treated fully and must now be left with little or no mention. . . . [A]ttribute the limitations to her whose privilege and responsibility it has been to make ready the manuscript for publication." Olive Dame Campbell was confident enough in her professional experience to write the book, change its organization, focus, and even topics; yet she chose not to publish it under her own name—or, for that matter, even to appear as its co-author, making her an interesting combination of modern and traditional.[19]

The Campbells did the research for the book together in trips around the Appalachian mountains from 1908 through 1909; in two years, Olive Campbell traveled 1,500 miles and visited more than seventy schools. As a modern business traveler would, she regularly put aside the domestic for the professional. She kept meticulous (although often hurried and cramped) diaries of their journey. In addition, she photographed their trips, later supporting their written arguments with the pictures. After her husband's death, she founded and ran the John C. Campbell Folk School near Asheville, North Carolina, collecting mountain ballads and working for rural education in general. Single career woman, author, intrepid traveler, privileged researcher, photographer, and teacher, Olive Campbell was a modern woman who both benefited from and gave back to the communities of Appalachia.[20]

That newly educated, professional, savvy women were so present in politics and Progressive activism at the turn of the century meant that the United States had to come to terms with new ideas about what a modern woman was. Appalachia was no exception. Mary Noailles Murfree (1850–1922) revealed in 1884 to shocked critics that the virile stories by "Charles Egbert Craddock" were written by a woman; by this time, most women felt comfortable being female in their public personae. Further, they challenged U.S. society to accept them as they were, not as ideal images suggested they should be. Virginia Amelie Rives Troubetzkoy divorced her first husband and later married a Russian prince she met through her friend, Oscar Wilde. Her first novel was notorious for its frank discussions of sexuality and women's desires; her Appalachian work, *Tanis, the Sang-Digger,* alludes blatantly to women's orgasms ("sparks o' fire was pourin' over me, an thoo me, same ez they does up th' chimbly when yuh beats on smoulderin' wood"). Later in her life, Troubetzkoy wrote about women's addictions to prescription drugs. Women connected to Appalachia, such as Troubetzkoy, thought about their sexuality and reproductive choices; they wanted companionate marriages that would support their careers, hopes, and dreams. If appropriate partners did not live up to their promises or never appeared, modern women got divorced or never married.[21]

In her diary, Tennesseean Emma Bell Miles speaks forthrightly of birth control, divorce, and the particular burden marriage could place on women's bodies. In 1914, she writes, "I have tried every way I can think of to escape what is coming, but for some reason the usual methods failed. . . . It drives me wild to remember how, from the time Joe was born, I have begged Frank not to lay this burden on my sick body, and overworked hands; and how at each of the two births and three miscarriages since then I have tried to make him understand that it is bound to kill me sooner or later." Her raw accounting of the day-to-day life of a marriage includes an entry seven months later, in which she laments that "he has been to a lawyer of his own, and has found that he can divorce me for the death of those unborn children—whom I loved and would have worked for when he would not. God, is there no justice anywhere for a married wife?"[22] Elsewhere in her diary, Miles remembers the shared intellectual conversations over which she and Frank fell in love; Miles's struggles, rather than being unique, place her solidly in the group of modern women across the United States at the turn of the last century.

Emma Bell Miles and her husband did not divorce, but Grace Mac-Gowan Cooke (1863–1944) joined Troubetzkoy as a divorced woman who continued a successful career after her marriage ended. After leaving her husband and their home in Chattanooga, Cooke experimented with co-operative living with other artists, lived in cities around the United States, and ended up in California working for motion pictures, those quintessential symbols of the modern world. Cooke never remarried, preferring to live with her sister at Carmel-by-the-Sea. Many women working at settlement schools and colleges never married or only married very late in life, a group that includes Katherine Pettit and May Stone. Such modern women were often labeled, by more traditional men and women in Appalachia, "quare" (queer) or "fotched-on," a label that speaks as much to their career choices as it does their sexuality and reveals the transitions facing not only mountain but also U.S. society at the turn of the past century.[23]

Women's Networks

Political, Progressive, college, and modern women and writers in Appalachia and the rest of the country formed extensive and sometimes surprising networks. May Stone and Sophonisha Breckinridge both attended Wellesley College. While Breckinridge worked with Jane Addams in Chicago, she and her sister-in-law, Madeline McDowell Breckinridge, were crucial early supporters of Pettit, Stone, and the camps preceding the Hindman School. Other women shared hometowns. Olive Dame Campbell was from the same town as Elizabeth Watts, and their conversations led Watts to the

Hindman settlement—where she stayed for forty-seven years. Women even shared households: Daisy Gertrude Dame followed her sister Campbell to do a stint of activist work in the mountains at Kentucky's Oneida Baptist Institute.[24]

Women's networks occasionally crossed racial, geographical, or class barriers, when women united over shared goals. For instance, Eleanor Marsh Frost (1863–1950), wife of the influential president of Berea College, William Goodall Frost, and an activist in the mountains herself, visited Margaret Washington, wife of Booker T. Washington, at Tuskegee in 1901 and discussed shared educational principles across races. Campbell's diary records many meetings with Frances Louisa Goodrich (who founded the Allanstand Industries in North Carolina after her experiences with suffrage in Sunday school elections), Katherine Pettit, and Eleanor Marsh Frost, despite working in different regions of Appalachia. Even the relatively isolated Mary R. Martin (1870–1936), who lived in the religious retreat of Montreat, met Goodrich; soon after, Martin wrote that she herself might take up activism. Martin ended her career as a schoolteacher in Appalachia.[25]

Other women met around their writing projects. While Lucy Furman (1870–1955) combined activism and writing by fictionalizing her experiences as one of Pettit and Stone's teachers, writers Miles and Cooke show indirect knowledge of activist women's work. In her 1913 diary, Miles writes: "I saw some chapters of [Furman's] 'Mothering on Perilous' when it appeared in Century, and envied the writer her grasp of mountain character and conditions. To one who has lived the life, the ordinary novel of moonshine and rifles seems merely newspaper twaddle. Miss Furman's work is heart-satisfying, and I am so glad to know more of her." Writers exchanged letters with others locally and across the country. For instance, Miles corresponded with Anna Ricketson, a member of an influential circle of New England writers. Appalachian women formed intimate relations with other writers— many of whom numbered among the country's most influential authors of the day. Cooke and her sister, Alice MacGowan, while staying in artists' retreats, lived with Upton Sinclair, Sinclair Lewis, Mary Austin, Jack London, and others; and both Cooke and MacGowan collaborated with Miles on writing projects. In other words, the Progressive, college, and political women teaching in the Appalachian mountains; the authors writing about the mountains; and researchers, readers, and authors around the country were aware of and connected to each other around a shared interest in Appalachia.[26]

Environmental Club Women

Elsewhere in the United States, some Progressive, political, college, and modern women were turning to environmental work as well. Vera Norwood, studying the female tradition in American nature study, argues that "American women's most significant contributions to nature study, conservation, and the environmental movement have occurred during the same period as critical developments in feminist activism." Scholar Carolyn Merchant is more specific; she finds: "Nowhere has women's self-conscious role as protectors of the environment been better exemplified than during the progressive conservation crusade of the early twentieth century."[27] Many used the same clubs that had been doing feminist work and simply added environmental projects to their agendas.

In 1900, Mrs. Lovell White of San Francisco "took up the cause of forestry" with the California Federation of Women's Clubs. She named as her inspiration women working to save the Palisades in New Jersey and cave dwellings in Colorado. Other club women were inspired by Florida women who in 1905 created the nucleus of the Everglades National Park. The garden club movement began in Georgia in 1891, and many other women worked to preserve historical sites as parks. Women's clubs were instrumental in the passage of a federal bill to preserve watersheds and navigable streams, the establishment of the National Park Service in 1916, and the first federal conservation measure, the 1900 Lacey Act targeting endangered animals. By 1910, as many as 283 women's clubs reported sending petitions on environmental issues to state or national governments, and 250 reported working for bird or plant protection that year. In addition to their multifaceted club work, women founded and flocked to organizations specifically dedicated to environmentalism, such as the Women's National Rivers and Harbors Congress that began in 1908 and had thirty thousand members only two years later.[28]

There is no denying that Appalachia was struggling with environmental questions. Around 1900, the Appalachian situation was a potent mix of logging, mining, poverty, and tourism. Environmental historian Albert E. Cowdrey describes it as an era of "exploitation unlimited" in the South, as business interests shamelessly coveted the region. Henry Grady, editor of the *Atlanta Constitution* and champion of the "New South," targeted Appalachia for exploitation, saying its mountains were "stored with exhaustless treasures." Capitalists were listening. Appalachia saw logging reach its peak between 1880 and 1909, which helped bring about an alarming amount of regional wildlife extinction. Additionally, much of Appalachia's valuable acreage was sold off to outside interests during the era, especially corporations bent on resource extraction. On the national scale, Jennifer Price suggests the economy was "on the brink of tremendous increases in production and consumption—and therefore the harvest, industrial transformation, marketing, purchase, and use of natural resources." For the same era, David Whisnant focuses on the Appalachian region to describe it as "a frontier on the verge of convulsive industrial development." Jacquelyn Dowd Hall, in her study of later industrial strife, argues that "the key to modern Appalachian history lies not in the region's isolation but in its role as a source of raw materials and as an outlet for investment in a capitalist world economy." Combined, the forces of industry and resource extraction radically reshaped the Appalachian environment.[29]

How women participated in conversations about environmental changes in Appalachia is an unsettled question. Merchant and Norwood have written the two most comprehensive books on women's environmental activism in the United States, yet neither spends much time on Appalachia. Should letters from Appalachia's women's clubs be added to the ones Merchant lists sending petitions, working for plants, or trying to save birds? Should Appalachian women be included among the illustrators, gardeners, and wildlife activists Norwood profiles? What local issues did environmental club women in Appalachia identify? Who emerged as their leaders? In what ways were Appalachia's middle- and upper-class activists indebted to the extractive industries? The detailed history of Appalachia's environmental club women's activities lies buried across the region, waiting to be unearthed. However, even if their clubs' histories have not been researched, individual women's writing and activities are available. Fortunately, those texts are also an important kind of evidence; in their writings, women work out their philosophies, assumptions, and ideas about feminism and environmentalism.

Nationally, environmental activism proceeded on many fronts, and fierce debates surfaced among activists. One of the most public was the philosophical divide between conservationism and preservationism. From 1908 to 1913, Gifford Pinchot, a conservationist, and John Muir, a preservationist, conducted a highly visible struggle over the future of Hetch Hetchy, one of San Francisco's watersheds. Although women were on both sides of the debate, club women generally sided with Muir and his efforts to preserve the watershed as it was. Pinchot and his allies argued for managed resources, scientific forestry, and conserved land that could be used for profit. Muir and the General Federation of Women's Clubs lost the effort, and Hetch Hetchy was logged.[30]

Locally, in 1934 the first southern and only the second East Coast national park was established: the Great Smoky Mountains National Park. The fight over its founding is an East Coast example of the Hetch Hetchy philosophical struggle. The idea of an Appalachian national park had been discussed as early as 1899 by a committee formed in Asheville, North Carolina. At the turn of the last century, however, this first attempt to create a park did not get far in Appalachia. Pinchot began his career in the Appalachian mountains; his influence toward conservation over preservation was partially responsible for the delays in the founding of a park, as the nation debated which system would best serve the country. In 1913, Margaret Morley was part of a group of conservationists (arguing both pleasure seekers and lumbermen should "use" the forest) advocating for the creation of what she called the "Southern Appalachian National Park." She argued that "there has grown up so urgent a demand for a national forest in the East ... whose function shall be forever to protect the cradles of the great rivers that are born on the slope of these mountains"; unfortunately nothing came of her efforts until 1924. In a much repeated story, Mrs. Willis P. Davis, the wife of a Knoxville, Tennessee, businessman, viewed Yosemite and told her husband that the Appalachian mountains were just as worthy of being preserved as anything in the West. Her husband joined a growing group of people interested in the project; their critical mass resulted in a final, successful push for the preservationist's park, which quickly became (and remains) the most visited park on the East Coast.[31]

Before the controversies between Muir and Pinchot and well before the Great Smoky Mountains National Park came into being, a campaign that dwarfed all others in its intensity was played out on women's bodies. The bird-hat campaign centered on the East Coast, featured the women-dominated Audubon societies, and had startling success in changing the nation's conversation about nature. Price credits it for framing twentieth-century environmental organizing and characterizes the bird-hat campaign as an argument that "it was wrong for higher-class women of superior morals to let lower-class men kill mother egrets, particularly for mothers" to wear. "Birds on hats" is a literal description of women's fashion at the turn of the century. Entire birds, birds with nests, and arrangements of feathers gathered in such a way that the birds died in the process were all commonplace—and big business. Several species of birds faced near extinction from ladies' fashion. The Audubon societies that began in the 1880s had collapsed by the early 1890s, but they gained new life around the topic of women's fashion for wearing birds on their hats. Many college, Progressive, and political women whose colleagues worked in Appalachia participated in local Audubon societies and anti-bird-hat protests. The campaign against birds on hats was not simply an all-white campaign; African American women could read in the *Richmond Planet* an article, "Appeal for the Birds," in 1903, arguing black women should limit their wearing of hat plumage in order to help save birds. Although there is not a lot of evidence about Appalachian women's participation, the philosophical assumptions Price outlines about womanhood and the role of proper mothers in saving mother birds shares much with Appalachia's social crusaders who wanted to improve Appalachia through its women's morals.[32]

Although the birds-on-hats campaign was argued on the individual level (in other words, what a moral woman should wear on her head), some Appalachian sources give glimpses of women making more structural critiques of environmental issues. Pettit asks in 1913: "Are the coal companies who own the mining towns organizing them with any view for the welfare of the people?"—a question that could lead to environmental as well as social concerns. Yet, Whisnant's research shows, in that same year, 76 percent of Pettit's school's endowment was coal company money. She accepted a donation of $25,000 of stock in the Elkhorn Fuel Company alone. Later in her life, Pettit endorsed the Save-Kentucky's-Primeval-Forest League, an organization chaired by naturalist E. Lucy Braun, that realized "the rapidity with which the last remaining stands of virgin forest are falling beneath the ax" and was dedicated to acquiring "the best remaining tracts of virgin forest to be maintained for all time as inviolate preserves." However, the league was only being organized in 1936, years past the time when women in other parts of the country began similar projects.[33]

In an obituary of Pettit, Furman says, "Always she distributed, along with the inevitable package of flower-seed, and a Gospel or testament, agricultural, sanitation, health, temperance and forestry bulletins"; the combination suggests Pettit in some way connected social issues with environmental concerns. Furman alludes to the Primeval-Forest League brochure, saying, "Conservation of soil and of forests has been one of her life interests. The past two years she has made heroic efforts to save the big trees on Lynn Fork of Leatherwood creek in Perry county—almost the last surviving remnant of the magnificent primeval American forest. But the effort may be in vain; already the lumber company that owns the trees is cutting in the next branch." In fact, Pettit's efforts were too little, too late; the tracts of land in question were logged by the early 1940s.[34]

Activist Eleanor Marsh Frost also begins a structural environmental critique of industry. On a trip around the region in 1914, she notices: "Farther up the water of this lovely stream grew dark as though dyed. This we learned was caused by the sawdust of the mills." She continues, "Formerly there was a law compelling the lumber companies to remove the sawdust from the edge of the stream. But companies had brought pressure on the legislature, and the law was repealed." Upon concluding her trip, Frost acknowledges the complexity of the Appalachian situation: "This summer's experience is one of many that reveals how very difficult it is to tell the truth about anything." Frost, much like Pettit, seems not to have done much beyond noticing extractive industry. Fortunately, in the texts of women who write the roots of ecological feminism in Appalachia, such structural critiques find full expression.[35]

Writing Women

Many political, Progressive, college, modern, and environmental club women coupled their activities with writing. With that choice, made possible by trailblazing women earlier in the century, they participated in a popular trend for women at the time. After the turn of the century, literary fashions were favoring masculine adventure and hunting stories like those of Jack London, Theodore Roosevelt, and Edgar Rice Burroughs; nevertheless, women such as Mary Austin made careers out of contemplative nature writing. They were following in the footsteps of female writers such as Susan Fenimore Cooper who popularized the genre and established its wide readership. Austin and Cooper joined other diverse literary regionalists such as Harriet Beecher Stowe, Sarah Orne Jewett, and Zitkala-Sa. Literary regionalists were selling well, which meant that across the country, people were participating—even if only from their armchairs—in women's conversations about environmentalism and feminism, many of which were led by writing women. Further, in part because they were telling stories about distinctive places, Appalachia was one of the most popular settings for stories at the turn of the past century.

Even women who did not attempt to publish their works in mainstream venues wrote. They viewed their writings as something more than private. For instance, with letters addressed to family, they say, as Daisy Gertrude Dame did, "As this letter is to be a 'pass-along,' I trust a great many people will see it or hear it." Some collections, such as the papers of Laura Maria Miller Grout, show evidence of careful crafting by the author—editing, revision, and recopying—demonstrating that the constructions of the texts are intentional and at least semipublic. In addition, many writing women took one further step and turned their diaries and letters into published memoirs or thinly veiled fiction that was privately or professionally printed and used for fund-raising purposes, such as Grace Funk Myers's privately published 1911 memoir, *"Them Missionary Women"; or, Work in the Southern Mountains.* Similarly, Martha S. Gielow's 1909 novella, *Old Andy, the Moonshiner,* asks at its end for donations to the Southern Industrial Educational Association of Washington, D.C. ("incorporated and organized for promoting industrial education among the impoverished, uneducated mountain people of the Appalachian region"), and Meta Townsend's 1910 novel, *In the Nantahalas,* was written to benefit the Methodist associated Brevard (North Carolina) School. Not only do the texts *reflect* contemporary discourses, but also they *enter* and *shape* that public discourse by their semipublic nature.[36]

Just as public and private blurred in the minds of writing women at the turn of the last century, so did the lines between fiction and fact. Bertha Daisy Nickum, a student at Berea College in 1901 and 1902, wrote home to her mother and family in Ohio. About the family of a fellow student, she says: "They are down right Southerners from Lexington and one could almost imagine themselves in story book land in their home." She continues, writing that "they are so much like the people we read of in Southern stories." Months later, Nickum is still comparing the people and places of the mountains with "story books"; about a planned expedition to Cumberland Gap, Tennessee, she writes: "I do hope she will let us go for it is just like reading a story book to visit there. They are such true old fashioned Southern people." Although she does not spell out all of the southern stories she and her family have read, she does give a hint about the kind of stories she judges to be true. Describing a trip to a local photography studio, Nickum asks her family: "Do you remember in *Uncle Tom's Cabin* the little Harry Eliza's baby whom she carried across the river?" Demonstrating an unswerving devotion to the truth of fiction, she continues, "He is a very very old man now and lives near here they have his pictures also [*sic*]."[37] For Nickum and other writing women, perceptions of facts about the mountains were held up against the truth found in stories.

The counterintuitive practice of judging the truth of an experience by how it matches with a fictional description (rather than judging the realism of a piece of fiction by one's personal experiences in that place) extends to other visitors to the mountains. Daisy Gertrude Dame compares her first days in Appalachian Kentucky not just to southern stories but specifically to southern *mountain* stories. She says, "I really felt as if I were living in a story-book when I saw real log cabins, sun-bonneted women, men tipped back against the houses in mountain chairs smoking—for it was Sunday—pigs in great profusion quite at home, and an infinite number of children." In addition, she finds the setting to match her expectations of mountain life: "The hills were beautiful. . . . The country was very green and fertile; corn fields clear to the very tip-top of some of the hills; others heavily wooded; fords to cross, blackberries to pick, women riding on mules double often-times, and all the regulation sights and sounds!" The strong sense of convention (of "regulation sights and sounds") gets further comment when she tells her family about her visit to the site of a moonshine still: "It is a really romantic spot, trees and green moss, a sloping hill covered with timber, and the afternoon sunlight streaming in. As a stage setting it was perfect—just what I had always imagined!"[38] Blurring lines between public and private, on the one hand, and fiction and fact, on the other, resulted in similarly blurred lines between genres and texts; any mountain story was fair game for theorizing, using as memoir, and supporting arguments.

Finally, many women note the specific mountain books they have been reading as research about Appalachia. For instance, Eleanor Marsh Frost read *In Buncombe County,* by Maria Louise Pool. Olive Dame Campbell, even as she is journeying hundreds of miles on foot, horse, wagon, and train to gather "facts" about mountain people, notes that she is reading Alice Mac-Gowan's *Judith of the Cumberlands*—which has its own description of a woman's research journey. Daisy Gertrude Dame passes on to her brother her sister Campbell's recommendation to read "The Dark Corner," which she describes as "a story of two sisters brought up under contrasting conditions—especially a story of the Carolina Mountains."[39] More than entertainment, Appalachian stories shape and reflect writing women's approaches to Appalachia.

Just because a writing woman goes to college, works in a settlement house, or earns money selling Appalachian stories does not mean that her philosophical assumptions are radical, transformative, or even helpful for other women, men, children, or the nonhuman community in Appalachia. Sometimes she writes a literature of the voyeur that only sees the freakish in Appalachian women and nature. Other times, she writes a literature of the tourist that dwells on her own personal transformation with no thought for the human or nonhuman community around her. She may write a literature of the social crusader but be unable to break out of her complicity in status quo structures of power that exploit most Appalachian community members. Rarely, though, she writes a literature of early ecological feminism, a radical, transformative vision for sustainable, diverse communities.

Feminism, environmentalism, and Appalachia have existed in a complicated relationship to each other at least since the turn of the last century. Literary, historical, and social conversations about human and nonhuman communities lie underneath the surface of texts written by Appalachia's different kinds of women—political, Progressive, college, modern, or environmental club women. Reading them closely unearths the tangled roots of feminism, environmentalism, and literature and exposes the forgotten legacy of ecological feminism in Appalachia.

CHAPTER TWO

Voyeurs and Tourists

Appalachian Women in
Sketches and Stories

IF YOU WERE a fashion-conscious American at the turn of the century, if you wanted to keep up to date on the latest fiction, if you loved to dream about traveling, if you wanted to read essays from Henry James and other literary lights, you had to have a subscription to at least one of the monthly magazines—*Century* or *Lippincott's* for the family, the *Atlantic Monthly* or *Harper's* for the evening. A character in Grace MacGowan Cooke's *The Power and the Glory* comments: "Illustrated magazines go everywhere in these days," and thus explains how even someone in oh-so-remote Appalachian Tennessee could know the latest designs of automobiles and driving fashions. Cooke is the exception, however; most writers decidedly did not have the Appalachian *reader* in mind. Instead, from your armchair in Wisconsin, New York, Florida, or California, you read about "Little Kaintuck," *In the Tennessee Mountains,* or "The Home-coming of Byrd Forebush: A Love Story of Little Turkey Track."[1]

In other words, rather than the audience, Appalachians were most frequently the characters in the magazines' sketches, as well as the novels, short stories, and poems published in the United States about Appalachia.[2] As a character in an 1898 novel, *Cis Martin, Or, The Furriners in the Tennessee Mountains* by Louise R. Baker, says: "I was of the opinion that a well-told descriptive article of life in the Tennessee mountains would meet with ready sale." Ready sales were so tempting that marketing departments at presses

willingly stretched the boundaries of Appalachia to fit a novel or story into
it. For instance, the action in Annie Maria Barnes's 1899 *The Ferry Maid of
the Chattahoochee: A Story for Girls* occurs in Marietta, Georgia, but the
novel was marketed and recorded as an Appalachian novel, arguing that
seeing the mountains in the distance is sufficient to make the residents
"mountaineers." (Having lived near Marietta, I admire Barnes's characters'
eyesight.) Similarly, the labor exposé from 1905, *Amanda of the Mill* by Marie
Van Vorst, has 57 pages set in the mountains of South Carolina (which, as
in Marietta, can be hard to find) and 283 pages set in the piedmont of that
state; it, too, appears as an Appalachian story. A large number of women
authors rushed to fill the market with Appalachian tales; even after dis-
counting works that were not set in the present—revolutionary war stories
and noble settler stories, for instance—and after keeping only works published during the time (not, for instance, memoirs looking back from a
distance of forty or more years to the turn of the twentieth century), a significant body of work remains. Most are out of print now, but many sold
out several editions when they first appeared.[3]

Reading the stories, novels, and poems is fun, teasing, and frequently
frustrating. The spirit of the young, female heroines (and they almost always
are) as they set off on adventures is infectious. Where will they go and
whom will I meet when I go along from my armchair? The melodramatic
situations are mesmerizing, and one turns the pages both to see if the heroines will resolve the situations alone and to see who and what are not as
they initially appear. For a reader like me who is from the places in which
these stories are set, there is also the excitement of what I will recognize,
as I read, for instance, to see if these characters will take the same hikes I
do. I wonder if they too will find that standing on Mount Pisgah is like
standing at the center of the world. I want to know if they also love to swim
and wade in a mountain creek and what they will wear when they do.

Frustration quickly follows, because I have not come to look at the
"weird" locals, for a vacation, or to sacrifice self to teach the "needy." I am
neither a voyeur nor a tourist, nor am I a social crusader in Appalachia.
Rather than identifying with the subjects of the texts, I am closer to the
objects—the local women encountered in the adventures. Yet even reading
subversively—looking beyond the heroines and narrators and looking for
local Appalachians—does not end the frustration. My high school in the late
1980s was more than 15 percent African American—and that is not new to
the part of western North Carolina in which it is located. But local black characters who are anything more than set markers ("You know it's *southern*

Appalachia because there's an African American here," the stories seem nervously to insist) are maddeningly absent.

My hometown also has a long history of Hispanic residents; and Eastern Band Cherokee were organized and visible enough at the turn of the century for a case to be argued successfully before the Supreme Court of the United States for reparations from the Trail of Tears. Yet Hispanic and Native American Appalachians are virtually invisible in this body of literature. Despite the rich complexity of mixed Appalachian families, authors reduce stories of intermarried Native American, African American, and white European families to dismissive insult. There are few light-skinned African Americans, and shared surnames between white and black Appalachians are similarly minimized.

Rare also are Jewish, Greek, and Italian communities, despite historical evidence that they were established in the region at the time, not to mention well-educated Appalachians and cosmopolitan resort residents of Asheville, North Carolina, or Tallulah Falls, Georgia. Local Appalachians who were prosperous farmers, independent business people, local developers, debutantes, and intelligentsia get pushed to the margins in story after story. One must read very closely to find the mountains' contemporary crises—local resistance to exploitative mills, coal mines, or railroad companies, for instance. The structural, social, and institutional pressures informing divisions between characters are deeply buried in the stories.

Appalachian literature of the turn of the last century has been analyzed by scholars for various thematic concerns, especially the construction of myths about Appalachia. Henry D. Shapiro argues that the idea of Appalachia has been invented and reinvented countless times and for various self-serving political and social purposes. Less understood, however, is why the women who came to Appalachia with college educations; friends working in settlement houses, Audubon clubs, and women's clubs; and a genuine love for the mountains did not write stories arguing for the continued well-being of the place and the people in it.[4]

Despite the previously discussed larger cultural overlap between women's rights advocates and environmental preservationists among women at the turn of the past century, much women's writing about Appalachia ultimately supports status quo structures of power that privilege certain humans over others and the human over the nonhuman. Especially with constructions of "women" and "nature," these stories employ essentialist hierarchies. Readers get plots that hinge on drama between individuals who are easily divided into insiders, outsiders, subjects, and objects. Self-Other thinking is firmly in place in a high-stakes battle that plays out on women's bodies. Mapped as the literature of the voyeur and the tourist, these texts are closely related to the literature of the social crusader (which chapter 3 examines). The writings of Emma Bell Miles, Grace MacGowan Cooke, Mary Noailles Murfree, and Effie Waller Smith push at the boundaries of all three (voyeur, tourist, and crusader) to propose radical theories that are the roots of ecological feminism in Appalachia. Voyeurs, visitors, and crusaders surround Appalachia's early ecological feminism.

Literature of the Voyeur

Then a figure slid down the rocky bank at his right, her one garment wrinkling from her bare, sturdy legs during the performance.

Gilman had never seen anything like her in his thirty years of varied experience.

She was very tall. A curtain of rough, glittering curls hung to her knees. Her face, clear with that clearness which only a mountain wind can bring, was white as a sea-gull's breast, except where a dark, yet vivid pink melted into the blue veins on temples and throat. Her round, fresh lips, smooth as a peony-leaf, were parted in a wide laugh, over teeth large and yellow-white, like the grains on an ear of corn. She wore a loose tunic of blue-gray stuff, which reached to the middle of her legs, covered with grass stains and patches of mould. Her bare feet, somewhat broadened by walking, were well-shaped, the great toe standing apart from the others, the strong, round ankles, although scratched and bruised, perfectly symmetrical. Her arms, bare almost to the shoulder, were like those with which, in imagination, we complete the Milo. Eyes, round and colored like the edges of broken glass, looked boldly out from under her long black eyebrows. Her nose was straight and well cut, but set impertinently.[5]

Scientific specimens, a zoo of human animals, sexually depraved white (but not quite) people, noble (always already) vanished Native Americans, comic black characters rendered "safe" from the racial tensions of the Reconstruction South, girlish men and mannish women—Appalachia, in the literature of the voyeur, is full of sights "never seen" in "thirty years of varied experience." There is much for the voyeur to view in Appalachia.

Figure 1. Amelie Rives [Troubetzkoy] with two dogs. At least for this photograph, Troubetzkoy has eschewed restrictive fashion, much as her character Tanis does. The photograph is located in the Amelie Rives Papers in the Rare Book, Manuscript, and Special Collections Library, Duke University, Durham, N.C.

see description of orparim, p. 22

Literature of the voyeur (as well as that of the tourist and social crusader, for that matter), as I use the term, is not an absolute category. It does not signal a formula *per se* for the fiction. Instead, it describes attitudes and structures of power informing stories told in a variety of ways. A character is a voyeur's object if she or he can exhibit no or severely limited agency. Literature of the voyeur can be signaled by a voyeuristic subject's presence in the text, but it can also emerge from the position the author provides for her reader.

The objects (who and what are viewed by the voyeur) in the literature of women writers about Appalachia are entwined in the various languages of "nature," with all its ideological baggage, but no agency. In other words, along with race, class, and gender, which are also operating, nature too becomes an inseparable category of power and identity. Some authors create explicit hierarchies of nature in which objects are closer to and subjects further from what is wild, untamed, and out there. Others use the flexible question of what is "natural" to set up an object lesson of the dangers of not embracing Progress, Civilization, and Capitalism. All try to maintain clear boundaries between who is viewing and what is being viewed, between spectator and spectacle. They trade on shock value—freaks, oddities, and unnatural beings work to hold reader and author/narrator superior from the objects in the stories.

Amelie Rives Troubetzkoy's 1893 novel, *Tanis, the Sang-Digger,* demonstrates the extremes to which the literature of the voyeur could be taken. Her novel concerns the Appalachian mountain people who made their living by digging ginseng ("sang") in Virginia to export to China as a medicinal herb. From her home at Castle Hill, near Charlottesville, Virginia, Troubetzkoy may have observed firsthand people who gathered ginseng for a living. During the harvest, she could see bunches of the roots hanging in general stores, waiting to be shipped; inflated prices made it a lucrative job. Because American ginseng has never been completely domesticated, a gatherer had to spend many hours and miles wandering in the woods to find it. With a local woman as the title character and the lower-impact industry of wildcrafting ginseng at its core, the novel could advocate for the overlap of environmental and feminist activism to support women like Tanis. Rather than admire the resourcefulness or potential profits of the career, however, Troubetzkoy seems to have nothing but contempt for ginseng-diggers as a whole. The objectified bodies and the circumstances of "nature" that have created and sustained such bodies make *Tanis, the Sang-Digger* a classist, racist, status quo argument for environmentally damaging, large-scale extractive development.[6]

In the melodramatic plot, Tanis meets George and Alice Gilman, middle-to-upper-class northeasterners who have come to the mountains for George's job and Alice's health. Claiming she wants a better life, but meaning that she wants to model her own love life on that of the Gilmans, Tanis goes to work as their servant. Tanis decides that her boyfriend, Sam, is never going to live "morally," particularly in relation to women—he's "ruined" three, with the result that "[o]ne uv 'em drownded herse'f, an they ole Grandad druv th' other two away tuh th' city. Po' things!" (Troubetzkoy, 57); he pressures Tanis for sex, saying, "[S]ay, honey-gal, a love yuh. . . . Doncher know a cud hole yuh an' tek a kiss anytime a'd a mine tuh?" (63); and is caught by her kissing another woman (130). Trying to escape him, Tanis tries several strategies to free herself. These include herbal potions, praying like Alice does, and spurning him. All the while, her worship of Alice increases. Eventually Sam and the other sang-diggers kidnap Alice; Tanis promises she will marry Sam in exchange for Alice's freedom. Because she has learned so well from Alice how to be a true woman, Tanis keeps her promise even though the Gilmans offer her means to escape. With images of a frozen world and an inert Tanis, Troubetzkoy strongly implies that the fading Tanis will soon die from the turn of events at the end of the novel.

The novel depends on class-based definitions of "mountaineers," sang-diggers (a subset of mountaineers), and outsiders who have come to develop the mountains; readers are held in the position of the Gilmans before they came to Appalachia, voyeurs of the Appalachian bodies encountered by their emissaries, the Gilmans themselves. As should be obvious from the excerpts I have included so far, one of the strategies Troubetzkoy uses to separate voyeurs from Appalachian objects is the egregious, stereotypical, and frankly awful dialect she gives the sang-diggers. Tanis may eventually work for the Gilmans and dress more conventionally, but her dialect never improves. The voice and body of the novel's main female character are sites for troubled intersections of race, class, gender, and nature in Appalachia.

Troubetzkoy builds a hierarchical class structure based explicitly on closeness to nature. All characters are identified by their closeness to and contact with the world around them—and that closeness is then directly correlated with the economic, social, and material elements which make up one's class. The hierarchy begins with the sang-diggers such as Tanis and Sam, who live outside and earn their money from gathering plants in the wilderness; they are the least empowered, most degraded people in the community, objects of pity and fascination. Sex, drugs, and animal passions are their domain. Above the sang-diggers are the agricultural mountain people who have roofs over their heads but little else; then come the various white mountain residents and African American men working on building the new railroad, who live indoors in the camps and do not earn their money directly from the land. After appearing in the first scene of the novel, African American men completely disappear from *Tanis, the Sang-Digger,* making it unclear whether Troubetzkoy follows through on placing certain white people below certain African Americans in the power structure of her novel. Ultimately, one's position in society is solely determined by one's closeness to nature, which replaces all discussion of race in the novel and in so doing erases all evidence of racial diversity in Appalachia.

Above the railroad men, Troubetzkoy presents the country doctor, who can speak with the mountain accent when he needs to, but who dismisses any natural and local ways of healing and who lives in town in the hotel. He is just slightly below the class of hotel tourists who are neither of the place nor dependent upon the place. Near the top of this hierarchy stands George, educated elsewhere and charged with applying that outside knowledge to build a railroad through the sang-diggers' wilderness; he is paid by an outside company and provides a home well-insulated from outside elements. His wife, Alice, who is in the confines of this home for almost all the novel, is independently wealthy, is distanced from any engagement of the out-of-doors, and is the most sophisticated of any of the novel's characters; she tops the novel's hierarchy. Literally an armchair observer of Appalachia, Alice stands in for the voyeur readers of the novel. Alice is, in fact, threatened (by her kidnapping, which begins with a throw from a horse) the one time she is outside alone—the one time she could move from voyeur to participant in Tanis's social and natural world.

Voyeurs, Natural Bodies, and Scientific Classism

"Did yuh ever see har [hair] no prettier nor mine?. . . We be reel chummy, muh har an' me," she went on. "When hit tuns cold in th' mountains, a wrops hit 'round me, an' hit kynder comforts me. A nusses hit on muh bres, like a baby, sometimes. An' a talks tuh hit. Seems like hits a critter, all tuh hitself, muh har does. Sometimes hit wone skars curl, tuh save muh neck. . . . Mos'ly hit's like hit is now, but sometimes hit's percisely like raw wood in the sunlight, when them little red, shiny flames is beginnin' tuh lick roun' hit. Hit's got streaks in hit, too, mos' zackly like a new silver quarter. See?" (23)

For Tanis and her "class" (for sang-diggers are discussed as consti-
tuting a class on their own [17]), closeness to nature is signaled by their
relationship to plants and animals. The plants mark what Tanis does for a
living; both her mind and body (not to mention her hair) are compared with
animals. When George Gilman first sees Tanis, parts of her are described as
like seagulls, peony leaves, and grains of corn (8–9). Later that day, Tanis
wears "bright crimson stuff about her shoulders, and a man's soft hat orna-
mented with a deer tail," which she has dyed herself with pokeberries. Tanis
not only wears symbols of animals, she moves "like a deer" and is described
as an animal. Tanis bounds about, speaks with "explosiveness," and yells
in "wild whoop[s]"; she considers her own long hair to be a "critter" that
keeps her company. As one of the other mountain people says, "[S]he was
a sang-digger. . . . They're a awful wild lot, mostly bad as they make 'em,
with no more idea of right an' wrong than a lot o' ground horgs." This
higher-class mountain resident (who still has the dialect but is one of the
men working on the railroad) clarifies: "We call 'em 'snakes' hereabouts,
'cause they don't have no place to live 'cep'in' in winter, and then they go
off somewhere or ruther, to their huts" (15–23). If nature and the nonhuman were respected, active community members in Troubetzkoy's novel, comparing the sang-diggers with snakes, groundhogs, deer, and various plants
might signal interesting coalition building or human-nonhuman relationships; but instead Troubetzkoy groups sang-diggers and the nonhuman
together as worthless, passive, degraded elements of society, who can be eth-
ically oppressed and dismissed.

More disturbingly, the sang-diggers (and only the sang-diggers) are so
connected to nature that at times it seems they will die if separated from it.
Sam says of Tanis, "[Y]uh be a mountain gal, yuh be wile an' na'chul ez
them vines an' things you're a rollin' on. Yuh 'on't nuvver git used tuh livin'
onder a roof, Tanis. Yuh 'on't nuvver larn tuh walk easy in city duds 'n' shoes
like these hyah." He continues, "Yuh be free an' wilful ez that water yonder, yuh 'on't nuvver wuk onder saddle no mo'n a wilecat 'ud. Why cyarn't
yuh love me an' give yuhse'f tuh me, and come back tuh the hills an' be
happy 'n' yo' own way?" (116). Tanis herself admits: "A cyarn't stan' hit much
longer—a cyarn't. A wuz bawn i' th' mountains. We b'longs tuh each other.
Seems like that thar house 'll kill me, sometimes. A wan't meant tuh live in
a house, no more'n that deer wuz meant to wear a shell like a snail" (71).
In these Appalachian mountains, even the female sang-diggers simply "stop
where night ketches 'em" (18). Contemporary authors such as Jack London
(and his precursor, James Fenimore Cooper) were celebrating the heroic

skill of white men who could live so seamlessly in the woods; Troubetzkoy repeatedly emphasizes the savagery and freakishness of women who could do the same.

Faced with this unusual figure, the Gilmans try to sexualize Tanis in particular, mainstream ways. George says upon first meeting her that Tanis's brother "shouldn't let you scramble about these lonely woods, by yourself, with only that one piece of clothing on" (13). Tanis makes it clear that, first, the forest is not a problem; rather, men associated with Gilman are, which is proven later, when one of the railroad men leers, "But some o' them sang-digger gals is awful pretty, though they go half naked in summer time an' are mostly mighty dirty" (18). Second, Tanis asserts she is perfectly capable of protecting her own sexuality and does not need his help: "[A] hain't nuvver hed a feller yit. . . . When they tries thar fool tricks wi' me a smacks 'em upside down" (20). She does, however, muse about Sam, "Sometimes, i' th' dark, a've thunk ez how yuh kissed me, an' it seemed like sparks o' fire was pourin' over me, an thoo me, same ez they does up th' chimbly when yuh beats on smoulderin' wood" (97). With other novels, Troubetzkoy landed in the midst of scandal for openly discussing women's sexuality; Tanis's orgasms in the dark reveal kinship to those books. Here, her status as an oddity, an object to be viewed, makes her expression of sexuality unthreatening because it is so abnormal for the Alices of the world.[7]

Troubetzkoy crosses over into the language of scientific racism to emphasize further the difference of her sang-digger objects, using differences in skin color to argue about the inferior inner nature of sang-diggers. Despite being European Americans, Troubetzkoy's mountain residents are brown, dark brown, and tobacco-colored. A sang-digger herb doctor is described as having "a forehead as brown and shriveled as a dried tobacco-leaf" and "gorilla-like arms, reaching below her knees" (Troubetzkoy, 73). Troubetzkoy is not the only author to resort to this technique; for instance, an old mountain woman in Marie Van Vorst's *Amanda of the Mill* (the South Carolina mountains novel) has "a dark-tanned hide." Other authors conflate duskiness with a combination of dirtiness and romantic earthiness: Mary Nelson Carter's short story, "A Foggy Day," features "a dun-colored figure walk[ing] out of the fog. In bedraggled skirts and shoes heavy with mud, she looked of the earth earthy." But Troubetzkoy goes so far as explicitly to label these humans of European American descent "savages" (Troubetzkoy, 11) and "barbarians" (17) in contrast with the "civilized" northeastern U.S. society.[8]

In nineteenth-century America, all these terms were, of course, common pejoratives for African Americans, Asian Americans, and other people of color; in fact, earlier in the century European Americans were even unsure whether the new Irish immigrants were white or black. However, it is class that makes the difference between sang-diggers and the other mountain residents, so Troubetzkoy is proposing a "scientific classism" that, like scientific racism, suggests that the sang-diggers are oppressed because they are naturally inferior. *Tanis, the Sang-Digger* points to the extreme racism, classism, and divided communities that lurk below the surface of much early literature about Appalachia.

Tanis herself stands as a liaison between the pure white of the Gilmans and the brownness of the mountain people; rather than "gorilla-like," her arms are "as white as the lining of a horse-chestnut burr" (Troubetzkoy, 39). In a manner similar to discussions of "race mixing" and multiracial people at the turn of the past century, Tanis is "multiclass," which explains why, unlike the other ginseng-diggers, Tanis even thinks of living differently. Her long-deceased mother was educated and lived higher up on the novel's rigid social hierarchy. The genetic argument about class (i.e., Tanis has some higher-class blood in her, which makes her different) is not unique to *Tanis, the Sang-Digger.* For instance, genetics are integral to Martha S. Gielow's *Old Andy, the Moonshiner.* In that 1909 novella, the main character's father has different, higher-class blood. He is a literate, educated lawyer, although his identity is not revealed until the very end of the story. His daughter, despite being raised by lower-class mountain people, is noticeably different from the people around her. Thus, the daughter is able to "escape," become educated, and eventually return to "save" mountain people like Old Andy.[9] However, in Troubetzkoy's piece, Tanis is more comparable to the tragic mulatta figures in nineteenth-century literature; her "mixed blood" allows her to dream of another life, but she is doomed not to reach it. One of the last views the hotel residents have of Tanis inspires "a young artist" to say, "I swear that's stunning. It would be a good pose for a statue of Eve gazing back at the garden of Eden!" (Troubetzkoy, 183). In this novel, middle-class "civilization" is so endorsed as to be called Edenic, and so unreachable for Appalachians as to be after the fall from grace.

Voyeurs Find Bodies in Nature

Fashionable Alice participates fully in mainstream American ideas of the true woman, from her clothing to her behavior, but when Tanis attempts this, her body cannot sustain the effort. Mainstream clothes are a particular problem for Tanis, first because she finds they take too much time and effort to be practical: "Say! . . . how many o' these hyuh duds *be* thar, *any-how?* A hain't got room on me fuh any mo', an' ther's 'bout three lef' over" (29). Second, she finds them literally dangerous; Alice's corsets, she claims, are "too narrer. A could'n' breathe" (40). When Tanis dons mainstream clothes, she loses her voice—becomes "as a rule, rather silent" (45)—and her vitality. By the end of the novel, Tanis herself is coughing and "inert and listless" (185–86)—much like Alice always is. For a moment, it seems that Troubetzkoy intends a full critique of ideals of middle-class woman-hood: Tanis's uncontrolled, boisterous body highlights unfavorably Alice's corseted, regulated one, confined to her couch, pale and in need of smelling salts. Yet Troubetzkoy backs away from the criticism, and, in the end, Tanis is doomed to her class; not even her mixed blood can make her into Alice, and trying, the end strongly implies, most likely kills her. Although the character of Tanis allows Troubetzkoy gently to criticize mainstream gender roles and expectations of women, her rigid hierarchies of race, class, gen-der, and nature keep Tanis forever as an object, a source of pleasure and revulsion for the voyeur reader.

In contrast to Alice and the readers ensconced in the parlor, Tanis is most comfortable in the woods—to her, danger comes from the public world and from trying to escape one's position. Examples of these dangers to Tanis include the men who are working on the railroad construction (15) and the threatening crowds at the hotel whom she calls wolves when she is trying to sacrifice herself for Alice (166). Ultimately, however, Troubetzkoy absolves the Gilmans, herself, and the reader by suggesting the enforcers of social hierarchies are the fellow objects, in this case, the sang-diggers. Despite the fact that Tanis momentarily feels threatened by the hotel patrons, it is the ginseng-diggers who force her to remain where she began. Through the kidnapping of Alice, they demand the ultimate sacrifice from Tanis—staying with them in the mountains. Underneath the plot device of the lovelorn Sam is the sense that Tanis's attempt to escape her class is prevented by that class, not by the "innocent" upper and middle class rep-resented by Alice and George.

George Gilman, as Tanis puts it, is "one o' them fools ez reads books, an' thinks nothin' 'live's got any sense but yuh selves" (11). Absolved of com-plicity and sure of his superiority, he colonizes the mountains with a rail-road that brings tourists to their new hotels and picturesque sites. Because Tanis's class of ginseng-diggers is also positioned as savage and ignorant, Progress continues unquestioned and unproblematized in this novel. His-tory shows the Progress represented by tourism and railroads to carry a heavy price for the Appalachian region; yet, any discussion of regulated development is absent in Troubetzkoy's novel. Lacking any sustainable decision making that includes diverse human or nonhuman community members, Troubetzkoy's portrait of an Appalachian community erases all environmental and social justice issues. This has a logical coherence: if the least empowered people (the sang-diggers) are the most knowledgeable about place, then the preservation of that place is likely to be undermined. In the course of the novel, a railroad is surveyed and constructed (8), more tourists are arriving (163), and all these changes to the community happen without discussion.[10]

While George represents a masculinity marked by Progress and wealth, local male characters often are feminized in the literature of the voyeur: Uncle Lucy in Mary Noailles Murfree's *His Vanished Star*—so pretty in his youth his name was changed from Luther to Lucy; Grandfather Warren in Sarah Barnwell Elliott's *The Durket Sperret*—whose rheumatism has him passing his days sitting wrapped in a quilt, rocking by the fire; and a series of sensitive, artistic boys in books such as Maria Louise Pool's *In Buncombe County*, or Louise Baker's *Cis Martin*.[11] That the same characters are described anxiously (to the point of defensiveness) as patriarchal, noble, and virile heightens the strangeness of these objects.

"The Capture of Andy Proudfoot" by Grace MacGowan Cooke features a working-class Irish man, Kerry (with "the artistic temperament"), from the North trying to capture and claim the bounty for an Appalachian man running from the law. As the two become friends in the isolation of a cave deep in the mountains, the language Cooke employs is increasingly homo-social. From the Irish man's perspective she describes Andy Proudfoot's "sumptuous" eyelashes, the "splendid virile bulk of the mountain-man" as it "appealed irresistibly to the other's masculinity"; she says, "every day he tasted more fully the charm of this big, strong, gentle, peaceful nature clad in its majestic garment of flesh." After Andy volunteers to go peace-fully with Kerry, they both "slept profoundly, after their strange outburst of emotion." Again, Cooke emphasizes "the Irishman's temperament" as it responds "like that of a woman" to Andy, and Kerry realizes "he had con-ceived a love for his big, silent, gentle companion which rivaled even his devotion to Katy [his fiancée]."[12] In the end, the two decide to team up to meet with their girlfriends and live together on land in the West, choos-ing a familiar resolution to their exploration of marginalized gender roles; while the actions of the two men are clothed in romantic language, it is clearly implied that the location—the isolated mountain cave—facilitates giving voice to their feelings, which are sexualized at the very least. That the story centers on two minority figures (an Irish man and a mountain resident with a Native American surname) further separates them from reader-voyeurs.

The rather extreme examples of "The Capture of Andy Proudfoot" and *Tanis, the Sang-Digger* epitomize rigid subject and object positions that keep humans separate from each other in the literature of the voyeur, but the stories' structures are reflected in much of literature of the time. The separation, in turn, sabotages the possibility of a confluence of feminist and environmental activism; Troubetzkoy may have worked for suffrage for some women in Virginia, but her novel does not make space for such work with local women in the mountainous part of the state—nor does it suggest value or merit in preserving the wild land on which the sang-diggers roam.

Literature of the Tourist

Leaving the road, they entered deep silent gorges, and followed the bed of mountain-streams through canons walled in by gray frowning rocks, over which the sky bent more darkly each moment. At last there was a break in the gorge. About her was a world of gigantic mountains. There was no sign of human habitation—nothing but interminable forests that climbed the heights, and failing half-way, left them bare to pierce the clouds.[13]

In Rebecca Harding Davis's "The Yares of the Black Mountains," Mrs. Denby is the tourist finding adventure in a "world of gigantic mountains." The narrator in Pool's *In Buncombe County* is another tourist; she begins by noticing, "We were alone on the platform,—alone, save that we seemed to be eternally accompanied by the heaviest kind of satchels." Emily Wooten, another Davis character, wanders by herself in the forest, pleased to be free of the constraints of staying inside the home. Alice MacGowan writes an extensive foreword to her 1908 novel, *Judith of the Cumberlands,* in order to explain how she knows so much about "life in the more remote districts of the southern Appalachians." She explains that she lives in Chattanooga but has also taken a trip that covered more than one thousand miles all around the mountains. She says she acquired a "mountain-bred saddle horse" and "was more than eight weeks making this trip, carrying with me all necessary baggage on my capacious, cowgirl saddle with its long and numerous buckskin tie-strings." To make the point absolutely clear, MacGowan describes herself on this trip as "a young woman, alone."[14] The freedom she describes and that all these women share is the giddy joy of the female traveler.

The literature of the tourist shares with the literature of the voyeur a distance between local and foreigner. Attribution to literature of the voyeur or the tourist is, in part, a matter of degree. Both dwell on difference and exoticism. Tourists, however, emphasize the liberation and transformation of themselves as female subjects through travel and the resulting interaction with Appalachian others. Readers, too, are ushered closer to the Appalachian characters in literature of the tourist, as the armchair travels along with the intrepid subjects. Local Appalachians may still be objects in this literature, but the possibility of transformation brings the subjects' bodies more fully into the stories and therein erodes (even if just slightly) the superiority of those subject positions. However, the closeness is eclipsed by the narratives of individual transformation; Appalachian objects, whether catalysts, lessons, or assistants, fall away once transformation or liberation occurs.

Women authors, in depicting Appalachia, frequently display the "picturesque sensibility" Alison Byerly describes in "The Uses of Landscape: The Picturesque Aesthetic and the National Park System." Byerly traces the history of the picturesque movement through the eighteenth and nineteenth centuries and argues that its legacy "has taught us to value nature, but the criterion for evaluation is the quality of aesthetic experience a landscape provides." She points out that the viewer is absolutely necessary to the picturesque because the viewer must recognize and hence create the picturesque scene. Byerly's focus is the development of tourist attractions with specifically picturesque vistas and how the manipulation of wilderness has affected American ideas of nature in national parks, but her framework suggests how nature and certain people both become objects to be exploited in the literature of the tourist.[15]

That the picturesque aesthetic was present in Appalachia is evident not only in literature but also in letters and diaries. Writing women use the word in an offhand way, as if its meaning is sure to be understood by their audiences. Bertha Daisy Nickum, the Berea College student, asks, "Did you folks ever get a little book Picturesque Berea that I sent some time ago. Well Berea certainly is picturesque." Frances Louisa Goodrich, who would later launch Allanstand Industries for women in North Carolina, calls the whole mountain experience simply "picturesque" in one of her earliest descriptions. Olive Dame Campbell, doing social research in the mountains, finds that "[i]t was picturesque enough to see the night settle on the mountains—

till finally we could only see the high mountainside on our left." Not to be outdone, Katherine Pettit, in the early days of her settlement camp, writes: "This the roughest branch I know but very picturesque," and "Although we may miss the extended view from the mountain top, the picturesque one of hanging cliffs on every side is beautiful."[16] Behind the word hides a sense of ownership of and superiority to the nonhuman world (and any humans who get assigned to the picturesque scene).

Laura Maria Miller Grout, a teacher and lecturer about Appalachia, summarizes the picturesque aesthetic when she writes: "[B]ehold the beautiful valley through the trees. The stretches of wood land, and the rich meadows watered by the small streams make a picture which it is pleasant to study." Operating here is Byerly's assertion that "tourists' enjoyment of landscape was based less on an appreciation of nature itself than on the secondary image of nature that they themselves constructed—either literally, through their amateur sketches, or imaginatively, simply in the way that they viewed the scenery." Daisy Gertrude Dame, another young teacher, writes: "The 'redbud' is in full bloom in the gray woods, looking for all the world like pictures of Japanese plum trees, and yellow-green blossoms of the sassafras (big and tall here) and the white of the flowering dogwood made a picturesque combination." Buying pictures, making sketches, and taking photographs are all recurring themes in the literature of the tourist.[17]

Scholars Annette Kolodny and Louise Westling begin their studies of American literature with the insight that American authors frequently feminize "the land," rhetorically supporting the patriarchal project (especially connected to white middle- and upper-class masculinity) of colonizing and dominating that land and the people on it. When women wrote about the same land, Kolodny argues, they tended in the mid-nineteenth century to want to make small gardens out of the vastness (whether feminized or not) and therein create safe spaces for themselves. Westling finds the specific women authors she studies (none of whom write about Appalachia) still relying on a feminized landscape and retreating into a nostalgia for nature that erases culpability for its domination.[18] Both scholars' research suggests an anxiety about unfettered, undomesticated nature. But writing by women about Appalachia shows little such anxiety about nature—wild spaces do not have to be made into gardens; they are not generally nostalgically mysterious; they seem, in fact, rather tame. Even undeveloped, the landscape is a safe and appropriate sphere for women travelers. Byerly's discussion of the picturesque helps explain the assurance with which women traveled and wrote about traveling in rural Appalachia.

No character encapsulates the picturesque aesthetic and the literature of the tourist more than Rebecca Harding Davis's Miss Cook in "The Yares of the Black Mountains" (1875), a short story Davis chose to reprint in the 1892 collection *Silhouettes of American Life*. Davis's most famous work is "Life in the Iron Mills," an 1861 story of urban mill life, but she published widely from 1861 to 1910. Renewed critical attention to Davis recognizes her significance in the history of feminist thought, and her reputation continues to grow as an innovator of the American short story, American realism, and American women's writing. New definitions of environmental writing which include regionalist authors discuss favorably Davis's contributions.[19]

Despite the renewed interest in her works, Davis's significance to Appalachian literature is underrecognized. I agree with Kenneth Noe, although his focus on the Civil War in Davis's literature differs from mine, when he writes that "Rebecca Harding Davis's greater role in Appalachian mythmaking surprisingly remains sadly unappreciated if not ignored by mountain scholars." Although not all of Davis's stories are set in Appalachia, she is one of the few writers of nineteenth-century Appalachian literature who actually lived in the region (Davis lived in Wheeling from age five through her midthirties). Despite setting five of the thirteen stories in *Silhouettes of American Life* in the Appalachian mountains, Davis seems to have been surprisingly successful at making them stories of "American" and not Appalachian life.[20] Part of how she accomplishes this is through her participation in the literature of the tourist.

The Tourists to the Black Mountains

> The shackly little train jolted into the middle of an unploughed field and stopped. The railway was at an end. A group of Northern summer-tourists, with satchels and water-proofs in shawl-straps, came out of the car and looked about them. It was but a few years after the war, and the South was unexplored ground to them. They had fallen together at Richmond, and by the time they had reached this out-of-the-way corner of North Carolina were the best of boon companions. . . . "Civilization stops here, it appears."[21]

"The Yares of the Black Mountains" tells the story of tourists who have come to the mountains because of the lure of the post-Civil War South's "unexplored ground."[22] The two main characters in this story are women who have been living in the Northeast, Miss Cook, who earns her living by journalism and is seeking an adventure for her vacation, and a young widow, Mrs. Denby, who is traveling to the mountains and up through the "silent gorges" (Davis, "Yares," 255), in hopes of saving her infant son. Miss Cook encapsulates the liberation possible in the literature of the tourist as she consumes the sights, sounds, and Appalachian female objects and uses them to support herself, free of family, husband, and economic debt. Mrs. Denby suggests the potential transformation of the female traveler as her visit lengthens and her interaction with the women of the local Yare family becomes more profound.

The story begins with Miss Cook explaining, "I've only three weeks' vacation, and I can get farther from my usual rut, both as to scenery and people, here than anywhere else" (242). Scholar John Sears suggests that tourism in the nineteenth century provided "freedom from ordinary social relationships, hierarchies, and restraints";[23] and that certainly seems to be the perspective of Miss Cook, who is "tired of New York and New Yorkers. . . . To become an explorer, to adventure into the lairs of bears and wolves, at so cheap a cost as an excursion ticket over the Air-line Railroad, was a rare chance for her." The thoroughly modern, professional Miss Cook supports herself as a journalist of "political economy lately," speaks in slang, earns her "bread by [her] brains," and is in quite a hurry (Davis, "Yares," 242–46). Nevertheless Miss Cook has done her research, as do many tourists in this literature. Miss Cook is a writing woman, and just as her historical counterparts, she blurs the lines between fiction and fact, relying on fictional sources to tell her all she needs to know about Appalachia.

Miss Cook is not the only character to use fictional sources to know "the truth" about the mountains. The narrator and friend in Maria Louise Pool's *In Buncombe County,* while still endeavoring to get their satchels to a friend's house, have to spend a night in a local family's cabin. Their reaction is telling: "Of course we had read about these hovels before, but being in one and reading about one are two different experiences." Similarly, an article Miss Cook has read "in some magazine on the inhospitable region yonder, walled by clouds" has told her the region "was 'almost unexplored, although so near the seaboard cities'; the 'haunt of beasts of prey'; the natives were 'but little raised above the condition of Digger Indians.'" From her reading, she expects that the mountain residents as a group are the same as all southerners: they "are impoverished by the war, and they have an idea that every Northern traveler is overloaded with wealth and is fair game." The region is even described as "a strange country and strange people"

(Davis, "Yares," 246–50), echoing the famous naming of Appalachia as "A Strange Land and Peculiar People" in 1873 by Will Wallace Harney.[24]

Miss Cook wastes no time in confirming her expectations of the mountains and mountain women. When the two women tourists stop to rest an hour with a mountain family, Miss Cook judges the genealogical history of the family from the appearance of the hostess's face: "'Finely-cut face, that,' sketching it rapidly while the hostess hurried in and out. 'Gallic. These mountaineers were all originally either French Huguenots or Germans.'" Without interviewing the woman (scarcely more than bartering for the price of the meal), Miss Cook determines the woman's life, her ancestors' lives, and dismisses her on aesthetic grounds: "She would be picturesque, under a Norman peasant's coif and red umbrella, but in a dirty calico wrapper— bah!" (Davis, "Yares," 244). In such passages, Davis summarizes how the picturesque separates subject (artist) from object and expands beyond places to include people. Miss Cook's "superior" outsider perspective separates her from Appalachian objects, keeping self firmly divided from Other in the literature of the tourist.

Tourist Consumers in Appalachia

Davis soon reveals that Miss Cook is gathering useful information—defined as that which is in strict accordance to her expectations—for her own "summing up," her "estimate of the people" (249). In short, Miss Cook is drafting her own publishable sketch of the vacation. Miss Cook moves through her mental checklist of the elements of her future sketch. It begins as she says, "What a queer tribe we have fallen among!"—confirming that they are the strange and peculiar people she expected. She continues, "Why, it was only Tuesday I crossed Desbrosses Ferry, and I am already two centuries back from New York" (245)—finding these people are just as removed from the modern world as she had heard. She "jot[s] down in her notebook some of the young girl's queer mistakes in accent and a joke on her yellow dress and red ribbons" (249) when they arrive at the inn in Asheville and are greeted by a mountain girl. The next day, Miss Cook gets up early to do her research. Davis sums it up in one long sentence, its structure matching the research style of the character, rushing headfirst through the mountain experiences:

She had sketched the outline of the mountains that walled in the table-land on which the village stood; had felt the tears rise to her eyes as the purple shadow about Mount Pisgah flamed into sudden splendor (for her tears and emotions responded quickly to a beautiful sight or sound); she had discovered the grassy public square in which a cow grazed and a woman was leisurely driving a steer that drew a cart; she had visited four emporiums of trade—little low-ceiled rooms which fronted on the square, walled with calicoes and barrels of sugar, and hung overhead with brown crockery and tin cups; she had helped two mountaineers trade their bag of flour for shoes; had talked to the negro women milking in the sheds, to the gallant Confederate colonel hoeing his corn in a field, to a hunter bringing in a lot of peltry from the Smoky Range. (250)

Not only is Miss Cook rushing through her research, but she is also unconcerned with listening to her sources: "As they talked she portioned out the facts as material for a letter in the *Herald* . . . a sharp, effective bit of word-painting in her mind." Late in the evening, she makes "sketches to illustrate her article from a bundle of photographic views which she found in possession of the landlady" (250–52). Thus, Davis brings the scene full circle. Miss Cook has come to the mountains having read what to expect; she spends a day confirming her expectations; she ends by copying picturesque representations which are made to illustrate the sources of her expectations. The multiple layers of representations through which Miss Cook—and, by extension, the readers who follow her—views the mountains almost completely erase the mountains themselves and the mountain inhabitants.

Especially absent, except for the brief, derogatory (for all parties) reference to "Digger Indians," are Native American residents in the Asheville of Davis's story. In other writing by women about Appalachia, Native Americans are present but only in narrow, circumscribed ways. They remain objects; they are consumed by tourists and white mountain residents for their special knowledge; and they are quickly displaced into the background of the story or of history so that the reader's focus remains on the transformation and liberation of the tourists. Native Americans are rapidly vanishing emissaries of Nature or holders of the "right" knowledge about how to live with nature. In Mary Nelson Carter's short story "Old Times," from her *North Carolina Sketches,* a female mountain resident tells a female visitor to the mountains, "There was Indians round, too, when my folks come up here. They wasn't to say wild Indians. They was right peaceable. They mostly come up here to hunt and fish. There were right smart o' trout in the rivers them days. The sawmills has killed 'em out of sight, though." Absent in the passage is any discussion of why the "peaceable" Indians are no longer around. It is followed immediately by another distancing of the Native Americans. The narrator claims that even then, "Them Indians lived way off. They'd bring up baskets and sich they made theirselves and trade 'em for victuals and things the folks up here had."[25] Miss Cook's brief research trip, however, uncovers no such people.

After her one-day visit in Asheville, Miss Cook declares her research complete, explaining: "I've done the mountains and mountaineers. . . . I should not learn that fact any better if I stayed a week. . . . This orange I have sucked dry" (Davis, "Yares," 252). Early in the story, Davis establishes Miss Cook's crass materialism as she exults over how cheaply she can get food from the poor people who live in the mountains: "[H]er very portemonnaie gave a click of *delight* in her pocket. 'I heard that these people were miserably poor!' she muttered *rapturously*. 'Don't look so shocked. If you earned your bread by your brains, as I do, you'd want as much bread for a penny as possible'" (244, emphasis added). Miss Cook is so thoroughly a tourist that, even in exaggeration, the longest she can imagine staying in the mountains is one week. Here, the literature of the tourist liberates the subject through her capitalistic consumption of a people and a place for individual profit with a story published and sold.

Although Miss Cook has clearly benefited from women activists who have made it possible for her to be a career woman (and aside from the occasional empty gesture as when she helps the mountain residents barter as part of her research), Miss Cook feels no personal responsibility to help any of the women in "dirty calico" she meets (244); they are still, ultimately, objects to her. She makes jokes at their expense and turns profit from their portrayal. Even though she is emotionally moved by the natural scenes around her, she feels no responsibility to engage those places—a photograph will do just as well. The photograph will remain even if the aesthetic views of the place and the culture of its people are destroyed. Miss Cook's writings will remain even if the people and the scenic beauty of the places do not. Yet the experience of Asheville has been positive for Miss Cook; she finds the respite she sought, she profits from it, and she will continue to consume such people and places to create an independent and self-supporting subjectivity for herself.

The title character in Louise Baker's *Cis Martin* comes to the Tennessee mountains after three years at a "select school for young ladies." She enters the mountains planning to "gather together anecdotes and funny little sayings of the people who eat snuff and were Aunt Lavinia's abomination," thus

suggesting Cis's literary kinship with Miss Cook. Cis's family suffers financial problems (explaining their temporary residence in Appalachia); Cis
says, "I understood more and more plainly every day that the finances of
our family were very low, and so I determined to try to make some money."
Her solution is Miss Cook's: "I should begin my career as a writer for magazines and weekly papers."[26]

She has her mother's blessing to be a traveler alone—"the mountains
were perfectly safe"—but encounters some difficulty finding "true local col-
oring." When her silk umbrella gets scorched because she placed it too close
to a cooking fire, she wonders, "How had I ever come to imagine that I
could make [mountain people] interesting by putting them, and their habits, and their homes, and their dismal 'deadnin's' [a way of clearing land]
upon one side of note-sized paper, and sending it unrolled to an intelligent
being in the outer world?"[27] Baker soon abandons the story of Cis as a
writer in favor of more action—a wolf attack, comic adventures in a school,
and a community corn shucking and taffy pull. But Cis and Baker, and thus
the reader also, remain tourists, profiting from their consumption of sights
and people in Appalachia; the novel's plot ends with Cis's family regaining
wealth and returning in triumph to "civilization" in the Northeast. Miss
Cook, Cis, and Pool's Buncombe County tourists find that the real profits
from tourism come in the form of their increased independence and
achievement. They are, of course, all white, middle-class, and from the population centers of the Northeast, and they all leave Appalachia behind.

Transformed Tourists

Mrs. Denby in "The Yares of the Black Mountains" and other characters
within the literature of the female tourist to Appalachia, in contrast, find
themselves more profoundly transformed by their time in the place; some
part of Appalachia stays with them, even if only as the long-ago catalyst of
their new way of being in the world. Like Miss Cook, Mrs. Denby is also
coming to a "strange country and strange people," but she is willing to live
in the mountains while her son recovers. Mrs. Denby feels that her journey
"is just as though I were coming among old friends." After staying for a day
in Asheville with Miss Cook, Mrs. Denby embarks on a journey deeper into
the mountains to "take Charley [her son] among the balsams" (Davis,
"Yares," 249–53). Jean Pfaelzer suggests that Mrs. Denby's journey on a cart
through the wilderness to the home of the Yare family functions as "a female
quest for wholeness and community in a rural world" that helps Mrs. Denby

to throw off erroneous interpretations of the relationship between humans and nature. The journey provides a change in her perception "from nature as luminous and sublime to companionable and familiar," in other words, from artistic (the sublime being an artistic term in currency at the same time as the picturesque) to relational, from romantic "Other" to something closer to "another."[28]

Mrs. Denby settles for an extended visit with the Yares, a mountain family with "a truthful directness of thought and speech which grew out of the great calm Nature about them as did the trees and the flowing waters" (Davis, "Yares," 259). As one of the Yare women explains, "The Yares hev lived on the Old Black for four generations, Mistress Denby. It wouldn't do to kerry us down into towns. It must be powerful lonesome in them flat countries with nothing but people about you. The mountings is always company you see" (267). Although reminiscent of Tanis's sang-digger beliefs, the Yares are given a dignity and agency never afforded the sang-diggers. They—almost—become subjects in their own story. The story ends with Mrs. Denby still in the mountains, still a visitor, but with a focus on her healthy son, healthy self, her new eyes, her acquired peacefulness. The Yares drop away as the reader is left to wonder what will happen to the young widow. In the end, if one must live in the mountains in order to know the mountains (and have the mountains know you), then what the reader knows from reading Davis's story (being an armchair adventurer) is suspect. The literature of the tourist brings closeness but keeps otherness in subjects and objects in literature by women about Appalachia.

Emily Wooten, in another of Davis's *Silhouettes of American Life* stories, "A Wayside Episode," also is transformed by her tourist experience. In the beginning Emily is described as "cow-like" and describes her life so far as like "gold-fishes and minnows," evocative choices since cows and these particular fish are herded, confined, caged creatures just as women in the upper-class ideology of separate spheres are equally confined. In contrast, once she is in the mountains, Emily dreams that she "was a squirrel, or fox, or wolf,—some wild creature that could go up that path into the woods and stay there. I should like to know what the life of an animal has in it." Two pages later, Emily elaborates on what it is about these animals' lives that she envies. These are thoughts she keeps to herself; in fact, "Usually she held [her thoughts] in check, even without her own knowledge." But now, looking out into the woods, she thinks: "For one day to be alone, to climb the mountains, plunge into the rivers, to be man, beast, anything that was free to gratify its own instincts and passions, good or bad!" She describes her longings as wanting "to run wild like a stag or a satyr"[29]—thoughts of being as free as the men around her, thoughts that happen only as she is traveling in Appalachia.

A "man of the woods" appears whom she finds much more exciting and challenging than her preening husband or the upper-class boys with tiresome crushes on her. This woodsman awakens confusing, explicitly sexual desires in Emily when he asks, "Don't I remember society? . . . Don't clever women tire of their stupid husbands and grope about for congenial souls?" The comment makes Emily feel "as if the man had come close to her and put his hands upon her." Without him actually touching her, Emily begins to be aware of her own body and its integral role in her life. The encounter prompts her to go "down through the camp to a great rock by the creek and hid[e] behind it." First, the mysterious man and then nature itself serve as catalysts for Emily's transformation.[30]

"A Wayside Episode" becomes the story of one female tourist's transformation in Appalachia: "Now she was alone. Nobody could drag out her naked soul in public here." Emily stays by herself for most of the night. She wrestles with the thought that perhaps she is "tired of her husband and groping about for a stronger man to love." Her aloneness cannot occur outside of her body, and it is, in fact, with thoughts of her female, embodied desires that she struggles. She considers "[t]his horrible emptiness of life" and wonders if the emptiness is caused by "the want of a real support, of a live love?" She emerges transformed, ready to consider the "drama of love with some other man," but, in fact, to start her life anew with the transformed husband waiting for her (while she is at the rock, he discovers that all their money has been lost through bad investments; a discovery that strengthens his mettle). Emily Wooten finds, in the end, a transformation that brings peace and the ability to be in wilderness (at the end of the story it is the American West, not Appalachia) with dignity.[31]

In some ways, Davis writes the smartest literature of Appalachia in this early period. Since she is not part of the North Carolina community of Asheville and Black Mountain, she does not presume to understand it best—she leaves that to the Yare family and does not speak for what she does not know. In "A Wayside Episode," she lets the focus move to Emily and her body; Davis does not pretend Emily's transformation is available to everyone or everything. Like many other modern readers of Davis, I find her writing challenging and exciting; the brief discussions of her short fiction I have provided here only scratch the surface of the stories. Yet Davis's Appalachian stories are tenuous foundations on which to support feminism or other analyses of social or environmental justice issues. Her tourists rarely notice or speak for the well-being of people or places in Appalachia; they pass through and on, leaving Appalachia as soon as it has been useful and used.

All the literature of the tourist by women about Appalachia thus protectively supports and surrounds the middle- and upper-class (or striving to be) reader. It allows for armchair adventures and models independence and transformation for women travelers. While the literature of the tourist can provide hints of the wisdom or guidance human or nonhuman Appalachian characters embody, the subjects of the stories eventually and inevitably eclipse local mountain residents and places. Space between subject and object may erode slightly, but characters are still held as subjects or objects, depending on circumstance of gender, nature, class, and race. The focus on individual bodies also means that larger social or environmental justice issues never appear in the literature of the tourist.

In the literature of the voyeur and tourist, whether a woman is closer to or further from "nature," including plants, animals, and even dirt, helps determine her race, class, and potential to live as a successful, ideal, or "true" woman. The freedom a woman feels in her body, often transformed by her experiences of Appalachian nature, helps determine her view of herself and of nature around her. Most of these stories suggest that social arrangements in Appalachia and elsewhere in America are inherently "natural" and do not need to be changed. Indeed, sometimes Appalachia can be empowering to individual characters. During her trip to the mountains, Emily Wooten finds a new way to be in her body that transcends the confines of upper-class women's social spheres. Miss Cook, Mrs. Denby, and Cis Martin find economic and psychological freedom in Appalachia.

More often, however, in the literature of the voyeur and tourist, the knots of woman and nature are mutually exploitative and support essentialist status quo structures of power. Miss Cook, Pool's Buncombe County tourists, and Cis Martin apparently do not turn beyond their own concerns to extend the hard-won freedoms to many others. Emily Wooten's and Mrs. Denby's freedom seems to be only for them, or at least only for women of similar social and economic classes. Troubetzkoy's *Tanis, the Sang-Digger* creates an inviolable distance between the reader and Alice Gilman, on the one hand, and Tanis and the sang-diggers, on the other; despite slight criticisms of mainstream women's fashion, the dying Tanis at the end of the novel leaves little possibility for either the Tanises or the Alices of the world.

The female bodies, middle-class, white nonlocal subjects and invariably poor, ill-educated, and (not quite) white Appalachian objects support the sometimes subtle, sometimes overt project of the monthly magazines and the publications emerging from them to make white people feel superior inside the idea of the "American." Appalachia and Appalachians were the exceptions to prove the rule: "What made Appalachia interesting after 1890 were the implications which the fact of its existence held for an understanding of America itself," according to Shapiro.[32] Perhaps one reason why environmentalism and feminism did not appear together in Appalachia as they did in other parts of the country is that middle-class (or aspiring middle-class), white, women writers felt (or created) a great deal of freedom for certain women's bodies in Appalachia as they imagined it already to be. Perhaps the ways middle-class, white women in Appalachia created authority and legitimation for themselves in their texts made them too complicit in environmental and social injustices for any other consciousness to be written into being.

In any case, Appalachian objects and American subjects remain opposites of each other in the literatures of the voyeur and the tourist. Both literatures turn inward on themselves to preclude the possibility of ecological feminism's emergence at the time. In fact, intersections of feminist and environmentalist concerns will only appear in writers who erode the divisions between subject and object and take seriously the deep influence of humans and nonhumans on their characters and their own writing. But first, a final form of literature by women about Appalachia must be unearthed before ecological feminism's roots become visible. The next chapter turns to the writers who entered the mountains as women influenced by Progressive and feminist ideas of activism for the mountain inhabitants; they create the literature of the social crusader in Appalachia.

CHAPTER THREE

Literature of the Social Crusaders

Letters to "Civilization"

And here they be, doing not only for the
young, but for every age. . . all hands is
a-larning civility.

—Lucy Furman, *The Quare Women:*
A Story of the Kentucky Mountains

THE SOCIAL crusader left fashion behind. She slept in tents instead of a "proper" bedroom for months on end; she learned to forgo the sidesaddle and ride astride (and once she changed, she never wanted to go back). One cold morning, she figured out how to assemble the wood stove that would be her sole source of warmth for the season. She nursed the sick and cooked what she believed was healthier food for the poor. She taught classes under trees, in churches, under tents. She braved fleas; embarked on all-day hikes; and endured gossip, loneliness, and moonshiners with guns (whom she found both frightening and fascinating). She also spent time identifying new plants, drawing the wildflowers around her, taking photographs, and adventuring on horseback—occasionally even by herself. She saw fantastic views that no one in her social circle could imagine without her help. Although she sometimes had to balance her writing desk on her knees or write by candlelight outdoors, she wrote and wrote—letters asking tactfully for money to continue her crusade; novels that could be sold to raise funds; exposés of the conditions she encountered; profiles of the women who inspired her; and public diaries because she sensed her work was important.

In archives across the United States today, the writings of social crusaders to Appalachia wait. Libraries hold their published stories, novels, and poetry. More so than the literature of the tourist and the voyeur, this body of literature is truly interdisciplinary, in that the writing women who were social crusaders wrote in and mixed together whatever genres seemed most useful to them for the story they needed to tell; accordingly, they produced letters, diaries, postcards, scrapbooks, research reports, and photographs. Their photographs are carefully composed; their photo scrapbooks are edited and revised. By defining "texts" broadly, all the documents they produced can be read as a cohesive body of literature. Reading the interdisciplinary texts of the social crusaders with the literature of the voyeur and the tourist provides a deeper sense of both women's activism and their sense of adventure as writing women.

As did the literature of the tourist and voyeur, the literature of the social crusader overlaps with the previous two categories. None of the terms is meant to be exclusive. Yet, unlike the literature of the voyeur and the tourist, the subjects in the literature of the social crusader—whether photographer, letter's author, or spunky heroine modeled on the author-activist—intend to get involved in the communities of Appalachia. They try to erase the distances between subject and object. As discussed in chapter 1, they were influenced by, supported by, or trained in the Progressive ideals and organizations that emerged from midcentury women's rights movements and were becoming early-twentieth-century feminism. They or their friends were environmental club women, political women, modern women, or college women; all were writing women.

More than the voyeurs or tourists, the social crusaders linger in their writing over Appalachia's trees, mountains, rivers, and gorges. Rather than serving as mere set pieces, Appalachia's environment and a concern for it enter more significantly into the literature of the social crusader. The tangles of environmentalism, literature, and feminism in Appalachia become more complicated here. However, the social crusaders are ultimately so crippled by essentialist views of both women and nature that their literature, instead of being revolutionary for the people and places they have come to change, ends up supporting a mainstream status quo in Appalachia and the nation. Ultimately, the literature of the social crusader never challenges the environmental and social justice issues facing Appalachia. That task will be left to writers such as Emma Bell Miles, Grace MacGowan Cooke, Mary Noailles Murfree, and Effie Waller Smith, most of whom studied carefully the literature of the social crusader.

The Progressive era's fervor for social uplift, combined with its extended roles for young women, translated into an influx of women reformers into Appalachia. For this reason, this chapter contains a lot of names. Although some of the women will be familiar to Appalachian scholars, many will not. It might have been clearer and certainly would have been simpler to choose one or two women on whom to focus. Yet the risk of oversimplifying, of tokenizing, was too great. The multiple voices of the women provide context for each other. I do not want to suggest that a single person completely dominated Appalachian work at the time, but I do believe shared philosophical outlooks emerge in the writing of diverse women doing "mountain work" in Appalachia at the turn of the last century.[1]

The twelve women discussed here defined activism differently—some, such as Katherine Pettit, May Stone, and Lucy Furman, were teachers modifying Jane Addams's settlement house model. One, Olive Dame Campbell, was a researcher gathering data (stories, sociological numbers, photographs) for presentation to national groups and organizing other activists into networks; only later in life did she found her own community school in the mountains. Some women were teaching at schools supported by religious organizations, such as Daisy Gertrude Dame and Frances Louisa Goodrich. Some, like Eleanor Marsh Frost, Bertha Daisy Nickum, Mary R. Martin, and Sarah Barnwell Elliott, were affiliated with the region's colleges or (later) public high schools. Finally, some were more loosely associated with benevolent work in the mountains—Meta Townsend and Margaret W. Morley, for instance.

At the time of their writing, they stood at various points in their careers—ranging from being in college learning to be a teacher or recovering from an illness and considering taking up "mountain work," to being committed to the work but looking for a focus, to being fully committed to and engaged in directing ambitious activist projects. They are overwhelmingly well educated and from middle-class backgrounds (with both the means to be educated and the means to get to the mountains), but they were not generally independently wealthy. Almost all came from northern families; all were of European descent. Although certainly nonwhite female teachers and nurses were active in Appalachia at the time, the outlook I am calling social crusading is very white, built ultimately on privilege and complicity. White social crusaders to Appalachia deeply influenced activism, feminism, and literature for diverse women across the region. Some lived the rest of their lives in the mountains, but some left after one or two years of "mountain work." All of them comment on their position as (at least initially) single or working women; they all draw attention to the women they meet in the region.

I admire the dedication of many of these women. I sincerely enjoyed finding them in archives, having the visceral pleasure of touching the postcard they sat by a waterfall to paint, and thumbing through the road-stained journals that accompanied them on their adventures. Because their letters have been mostly forgotten for so long, and because I have now spent so much time with them, criticizing them can feel like being a bad friend. Yet, the value-laden, oppressive, hierarchical assumptions they made, specifically those concerning nature and gender, were frequently short-sighted, often self-serving, and helped to set up the mountain communities for the social and environmental challenges of today. Understanding those assumptions—making them visible—helps me, first, to understand what was truly different about the models proposed by Miles, Cooke, Murfree, and Smith, and, second, to participate in developing solutions for my own era.

Other studies have been written and the debates in homes, newspapers, and families are long-standing about whether activists to the mountains were an overall benefit or harm to the people of the mountains. In these debates, sometimes the focus is on economics, sometimes on the intellectual legacy, and sometimes on cultural colonialism; I do not intend to recover that ground. Here, the focus is on what these women wrote as women, how they say what they say, what they say and what they do not say—about the human and nonhuman world around them. More explicitly than in the previous chapter, the question becomes not just what happens to people like Tanis when she is compared with snakes and groundhogs but also what happens to the snakes and groundhogs. Putting the ecological community at the center of analysis extends the previous chapter's exploration of subject-object relations and gives added resonance to the activists' repeated phrase, "mountain work."

Social crusaders share a basic belief in what people at the time called "mountain work"—that is, that the mountains and the people living in the mountains needed to be worked on, that women could be effective workers in the crusade, and that social values from elsewhere could improve society in Appalachia. As Margaret Morley, the naturalist who also commented on mountain work around her, wrote in 1913: "Every one who has come from the outside world to live in the mountains, and who has employed or taught, or come in any kind of real contact with the native people, has had a share in their advancement." Those who participated in this movement carried flags of domesticity, women's rights, and an unshakable belief that "[n]othing can stay the march of progress that has now begun"; their anthem touted nationhood, womanhood, and enlightened education. In short, they were ready to sacrifice much to bring a social crusade to Appalachia.[2]

Many believed with Morley that the mountains needed to "continue to develop in the direction of sanitation, safety, and ever-increasing beauty."[3] Morley may be unique in her emphasis on developing the beauty of the mountains; yet, she shares with female social crusaders to Appalachia the desire to explore how the beauty of Appalachia could be both personally freeing and politically useful in their writings. They use techniques from nature study to categorize the Appalachian world around them, including its people. And they are overwhelmed by the dirt, dust, and fleas they find or create in their new mountain efforts. The writers use Appalachia's beauty, insights from nature study, and the mountains' supposed dirtiness to justify their own presence in the mountains, judge the success of the work they are doing, and ultimately keep themselves separate from and superior to the people and places they are experiencing.

A World of Green Loneliness and Wild Beauty

After they had pulled through the deep mudholes in the town, they turned into a creek-bed, and plunged at once into a world of green loneliness and wild beauty. All day long they either "followed creeks," or wound around the sides of steep mountains, with sheer drop-offs below the narrow trail. . . . Often it seemed that they must go over the edge, or that the mules could not climb the steps of rock up which they had to pull the heavy wagon; but always the danger was safely passed. Isabel wished, however, that she had four hands instead of two, to hold on with.[4]

Traveling to their new schools or camps in Appalachia involved railroads, carriages or wagons, horseback rides, and hikes. As historian David E. Whisnant argues, "Among women drawn to settlement work, there also appears to have been something of a pattern of seeking out new 'needy' areas—both urban and rural—where settlements could be started." Defining "needy" in such an adventurous way led to settlement schools being located in some of the more remote areas of Appalachia. In Lucy Furman's _The Quare Women: A Story of the Kentucky Mountains,_ a fictionalized account of the early years of the Hindman Settlement School at which Furman later taught, it is a young teacher on her way to her first school who comments on plunging "into a world of green loneliness and wild beauty"; and it certainly must have felt this way for many.[5]

History also suggests that the social crusaders' destinations were not always as remote as they sound in their letters, diaries, journals, and novels. This is the same era that bride Gladys Coleman from Asheville, North Carolina, was on the cover of the *Ladies Home Journal,* as the height of fashion that season. It is also the same land that Rebecca Harding Davis's Miss Cook rejoiced over being able to reach in just a day by rail. Appalachia's social crusaders may not have been above exaggerating their adventures in letters home or fictional accounts. For instance, even though Hindman was a small town of 400 people and Hazard, 600, they were nevertheless towns. Yet when Pettit and Stone arrive, they go out of their way to exaggerate their camps' isolation by refusing to summer in the buildings the community offers. Later in the summer, their journals reveal them teaching outside—in front of public churches and school buildings—and the texts consistently emphasize the outdoors and gloss over the buildings, furthering the impression that they are women alone in the wild.[6]

As do other social crusaders, Stone and Pettit enjoy describing in detail the extent to which they are "roughing it" in the Kentucky wilderness and the outdoor adventures they successfully survive as a result. The camp format they initiate for the settlements, chosen in part to emphasize the temporary nature of their efforts (at first) and to avoid threatening existing teachers, doctors, and other social welfare agents, nevertheless contributes to the women-in-the-wilderness theme of their journals. They choose to live and teach in tents they pitch. The first tent community is on a mountainside; the next summer they pitch tents at the joining of two rivers—both sites of green loneliness, if only one ignores the nearby town. Such social crusaders were deeply invested in describing the mountains, gorges, rivers, and rocks around them, to the pleasure of their readers.

All parties involved were disdainful of the resort tourist of leisure or the armchair voyeur. In fact, many of the era's mountain people are also leery of tourists and question all visitors' motives; Pettit reports one woman who asks: "Wimmen I jist want to know, what air ye all in these hyar parts fer, hev ye any business, did ye jist come up to look around fer a spell and then go away and never come back?" Despite being recounted in dialect, the message is clear that simple tourism and short-term activism are neither trusted nor desired by the mountain residents. By telling the story, Pettit marks her own distrust of tourists and uncommitted activists. It is her way

of separating herself in her letters from others and allying with the questioner; because she can answer "no" to the mountain woman's question,
Pettit is therefore the most dedicated; hers is a true crusade.[7]

Personal Liberation through Hiking Appalachia's Wild Beauty

Despite the occasional exaggeration, Appalachia's wild beauty frequently
was sincerely personally liberating for women coming to Appalachia. The

Figure 2. Olive Dame Campbell on an overlook in Appalachia.
The photograph is located in the John Charles and Olive Dame
Campbell Papers #3800, Southern Historical Collection, Wilson
Library, University of North Carolina at Chapel Hill.

sense of wonder at the scenery around them is palpable in the writing of the social crusaders. More importantly, the women marvel at their own physical, emotional, and even spiritual achievements in accessing those scenes. As a reader, I find myself cheering Katherine Pettit up a washed-out path, holding my breath as Mary Martin slides across a log over a flood-swollen river, and admiring Margaret Morley's courage at joining mountain climbs. Nevertheless, the political uses to which those scenes are put by the social crusaders as authors also cannot be denied. What can seem like simple description serves to convince readers, some of whom had the power to fund whole schools or research trips and some of whom were simply worried family members, that the authors or main characters are physically capable, safe, ambitious, observant, and not given to wasting time or money. The message frequently comes at the expense of the people who and places that are "conquered," "subdued," or "won."

One such observer of her own increasing capabilities was Mary Martin, who came to the mountains of North Carolina in 1898. She was twenty-eight years old and needed to recover from the stresses of college and caring for invalid parents. She visited and loved the religious settlement that was to become Montreat, North Carolina; within a year she took up permanent residence there until her death. Soon after moving to the region, Martin felt healthy enough to begin teaching; over the course of her career, she taught at Montreat High School, Wildwood, and the Montreat Normal School. Her letters of 1898 and 1899 to her mother and sister in Philadelphia give us insight into a woman who came to the region and was affected enough by it to become an activist. Given that early Montreat settlers, as Martin describes them, were predominantly women, her letters provide a window into a women's community at the turn of the twentieth century.[8]

The wilderness trips Martin takes on her first visit to Montreat are the subject of many of her letters home. At first she is quite worried about her physical capabilities, writing: "On Friday morning we climbed part way up one of the mountains & got a most beautiful view—even taking in Mr. [sic] Pisgah & the Rat which are way beyond Asheville. Climbing does not agree with my shoulder, so hereafter I am to go on horesback" [sic]. On another day, she describes how "six of us went for a walk in the beautiful woods. We just strolled along at our own sweet will, and spent a great deal of time sitting on mossy logs, or on great rocks out in the stream. How I did want to fall into the water! It was so warm and the water looked so cool, but I managed to refrain."[9] Although she assumes in these early descriptions that "strolls" are more appropriate, a hint of the adventures to come hides in her "desire." Soon, she will metaphorically jump into Appalachian nature as she becomes an active subject in her story.

Once she is comfortable strolling along the valley, Martin becomes more daring (and she never mentions her hurt shoulder again), as she describes a harrowing trip up Brushy Knob and then down a route that included a spur "just like a cone of ice cream turned out on the edge of the mountain, & the trail goes directly over the point." She admits, "If any one had told me of all these places and that I would be able to take the trip, I shouldn't have believed him." The emphasis Martin places on these outdoor adventures in her letters suggests that the trips and her growing belief in the capabilities of her own body help her decide to get two lots in Montreat, assemble her own wood stove and "build my shanty on the winter side, and then if it is too warm there in the summer, put a tent on Mother's lot and so get a summer's outing." "What is more, I hope to go again some day, and shall probably take the all-day trip to great old Gray Beard some time in the future. I've lost my heart to these beautiful mountains,"[10] she tells her mother. The spiritual growth of falling in love with the place and the physical growth of healing her body and pushing its capabilities allow Martin to embrace her emotional thrills. Despite feeling geographically isolated, Martin finds personal mobility and freedom, and it broadens and deepens her sense of self.

Naturalist Margaret Morley describes a similar sense of personal freedom, acquired, in her case, through adventurous hikes. She speaks directly to how short hikes can lead to longer hikes, which can result in personal liberation for women new to Appalachia. She writes: "And so you return to Blowing Rock after days of wandering, only to rest awhile and start again, gaining endurance with every trip until the ten miles' walk that cost you a little weariness becomes the twenty miles' walk that costs you none. You cannot tire of the road, for every mile brings new sights, new sounds, new fragrances, new friends, new flowers." Twenty miles in a day is a respectable distance for hikers today; when done in skirts, without hiking shoes, and frequently unaccompanied, it is quite an accomplishment. For many social crusaders, being able to hike twenty miles in a day or up a challenging grade stands in for being able to live on one's own, run a settlement house, or be an expert on an area of the country. Morley took to heart not only the physical freedoms of which she speaks but emotional and mental ones as well. Even as she describes her solo adventures in *The Carolina Mountains,* she also wrote books explaining science to children, and even created publications on sexual education for young boys and girls.[11]

"Everyone Here Rides Straddle": Social Crusaders' Personal Mobility

For many of the social crusaders, life so far had been very urban; they had little or no experience with homesteading or with the animals upon which rural life depended. In their writings they transition from iron horse to actual horse or from bicycle to mule. The artificiality of the technological world gives way to the natural world's equivalent animals, and the city-bred women frequently enjoy the process. For her first experiences with horses, Mary Martin's frame of reference is her bicycle back home. She says, "I took my first horseback ride on Tuesday afternoon. . . . I had expected to feel very high up and correspondingly uncomfortable, but I found to my surprise I hadn't any worse sensations than when on my wheel." She also finds: "It is such fun to roam around this country on horseback," and "I am so delighted to find that I haven't the slightest fear on horseback, even in the steepest places. It is a very necessary state of affairs if you are going to get any pleasure out of riding in this country." Martin moves quickly from comparing the experience with previous ones, to enjoying riding on its own, to developing her skill and daring.[12]

Figure 3. "The Greenhorn Brigade," according to the original caption. Notice that (at least) the two women on the outside are riding astride. The photograph is located in the John Charles and Olive Dame Campbell Papers #3800, Southern Historical Collection, Wilson Library, University of North Carolina at Chapel Hill.

New social crusaders to the mountains also move from being ones who must be carried to ones who ride. The transition from sidesaddle to cross-saddle riding expresses the subjects' increasing agency and freedom. Scholar Lila Marz Harper points out: "The sidesaddle seemed almost to require that a woman be accompanied by men, since mounting the sidesaddle was not something a woman could do alone. She needed a platform and at least one man to lift her into the saddle, while another held the horse's head."[13] In addition, for safety, sidesaddles benefited from specially trained or exceedingly docile horses, because the rider had less security and control on the horse. Thus, the transition to cross-saddle riding was literally the move from dependence to independence.

Martin's letters trace her path to independence. A few months after arriving in Appalachia, she writes: "Every woman down here rides straddle. Nothing one does or wears makes any difference." And a few months after that she is arguing: "I find straddle riding so much safer and more comfortable than a side-saddle. In fact, my ideas are becoming so degenerate that I now consider it the more elegant and ladylike way to ride." Finally, Martin relates an anecdote that illustrates how far she has traveled philosophically from her initial sidesaddle horseback ride: "One day when I wanted to ride horseback, I wore my divided skirt and walked down to get a horse from one of the natives. As I rode off I heard a man say, 'Jim, why didn't ya help the lady git on her horse' and Jim replied, 'If she's man enough to wear them clothes, she's man enough to git on her *own* horse,'"[14] which, apparently, she is, since Martin does not comment further on this anecdote. The process of coming into her own as an independent woman who was confident enough in her personal freedom and agency to help others begins, for Martin, on these hikes and rides around Appalachia.

Martin is not an exception, however. After a summer of outdoor adventures, Daisy Gertrude Dame writes home to Massachusetts: "I would love to be in a Utah Canyon for here it is not high and is quite warm."[15] Just as Martin never looks back once she begins riding horses and hiking, Dame feels ready to trade what she sees as safe Appalachia for the Wild West. The Appalachian mountains are no longer enough for her; she is ready for the Rockies. As she adjusts to an active, outdoor life, Dame believes herself ready to conquer any physical challenge. She sets her standard for adventure higher and is ready for more exploration.

A principal at Oneida Baptist Institute in Kentucky from 1909 to 1910 and the sister of Olive Dame Campbell, Dame writes frequent letters to her family in Massachusetts; the letters are refreshingly informal (for instance, men are often "chumps" and fun times are "killing"), and they are made enjoyable by her enthusiasm ("Dear Family . . . I am *busting* with excitement!"). Like Martin's, the letters are marked by her increasing confidence and freedom. In the course of a summer, Dame discovers the freedom of the regular saddle and writes home about it. A photograph early in her album labeled "The Greenhorn Brigade" with four women, some riding sidesaddle, and all new to horses, gives way later to photographs of women in divided skirts, riding proudly on lively horses. In addition to day trips, Dame takes "a two days" horseback journey with Campbell, Campbell's husband, and a Dr. Farrand.[16]

Dame, who is offhand about many of her adventures, writes about another trip: "We have had some delicious baths in the warm waters of Red Bird, some boat rides in the canoe and in some flat bottom riverboats, and the rivers are very beautiful." Along with the riding, boating, and swimming, she and her friends fish regularly (her photograph album and Campbell's contain several copies of a picture of a woman holding a quite respectable thirty-eight-pound catfish), and they come to enjoy long hikes, such as the one in which "[w]e climbed up the highest and steepest hill, but it was densely wooded, and the shade was very grateful, even if we did mud about a good deal."[17] Dame only stays at Kentucky's Oneida Baptist Institute for one year, but her sense of freedom allowed her to fit in many such adventures between her teaching and management responsibilities.

Some women were more dedicated to creating an image of themselves as courageous, serious reformers in their writing. Dame gets in trouble for smoking on the front porch at her school, but her sister, Olive, is a little older and much more serious. Although Campbell describes some pleasure trips such as a hike up Pinnacle Mountain to see the cornerstone of Tennessee, North Carolina, and Virginia, she is generally reticent about the 1,500-mile trip to more than seventy schools in Appalachia that she took with her husband. Most of her journal entries begin with a notation of travel, such as "to Hindman," but she gives readers only glimpses of the personal triumphs involved. A typical example is February 13 through February 27, 1909, during which time they crossed the Tennessee–North Carolina line five different times and forded the Nolichucky River at least once.[18] Campbell frequently expresses herself more fully in the photograph albums she constructed, which reflect experiences similar to those of her sister Dame and to those of Martin. She begins traveling riding double with her husband but soon moves to her own horse by riding sidesaddle. Not long after, Campbell adopts the independent cross-saddle and never looks back while in Appalachia.[19] Although accompanied by her husband, Campbell demonstrates her intellectual independence in her journals; after his early death, Olive Dame Campbell's continued work in the region suggests just how strongly she believed in her own abilities and freedoms. Her wilderness adventures in Appalachia are part of what shaped that belief.

"Not Half Way to the Sunday School": Keeping Adventures' Goals in Mind

Combining the approaches of women like Martin and Dame with the approach of Campbell and Morley, Stone and Pettit observe nature and enjoy its wild beauty without allowing readers to lose sight of their ultimate goals of reaching destinations. Stone and Pettit's journals, created in large part as public documents for the women of the benevolent organizations both downstate in Kentucky and in the nation who were fund-raising to support their summers, suggest that they had a self-conscious desire not to be seen as wasting time. Nature and wilderness were worthy of note and titillating to their readers; but, at least for these women, they were not means in and of themselves.

Figure 4. Daisy Gertrude Dame and her kindergarten class at school in Oneida, Kentucky. The photograph is located in the John Charles and Olive Dame Campbell Papers #3800, Southern Historical Collection, Wilson Library, University of North Carolina at Chapel Hill.

Stone and Pettit dwell in their writing on the paths they must take to the Sunday schools and day schools they were teaching. At one point, they begin with a treacherous crossing over water "so swift it made us dizzy and we had to slide over the rail [that formed the only "bridge"] side wise to keep it from turning with us." The women next must walk around a cliff. Pettit writes: "The recent rains have washed down the path in some places and it was very slippery all along but we clambered up, stumbling over rocks and fallen trees. The path zigzags up to a huge over-hanging cliff, over which the water was dripping. The path here is very narrow and in one place we had to slide down about three feet to get a footing." Pettit then steps away from the narrative of action to reflect: "When we had time to look away from our feet, we had a beautiful view of the winding creek." She notes the plants and geological features of the land before she jumps back into her narrative: "There were trailing vines and ferns growing in the crevices of the rocks, towering up on one side and on the other the hill covered with laurel and rhododendron." Finally, she says, "After climbing over more rocks and trees, we reached the creek where we sank to our ankles in soft mud and climbed a fence to escape deeper mud."[20] With Stone and Pettit, the language of wilderness adventures becomes that of conquering, subduing, and winning. The deep mud is no match for these crusaders.

Their "wilderness adventure" lands them merely at the home of their guide. After only a moment's pause in her narrative (and no paragraph break), Pettit announces: "But we were not half way to the Sunday School yet."[21] Such description makes for dynamic storytelling. But it also encodes assumptions about differences between teachers like Stone and Pettit and residents of the area in which they were teaching. Local mountain people, in the literature of the social crusaders, do not complain about the location of their homes; they do not seem to consider traveling to and from them to be an adventure on this scale. Although certainly people living in the mountains at the turn of the last century longed for better roads or easier access from home to school, one generally adapts to the conditions in which one finds oneself. Thus, what is wilderness for Stone and Pettit is, for the men, women, and children who live there, merely home.

Beyond emphasizing personal mobility and freedom, descriptions of wild beauty in Appalachia enforce hierarchies between the activist-authors and the mountain people and places that are objects in the texts. Alison Byerly argues that the picturesque aesthetic, upon which many of these descriptions draw, was "socioeconomically elite, because while artistic talent and original judgment were not required to participate in the picturesque, money was." In the mountains, it would be more accurate to emphasize the "socio" as well as the "economic" and include education and social class, but in any case, the activist women were privileged to have it and most of the mountain residents did not (at least according to the writings of the social crusaders). When Stone and Pettit return for a second summer of teaching, they comment, "Even our favorite view of the valley . . . was changed by the ugly new farmhouses that were dotted here and there."[22] As creators of wild beauty, Stone and Pettit will not admit to their own role in encouraging ugly new farmhouses or new cities. They do not seem to notice the tension in this comment between the former, picturesque cabins halfway to Sunday school and the new homes of people who are doing what the activist women have been educating them to do—using new building supplies, getting out of old cabins and into new houses, and embracing progress in all its forms.

Erasures and Absent Voices: Creating Green Loneliness

Martin takes a different approach as she creates a picturesque wilderness in her letters by simply erasing the people who live there. She writes: "I wish I could tell you more about the mountain people, but we see almost nothing of them."[23] This allows her to describe her singular adventures without the messiness of interactions with unfamiliar people. However, the assertion is undermined by all the points in her text in which she does interact with "the mountain people"—as her washerwomen, mailboys, men from whom she rents horses, firewood suppliers, and errand runners. They become so thoroughly objects that her increasing agency and subjectivity allows her to entirely look over them.

By erasing other mountain residents so completely, Martin exaggerates a choice made by many writers in the literature of the social crusader. In patriarchal systems of turn-of-the-century mainstream America, in which women were disenfranchised, paid less, and assumed to need male protection, the presence of powerful men could threaten the social crusaders' increased mobility and freedom—whether as sexual predators toward women riding alone, enforcers by social persuasion or political influence of traditional familial or societal arrangements, or simply rival leaders in mountain or Progressive work. To create a world of green loneliness and wild beauty, male power and influence, in particular, had to be minimized in these texts.

Unlike Martin, Stone and Pettit walk a fine line in their early journals as they both use male influence to justify their work and minimize the effect of individual men in the community to play up the sense of themselves as women adventuring in the wilderness. They do the latter by employing discourses of other hierarchies present in the United States to create their own social hierarchy in which the social crusaders remain on top. Thus, men appear but are disabled, elderly, very young, or feminine in the journals. As healthy, active, mature, adult women who are not disabled, old, or immature, Stone and Pettit follow the first three hierarchies without modification. But it is more puzzling that they would choose to feminize mountain boys who are their guides and helpers, in order to assure their own place at the top of a social hierarchy—for they themselves are also feminized by their writing and societies.

One of the most vivid anecdotes they tell involves their forcing a boy to wear a dress so that a mountain cow (who heretofore has only had women milkers) will let him come close. He seems humiliated by having to do this "women's work" in women's clothing, and, in fact, even though they say that "[i]n a short while he could milk alone," they admit "he never was a success"[24] and imply that a female maid takes the job back. This is not to suggest that an animal used to being approached by a certain kind of human—one wearing a dress, for instance—might not complain when approached by a different kind of human. Further, Stone and Pettit suggest that their intent is to give this particular work away from women whom they view as working too hard in the mountains and back to men. In western Kentucky, where they are from, milking is traditional male work; Stone and Pettit may simply be trying to shape mountain practices to be more familiar to them. However, the rhetorical effect of this episode is quite striking.

By the time Lucy Furman fictionalizes the scene in 1923 for *The Quare Women*, she has the boy *volunteer* to put on his sister's clothes, which suggests Furman was uncomfortable by the forced feminizing of this boy. In Stone and Pettit's journals, other boys worry they too will become metaphorically dressed in women's clothing, and thereby feminized, if they hang around the outsider women too much. The effect of the milking scene and others like it in the journals is to minimize the role that Jasper, their primary guide and assistant, plays. He is downplayed as a masculine protector during the women's adventures, which exaggerates the sense of women alone in the wilderness.[25]

Lucy Furman minimizes male influence in another novel, *Mothering on Perilous*, by suggesting the job of her main character, an activist woman teacher, is to watch out for some "big girls" and many "small boys." Martha

Berry follows the same practice in writing about her school for boys. Although not feminized to the point of cross-dressing, all these authors speak of asexual or feminized mountain boys in Appalachia's wild spaces but rarely include fully realized male characters who might challenge the work or presence of the social crusaders. The men who are erased by these strategies of enforcing a particular social hierarchy include the ones who grow up at Berry College, making it, as Campbell notes, "[h]ard to get good teachers. Many fall in love with the boys. Miss Berry has had same trouble." These practices also erase men like Yancey Lyttle, a university-trained lawyer living at home near Oneida, with whom Daisy Dame spends hours dancing, talking, taking day trips, and visiting his parents. When he confesses his love of her, she seems truly shocked that a man from the mountains would be so presumptuous. It is as if she cannot see him as a fully adult, sexualized male—because her social hierarchies (and those of activists like her) cannot allow such a thing.[26]

The cumulative effect of these strategies is for Appalachian spaces to become even more class and race inflected—in other words, the green loneliness and wild beauty is for middle-class white women at their leisure and for their adventures. The rhetorical strategies help explain how well-meaning activists, working very hard to improve life for mountain residents, can say with Eleanor Marsh Frost, "Personally I exulted in the poor roads that shut out automobiles, carriages, and dust and left this county an equestrian's paradise."[27] Social crusaders, under pressure from mainstream society because of their already radical choices, crafted in their literature an Appalachian nature that afforded them personal freedom, mobility, and social power. When they began to observe details of the wilderness around them, they continued to find ways to legitimate their own presence and their crusades.

Categorizing the Mountains

Hunting in these later days has been transferred almost entirely from the destruction of animals to the finer sport of finding and treasuring precious stones and rare or beautiful plants. The animals that once abounded here are practically gone. The crystals, hidden away in the recesses of the earth and affording more difficult hunting, are only beginning to be objects of interest. But the plants have long attracted interest . . . of every botanist who came hunting to this paradise of botanists.[28]

Reading archival sources and fictional portraits in the literature of the social crusaders reveals social crusaders to be accomplished amateur scientists, practicing botany and nature studies in Appalachia's "paradise of botanists." Women's participation in such sciences had flourished in the mid-nineteenth century. Influential texts like Susan Fenimore Cooper's 1850 *Rural Hours* and Harriet Beecher Stowe and Catherine Beecher's 1869 *American Woman's Home* popularized the idea that a knowledge and interest in the plants, animals, and geology of the world around them was appropriate and important for middle-class women. By the turn of the twentieth century, a generation of middle-class, educated women had been trained in such botany and study; from this pool of people, activists in Appalachia emerged.[29]

In one of her early letters home, Frances Louisa Goodrich writes: "I had a time botanizing on the way home, and filled the basket with ferns, and made a little sketch." Goodrich first came to the mountains of North Carolina in 1890 as a teacher for the Home Industrial Schools of the Presbyterian Missions. She taught for several years near Asheville; her letters reveal that, although Goodrich at first seems at loose ends in the mountains, she soon finds her calling in collecting and supporting women's local crafts. An artist herself, she recognized the artistic and economic value of women's work in the mountains. Goodrich eventually founded Allenstand Industries, a factory and distribution organization for the rugs, coverlets, baskets, and quilts. In the spring of 1891, however, her interest is in the world she observes around her: she writes that she has gone on a hike for some "pink moss," which is "a delicate pink on top and pearly gray below," the gathering of which involved her scooting across a log over a creek. Nature study gives Goodrich an introduction to the communities in which she finds herself.[30]

Goodrich is not alone in using her informal training in botany and nature study to categorize her new experiences in Appalachia. As Stone and Pettit pause to pitch their tents for the first "Camp Industrial" at Hindman, Kentucky (which would lead to the permanent Hindman Settlement School), they identify and report thirteen different kinds of trees and vines on their hillside: "sourwood, pawpaw, hickory, walnut, chestnut, persimmon, basket-oak, black oak, dogwood, redbud, wild grapes, sassafras, and sugar-maple." Early in her fact-finding journey, Olive Campbell records hurriedly in her diary that she is looking for someone "to refer me to people who can tell me of fruits vegetables etc. that onli [*sic*] grow in mts." After living in the mountains for only a month, Mary Martin writes her parents with a Christmas-gift wish list; even though it is December and she has yet to experience the wildflowers' blooming seasons, she requests they send

How to Know the Wild Flowers by Dana (Frances Theodora Smith Dana Parsons) "to ornament the house." Dana's book of nature study is the only book she requests, in company with essential items like handkerchiefs, cotton stockings, five yards of denim, and a table cloth.[31]

Eleanor Marsh Frost comments in her journals about her observation of animals rather than plants, but the philosophical outlook is the same. She notes: "Went out for an hour in the morning, watched birds, drank in freshness of everything, came into the house with greater peace than for long time." Scholar Vera Norwood argues that bird-watching was seen as an especially appropriate activity for women at the turn of the last century. Bird behavior was considered educational without being unsafe or improper; birds were "microcosms of human domesticity" to the late-nineteenth-century "bird ladies." Paraphrasing Emerson, Margaret Morley suggests in Appalachia people should "name the birds without a gun, love the wild rose and leave it on its stalk"; Frost would seem to agree.[32]

Teaching Nature's Categories

As they began teaching, many social crusaders transmitted their knowledge of nature studies to their mountain students. For instance, Olive Campbell relates how at one school, "The art teacher says she finds great appreciation of natural beauty, flowers, etc. among students as soon as their attention is called. Great desire to put it on practical basis." Frances Goodrich describes in *Mountain Homespun,* her interdisciplinary memoir that is part fiction, part scientific manual, and part autobiography, a scene reminiscent of her own moss and fern gathering: "Lois Rice had studied botany.... The smattering she had learned of classification came back to her now when she was in the real country, and she became keenly interested in the flowering plants and the trees and shrubs on Lonesome. Armed with her Gray's *Manual,* she spent many leisure moments in identifying the specimens gathered from the roadside." Goodrich then describes the specimens "brought to [Rice] by her pupils, who had grown interested in what they looked on as a new game of teacher's." The game for some was more unsettling than Goodrich could imagine.[33]

Writer Grace MacGowan Cooke strongly criticizes such school games, with a grown-up version of Goodrich's fictional students. Cooke's main character says in *The Power and the Glory,* "Miss Baird, that taught the school I went to over at Rainy Gap, had a herbarium, and put all kinds of pressed flowers in it. I gathered a great many for her, and she taught me to analyze them—like you were speaking of—but I never did love to do that." The character explains: "It seemed like naming over and calling out the ways of your friends, to pull the flower all to pieces and press it and paste it in a book and write down all its—its—ways and faults."[34] Cooke points to a violence inherent in botanizing, if one has a personal relationship with the specimen before it is collected. Despite such local criticisms, the practice of nature study in schools was a mainstream trend well established in the mountains, in part from the social crusaders' efforts.

In Meta Townsend's *In the Nantahalas* (much of which outlines the educational program of the Brevard School, a Methodist organization), the first thing Townsend's newly educated mountain heroine does to help "her people" is to engage a "nature-study teacher" who will teach "the young pupils some of the wonders of the nature-world." The wife of a Methodist preacher, Townsend was published by the Methodist Church. Thomas Ivey, in the preface to *In the Nantahalas,* asserts that Townsend has "demonstrated her ability to minister as a true wife and loving mother in a little parsonage home and at the same time to make the great outside world better by her thought-product." Although not much more is known about Townsend herself, her book suggests that—when properly educated—certain mountain girls could take up the mantle of nature study and botanizing and continue the work. Fictional or not, these teachers were participating in the nation's movement to increase nature study in schools, since, as Peter J. Schmitt argues, "nature-study offered children a watered-down version of biology, geology, chemistry and physics in an era when 'science' seemed more and more important."[35] Science was becoming more important as industrialization and modernization progressed throughout the United States.

Consistent with the Progressive activists' embrace of nationhood and progress, women could not engage in just any categorizing, and they especially could not use only local systems of knowledge. Categorizing the mountains had to follow the newest, latest scientific advances, as Mary Martin's request for Dana's wildflower book suggests. Social crusaders used books from northern publishers, written by people outside of the mountains. In so doing, they applied a general, national knowledge and dismissed local modifications in situations without examining whether the national knowledge was necessarily applicable. Apparently oblivious to the embedded criticism, Goodrich relates what the mountain students think about collecting specimens for Lois Rice: "'You know the names, and we know the things,' they said, as she named one of the plants so familiar to their eyes."[36] In terms of the long-term health of an ecosystem, a complex community of human and nonhuman members, knowing the thing proves more important in the long run than knowing a superficial name.

Yet social crusaders put great reliance on the "proper" names, a reliance that extended even to place names in the region. Katherine Pettit comments that what the mountain people call Ogden Mountain is wrong, because it is technically Audubon Mountain; she says this in reference to a trip over that mountain guided by a local man. His knowledge of the intimate mountain—whether named Ogden or Audubon—is what keeps her alive on that trip. Nevertheless, in her writing, Pettit privileges the scientific categorization of the place over the people's local knowledge. When Margaret Morley says offhandedly "Scape Cat [Ridge] has no name on maps, being one of the countless ridges which are waiting for some one to come and, discovering how beautiful it can be made, occupy it and name it according to his fancy," she encapsulates the colonialism, the superiority of outside knowledge, the passion for improvement, and the need to change local features that are behind many of these authors' reliance on national guidebooks.[37]

"It is Remarkable How Safe One Feels": Safety and Problem-Solving

Nature study and botany provided an important filter through which social crusaders made sense of their world. In their writings, however, its effect is more than just to mark their awareness of the nonhuman world. Authors use botanizing and nature studies to reassure readers of their personal safety as they exercise increased freedom and mobility in Appalachia. They can (although rarely) use it to develop local solutions to local problems. But they also extend the nature study and botanical tools of categorizing to apply them to the people lower on their social hierarchies. By lumping together people with nonhuman nature in Appalachia, the social crusaders undermine their own mission of bringing subjects (themselves) and objects (mountain people) closer together.

Although the women's new prowess in hiking, riding horses, or adventuring demonstrates personal capabilities, readers might still wonder about outside threats to these social crusaders. Categorizing Appalachia answers those questions as it extends the authors' spheres of comfort. With the world around them understandable through identification, reference, description, and categorizing, the women begin to say, as Mary Martin does, "It is remarkable how safe one feels in this wilderness. One can ride or walk long stretches without seeing a soul or even a house, but there is absolutely nothing to be afraid of."[38] For Martin, feeling safe in Appalachia must have influenced her later decisions to become more outwardly focused. Her teaching implies a shift to a political focus as she worked for the condition of the public, not just the safety in and of her own immediate (private) sphere.

The few times social crusaders mention elements of the world around them that might have been a threat to safety, categorizing becomes more literal. Wild or unsafe animals are almost always tamed, caged, or confined—much like pinned butterflies—as safe specimens. Frances Goodrich discusses bears in western North Carolina, but they are tamed, contained in an anecdote set in the past, and given as a retelling of someone else's story. She describes an acquaintance whose "mother tames bears. She gave one honey and egg and made it come down out of a tree backward. Once when they were taking one that she caught to Asheville to be sold, they had to take it on the hind end of a cart." She continues: "It got away and ran into a house where the dinner pot was over the fire. It knocked off the cover and stuck its nose into the pot and got burned. They caught it again and it was sold." Just as Morley suggests the wild animals that "once abounded here" are all gone, what could have been a significant threat is safely restricted to the structure of the story. Eleanor Marsh Frost, in Berea, also speaks of bears in the (more recent) past and a distance, saying, "Bears still live in the region. One was killed last year. I felt quite eager to see one—at a distance, especially when assured they never hurt anyone unless made mad." Daisy Gertrude Dame, from elsewhere in Kentucky, adds, "Mr. Burns told us later, after our danger was passed [hiking in the woods at night], that those woods were full of wildcats too!"[39] Despite their wanderings in the wild woods, these women do not write about encounters with unsafe people or animals, and readers should have no reason to question the competence of Appalachia's social crusaders.

At its best, categorizing Appalachia helped women focus specifically on the place. In so doing, it could lead to local solutions to local problems—modified agendas that reflected the specific places and challenges faced by people in those places. For instance, when Goodrich first arrived in the mountains around Asheville, North Carolina, she knew she wanted to help the mountain people. She began with a general solution popular at the time: teaching mountain youth through a church organization. After two years, she turned from this general activism to a more specific, local activism; she comments in her diary that she has decided not to teach as much because the women need as much or more help than the children. From then on, Goodrich focuses her efforts on the women of the region.[40]

Goodrich's collecting of ferns and mosses changes into noticing the herbal medicines used by indigenous doctors around Asheville (there are entries in her journals about "white lily root" and onion poultices, poke root poultices, and teas such as "tansy for the stomach, slippery 'elum,' for the head and mint for I don't know what"). Her interest in plants culminates in collecting herbal dyes used by women in the mountains in their weaving and sewing; Goodrich prints an appendix to her 1931 *Mountain Homespun* that lists twenty-nine plants, the part of them used in dying, and the material colored by that plant. She groups the plants by the color they give to fabric and tells us that she had these plants "identified in 1901 at the Bureau of Plant Industry in Washington, D. C." The list also includes two plants "identified by F. L. Goodrich."[41]

As *Mountain Homespun* chronicles, Goodrich's interest in plant-based dyes and women's weaving leads her to found Allenstand Industries, a "factory" of sorts that brought these local women weavers and artisans into the market economy. Although criticized for not living up to its egalitarian myth, Goodrich's solution did accomplish some ecological and feminist change—she preserved local knowledge, invested local plants with a value beyond aesthetics, and popularized and made exportable a local women's industry (one that was not extracting nonrenewable resources), in the process recognizing women's role in the mountains as contributors to the family economy.[42] In her writings, at least, her awareness of local communities stops with Allenstand; she seems not to have extended her focus to, for instance, preserve the places those dye plants grew or to advocate programs to ensure clean water and air for the communities in which her workers and nonhuman Appalachian nature might have been threatened. Part of why her promising start may have been cut short lies in her parallel willingness to categorize people along with plants.

"The Eyes Were Wild": The Dangers of Categorizing and Photography

Categorizing people like plants quickly increases the distance between social crusaders and Appalachian people and places—the opposite of what the social crusaders set out to do. Categorizing people depends on othering people—as if they too are specimens like the pink mosses and beautiful wildflowers. In the literature of the social crusaders, categorizing appears in descriptions of mountain types—sometimes contrary to the other evidence (such as of individuality or humanity) presented by the women. Although they participate to different degrees, the social crusaders' pseudoscientific descriptions of people align them with the era's overall fascination with eugenics, social Darwinism, and early sociology and anthropology. For instance, Goodrich says, soon after arriving in the mountains, about an unnamed mountain person she has met, "The eyes were full of expression and kind of wild like many of the people here." In Goodrich's language, the mountain person does not even own his or her own body parts (it is "the eyes" rather than "his eyes" or "her eyes" or even "John's eyes" or "Miss Smith's eyes"). About Bacchus Boone (son of the woman who tames bears), Goodrich claims, "He has a thin face like a weasel, the regular mountain type." Campbell similarly describes an anonymous mountain woman she meets on her research trip as having "a dark full blooded face.... They said they had come over from North Carolina. Mr. W[ebb] says they are the digger Indian type—the lowest of the mountaineers."[43] Neither Goodrich

Figure 5. The label of this photograph in the Campbells' album reads, "Part-Indian." It is on the same page with a picture labeled "Defective Family." Both captions are examples of the tendency in the literature of the social crusaders to categorize people. Since Native American ancestry is embraced today, this photograph does not carry the negative connotations that the judgmental term "defective" still holds. Out of respect to the families involved, I have chosen not to reproduce the second photograph here. Both are located in the John Charles and Olive Dame Campbell Papers #3800, Southern Historical Collection, Wilson Library, University of North Carolina at Chapel Hill.

nor Campbell questions social hierarchies in her writings. Racial and class hierarchies are seen, practiced, and written onto the physical bodies of mountain residents who are then further dehumanized by being dismissed as types or specimens.

The albums of photographs assembled by the Campbells in their research provide a particularly rich source to analyze the categorizing of people. These were assembled as alternative "texts" to secure more money for "mountain work." Most of the people pictured are captioned with descriptors rather than names: "Mission Barrel clothes, McKee, KY," a picture of five women; or "An Incident at Betty's Troublesome," a girl holding a banjo. Neither subject is afforded any biography other than what is frozen under the view's microscope. In other pictures, the caption pushes the viewer further into the position of a removed, dispassionate scientist: on the picture of a boy (whose name is given), the Campbells add, "note intelligence, if any"; with a girl, they comment, "note dirt on feet."[44] As the reader is addressed by the Campbells, the objects in the photographs are further silenced and made unable to act in their own behalf.

One ominous caption reads, "Defective Family, Caney Creek," on a page with a second picture, labeled "Part Indian." The effect of such labels is to define the nonwhite as defective by association. The Campbells reinscribe whiteness as the top of all social hierarchies by naming everyone else as exceptional or wrong. The captions illustrate how the confluence of mental, medical, and racial language at the turn of the twentieth century inscribed a very particular grid of power onto society. With today's eyes, the families neither look unintelligent, noticeably dirty, "defective," nor particularly racially "other." But as specimens in the Campbells' albums, they are categorized as such. Self cannot be any further from Other than here in the Campbells' photographs. To paraphrase Cooke's character in *The Power and the Glory*, the families have been named over and called out, pulled all to pieces, and had all their (real or imagined) ways and faults written down.[45]

The Campbell photograph albums indirectly reveal another effect of "scientific" categorizing. The power to photograph and then caption—that is, categorize—another person's image generalizes from an individual's image to that individual's society and inscribes social hierarchies on that society. This is what the Campbells were doing with their photographs. Lucy R. Lippard and the contributors to *Partial Recall* discuss similar manipulations of images of Native Americans in the United States. Lippard calls the working of power in photographs the "'right' to represent everybody, the 'colonial overview'"; although the Appalachian situation is a case of white people representing white people, the class and cultural differences are so stark that the comparison is apt. I also heed her warning that modern scholars run the risk of reinscribing equally arbitrary meaning to these pictures. Although I am as much a mountain person as anyone, I cannot know the truth of these photographs any more than anyone else at this historical remove. Did the person have a developmental disability? Did the children just return from a day playing outside in their old clothes, leaving their new clothes hanging inside? Had the father in the photograph fought in the Spanish American War or had he truly never left Appalachia? How do I know the girl had never worn shoes before? Lippard's concept of "partial recall" shows how in the "partial" the individual falls away, but the social memory remains.[46] Here the distance between the self of the social crusaders and the other of their Appalachian objects remains. The pictures illustrate the divide between social crusaders and the mountain people and places around them.

One album contains two photographs with men, women, and children in the picture; all are fairly well dressed. Their clothes are handmade, but this is not different from most of the pictures; the people are neat and looking attentively at the camera. Early in the album, the photograph is labeled "Georgia Mountain People." But at another point in the same album, the same picture—a duplicate copy of the same—is labeled "Georgia Moonshine Family."[47] There is no jug or bottle, no still, no visual indication of moonshine. The caption alone alters the people in the picture. Because there are no names attached to the picture, because the image has been removed from context, the only "truth" readers of the photo album have is the truth the Campbells give it. This mountain family—whatever its practices and whatever a "moonshine family" might be—has no control over its own story.

Once a person has been moved from full human status to that of an object of study or categorization (again, from a live butterfly to a dead and pinned specimen), issues of agency—the ability to act, speak, or effect change for oneself—shift radically. From the perspective of the social crusaders, a different ethics is followed once people become objects. For instance, a series of pictures in the Campbell albums is labeled "Walker & wife & two extras & their children and the valley residents. 1=legal wife, 2 & 3 illegal, x=father of most of the group and 'Patriarch' of my preliminary report. This picture difficult to secure, and under promise of not making public." Nevertheless, the photograph is placed in the Campbells' albums, the promise of privacy made to such categorized objects broken. Although the mountain family tried to resist being made into objects by extracting a promise of privacy, their efforts proved ineffective. However, the request is a clue to the awareness mountain people had of the uses to which their images might be put. Residents' awareness appears in fiction as well (usually meant as an illustration of the ignorance of mountain people); for example, Sallie O'Hear Dickson's *The Story of Marthy* includes a mountain woman who asks her child about a visiting social crusader, "Well 'en w'at she want you fur? I reckon she jist wanted somethin' ter laugh at, en maybe she wus tryin' ter git er pictur uv a mountain gall." Although Dickson quickly dismisses the mother as ignorant, the mother understands that pictures of mountain girls could be powerful objects in the power dynamics between social crusaders and the people they set out to help.[48]

The photograph album with the Walker family pictures seems to have been assembled by the Webbs, friends of the Campbells who were working in Tennessee.[49] That it ended up in the Campbells' papers, mixed in among albums presented to the Russell Sage Foundation, undermines that promise of privacy made to the pictured families—once captured by the camera, they become mere data to support claims, however well meaning those claims might be. Data are most useful as silent testimony; researchers can find it unsettling when data begin to voice an opinion. Throughout the albums, Campbell carefully excludes mountain people's opinions from the captions. Campbell is thus unwilling to question another activist teacher when one of the "specimens" is in the room: "A girl from the neighborhood was there most of the time, so rather hindered free questioning. When she left we asked a few questions."[50] The strong message is that the object has no proper say in his or her own life. The overall effect is to reduce the mountain person's agency both in analyzing his or her society's problems and in assessing the proposed solutions. Local solutions are essentially precluded when local voices are so silenced.

On the surface, class distinctions allow the categorizing that increases the distance between helpers and helped. But the situation is complicated (as always) by the genders, races, and places of the social crusaders and mountain residents. The middle-class, primarily northern, white social crusaders are still arguing for legitimacy as women in U.S. society, and they use the lower-class (because they rarely acknowledge that upper-class mountain residents even exist), southern, Appalachian "race" to help make their case. Through strategies of categorizing people, social crusaders manipulate class and race privilege to claim legitimacy for themselves as agents. As idealistic as these dedicated activists may have been, this was no happy sisterhood of equals between mountain women and activist workers.

I am not arguing that every teacher and benevolent worker categorized her world—humans, plants, and animals—and then made judgments out of that strict worldview. Nor am I arguing that even those who did, did not do important work or maintain good relations with individual mountain people. However most, if not all, of the social crusaders had to work in or against the discourse of pseudoscientific categorization. The practice of quick categorization shares much in common with the literatures of the voyeur and the tourist. The surface descriptions, stereotypes, and caricatures of George Gilman about Tanis and the sang-diggers, of Miss Cook about Asheville's mountain people, of Campbell's "Incident at Betty's Troublesome," or Goodrich's "regular mountain type" are strikingly similar.[51] But the overlay of scientific legitimacy lends additional weight to the judgments of the social crusaders. It furthers the definitions of them as more than authors; they are authorities, capable researchers, and independent women who are equipped to lead schools, settlement houses, and hospitals. In the laboratory of the southern mountains, social crusaders, with their botanizing manuals, were not simply looking at pretty ferns when they had time off from their teaching and benevolent work.

Nature, however, did not end when the social crusaders put down their manuals and sketchpads. It had a way of following them into their tents, into homes, and into their waking lives. Women like Olive Dame Campbell, Frances Goodrich, Katherine Pettit, May Stone, Daisy Gertrude Dame, and Mary Martin were challenged by an everyday nature that was not picturesque, not adventurous, and not at all romantic. They responded by using the dirt, dust, and fleas they encountered to solidify their own presence in Appalachia.

Dirt, Dust, and Fleas

The fleas began their work promptly, even before night, and three times in the night the girls had to light the lamp and have a flea-hunt, each sitting in the middle of her enormous feather-bed. They had already, at the women's cottage, become somewhat expert in catching the little torments and cracking them between their thumb-nails.[52]

The most profound experience of nature had by these activist women may well have been the day-to-day experience of the outside coming inside. Their new lives in the mountains involved close encounters with dirt, dust, fleas, and other "little torments." Stone and Pettit, for instance, say dryly, upon visiting a mountain family, "We were impressed by the bare, unattractive rooms and the quantity of dirt." After a visit to a local professional, they write: "We found the doctor, whom one would naturally expect to have clean and wholesome surroundings, living in the midst of as much dirt as the average mountaineer." They profess to be shocked by dirt, dust, and fleas throughout their letters and diaries.[53]

In the early summer sessions, Stone and Pettit find: "Sleep was interrupted many times last night by the fleas. The candle was lighted and the process of 'fleaing' gone through." The frustration remains with them all summer, as their strategies of carbolic acid and cleaning fail; Pettit says, "Miss McNab and I had another struggle last night with fleas. This is an absorbing subject now." When they finally ask a mountain woman how to get rid of the fleas, she (amusingly) tells them, "[J]ist keep from swearing, if you can." Whatever loneliness social crusaders felt for family, home, and daily routine was highlighted by the bugs and dirt encroaching on their sleeping arrangements. Upon being told that a particular church had a "million fleas," Pettit has all of the pews dragged outside before she will teach. On a warm day, with mountains in the background, whatever dust, bugs, and heat that they will endure outdoors is more acceptable than when they are indoors. Sitting outside on a bench on the mountainside to teach Sunday school was, for Stone and Pettit, a better solution than sitting inside with nature's dirt, dust, and bugs.[54]

Some of the crusaders clung stubbornly to the details of propriety from their home communities. Stone and Pettit, for instance, are inflexible about the proper degree of whiteness clean clothes should achieve—even if those clothes are washed in a creek; their journals contain numerous references to having to "teach" the local people how to wash properly. This is met with puzzlement (and occasional outright resistance) by the mountain residents and inspires one woman to comment after watching their elaborate preparations for bed, "Ye all must be a lot of trouble to yerselves."[55] Stone, Pettit, and the Hindman teachers insist on wearing white, full-length, properly petticoated dresses even though the rivers are swollen, the paths are muddy, and the days are exhausting.

Too Muddy for Fashion

Other women's experience with the dirt, dust, and fleas lead them to question mainstream fashion. Mary Martin, for instance, ponders a trip home to Pennsylvania and decides, "One thing I really dread, however, is having to fuss about clothes." Criticizing even average attention to fashion, she says, "I don't think we [her family] do a great deal of worrying about the latest styles, but it's a subject that takes a great deal of time and thought without that." She announces: "Down here it is of absolutely no importance what one wears. Dresses eight or ten or twenty years old would pass muster as readily as new ones. Indeed, they would cause much less comment. . . . When a skirt wears around the bottom, it is only necessary to cut it off and rebind it, the shorter the better" and concludes, "I hope the fashion of trailing skirts for street-wear will be a thing of the past when I come home. I'm sure I could never bring myself to wear such a thing."[56] Martin's concerns reflect the contradictory emotions she feels as she criticizes mainstream fashion without completely embracing the culture she sees around her.

Eleanor Marsh Frost expresses a similar criticism in an early letter from Berea: "The people do not pretend to know anything about ways and fashions of the outside world. I shall fall behind the times and old fashioned if I finally do emerge out from among these hills." Both women are helping to support the myth that Appalachia was a land out of time, a place caught in the past, but they are also using that impression to criticize the present in which they live. Frost extends Martin's argument to think about the consequences of not spending time on preparing and maintaining fashionable clothes. Frost concludes: "[B]ut I would not wonder if I shall be more truly useful and shall have made more real progress than I would have done in trying to keep up with the procession at Oberlin."[57] All the social crusaders were performing hard work in difficult conditions; their increased mobility pointed out how restrictive the era's fashionable clothing could be.

The criticisms expressed in letters for outside readers do not shake the social crusaders' fundamental belief in the superiority of mainstream fashion. Instead they argue for something more like exceptionalism, the freedom to take a personal break from fashion's dictates. They certainly do not embrace the fashions worn by the mountain women around them. If social crusaders comment on mountain women's clothes, it is only as they are consumable novelties. For instance, young Bertha Daisy Nickum writes: "I am going to get you a sunbonnet made from buckeye bark. The cooking teacher has one and it is the prettiest thing. The mountain women make them." When Nickum began her life as a student at Berea College, she wrote home often about the sights and sounds of Kentucky. From the big city of Cincinnati, Ohio, Nickum traveled to the Kentucky mountains for college. In her letters, she mentions that she hopes to use her college education to be a teacher or activist and lists the Rocky Mountains or China as potential posts. There is no direct evidence that she follows through on this plan; in fact, it is likely that she has tuberculosis ("I cough up great mouthfuls of blood all the time but I am so anxious to stay"). In any case, she does not return to Berea to finish her degree. She is a charming letter writer; most of the letters are addressed to family back in Ohio, and in most of them she is very much the college student (complaining about the food and dorm life, for example). Pieces of clothing developed in the region, for practical use by women working in the place, are only amusing to Nickum; she would never consider them seriously.[58]

In fact, activist women often rely on clothing as an easy way to judge whether their activism has been a success. If a mountain woman has given up her homespun fabric and is now wearing clothes from store-bought material, the work is declared successful. The before-and-after series involving the Walker family in the Campbells' albums shows a mountain family with store-bought clothes substituted for homespun and hair restyled to match middle-class standards of taste. The family is still barefoot in the after picture and is still living in the same low-quality housing. It is unclear what new dresses have improved for this family—except that they now are more recognizable to the social crusaders and their readers. Fashion becomes a peculiar double standard—in which mainstream clothes are judged too restrictive for the activist women but held up as an improvement for the mountain women.[59]

Cleaning Up Appalachia: Crusaders at Work

Certainly the northeastern cities and towns from which these women came were susceptible to dirt, dust, and fleas. In some cases, middle-class privilege may have sheltered the women from such intimate encounters with the messier side of life. Dirt, dust, and fleas could be some of the most damaging effects of poverty on health and quality of life. But the triad functions in symbolic ways in their writing as well. Repeatedly, the authors employ the language of Progressivism and its emphases on public as well as private domesticity, scientific housekeeping, and women's responsibilities to both family and nation. They use Progressive language to establish the continuing legitimacy of their work; they directly connect the cleanliness of places to the cleanliness of individual people in the places, the public to the

Figure 6. "Before" and "After" pictures. These two photographs appear on the same page of the Campbells' album. The first is labeled "Mary Stinnett's Family 'B' March 1902. Mrs. Bill Walker in the group, and a grandson of Mary Ann Moore. 1. Patriarch's legal wife, 2. Illegal wife." Although it is difficult to see, the older woman to the right is marked "1" in this, the "Before" picture. The second photograph is labeled "Mary Stinnett's family—August 1903." Both of these photos depict the same family group whose permission was "difficult to secure and under promise of privacy," as discussed in the text. Notice that in the "After" picture one wife is gone and the clothes are no longer homespun, but everyone remains barefoot and the living conditions have not changed. Both photographs are located in the John Charles and Olive Dame Campbell Papers #3800, Southern Historical Collection, Wilson Library, University of North Carolina at Chapel Hill.

private, exterior to interior. Daisy Gertrude Dame writes: "The women here are very ignorant, even about washing and ironing, not to mention cooking and the commonest facts of hygeine [*sic*]."[60] Dame leaps from criticizing the women for not knowing how to wash or iron according to the latest technological developments and standards embraced by Progressives to finding them personally, physically unclean.

More disturbingly, social crusaders equate outward, physical hygiene to inner, spiritual morality. Stone and Pettit make the comparison explicit when they ask: "Add to bad air, dirt, and bad cooking, the use of tobacco by men, women, and even children ... how can we expect good health? And without any regard to the laws of health, how can the people be strong mentally or morally?" Their argument is made visible in the Campbells' before-and-after pictures. Although the change in clothing was an important marker, the parallel concern is to disrupt a nontraditional family organization the Campbells find immoral. In the "before" picture, two women, elsewhere identified as wives of the same man, sit together, surrounded by children; by the second photograph, the older of the women has disappeared and only the younger woman and the children remain. What has actually happened to the older woman, viewers cannot know; but the implication is that along with new clothes and hairstyles, the family's morals have also been brought into agreement with those of the Campbells.[61]

Female social crusaders repeatedly targeted women in their judgments about outer cleanliness and inner morality. Allenstand Industries founder Frances Louisa Goodrich argues that women's religion should apply to family hygiene when she complains about a mountain woman, "She is a well-meaning woman, but her Christianity does not include good housekeeping and I fear never will." Identifying women's domestic practices as the key to improving society's health, morality, and intellect sets up the argument for why these activists are the best choice to live and work in the mountains, and it expands the scope of the "mountain work." The reflective Stone and Pettit make this an explicit goal, as they take as their mandate "To live among the people, in as near a model home as we can get, to show them by example the advantages of cleanliness, neatness, order, study along both literary and industrial lines, and to inspire them to use both pure language and to lead pure Christian lives; these should be our efforts."[62] As women, the argument goes, social crusaders will best be able to teach women; and as women with great personal freedom and knowledge of scientific categorizing, they will best be able to judge the women's success at their lessons.

Enforcing such ideas of cleanliness involves policing the female body. Emphases are put on both mountain women's bodies and the activists' bodies. Unlike Tanis in the literature of the voyeur, who is given a pile of Alice Gilman's cast-off fashionable clothes and must guess (wrongly, of course) what to do with them, issues of the body bring the social crusaders close to the objects in their stories. The object gets to view the intimate body of the subject and make comments; but in the process both subject and object bodies are policed. Thus, Stone and Pettit relate the story of a mountain woman who "came in while we were dressing and seemed pleased to see the way I buttoned my skirts to the waist; said she had always thought that women ought to dress 'more healthy, but never knew how.'"[63] Although the connection between a tightly corseted body and health might seem dubious today, in Stone and Pettit's journal, proper clothing metaphorically represent proper physical and moral states. Because the social hierarchies keeping women activists superior to mountain residents have been so well established in the literature of the social crusader, moments of intimacy such as this scene of dressing do not disrupt the basic arrangement of power.

At the same time, social crusaders are not free of the worry that mountain girls may want to transcend their social class. Goodrich writes: "As spring advances the sunbonnets come out. Miss Eva has one and we decided that she had better wear hers to school on the principle of encouraging what is unobjectionable in the peoples [sic] ways. We thought the older girls were getting too high and mighty ideas about dress." Dame makes a similar point when she says: "Mr. Burns does not want the dormitory luxurious, which might make the girls dissatisfied with their homes." As scholar Barbara Ellen Smith argues, "Class formation is a gendered process. It identifies women's (and men's) class positions by gendered markings, as Mother Jones pungently observed: 'God almighty made women, but that Rockefeller gang of thieves made the ladies.'" Although the social crusaders are dismissive of the ladies of the resort tourists or armchair voyeurs, they trade on a related sense of class privilege that could be threatened by an emerging social class of mountain women. Smith continues, "More importantly, [class formation] entails the construction of distinct positions and relationships based on gender within each newly emerging class."[64] Class anxiety is generally not expressed by female social crusaders that the men are rising up—rather, it is that the girls are getting too fashionable, too impatient with their roles. The stakes, after all, are high; if all mountain women suddenly achieved the same social class as the social crusaders, activists could find themselves out of work.

Figure 7. Washerwomen. These two photographs appear on the same page in the Campbells' album, along with a longer-distance shot of the group picture. All three are captioned, "There are some Negroes in the mountains—this is wash day near Manchester, Kentucky—which because of its salt works was settled by bluegrass families who brought their slaves with them." Copies of the same pictures also appear in Katherine Pettit and May Stone's papers and in Bertha Daisy Nickum's photograph album at Berea College. Nickum comments on the photograph of the single washerwoman, "A king might envy her content." Both photographs are located in the John Charles and Olive Dame Campbell Papers #3800, Southern Historical Collection, Wilson Library, University of North Carolina at Chapel Hill.

Pure White: Social Crusaders Confront African American Appalachian Washerwomen

The policing of female bodies in the literature of the social crusader also extended to strategies to ensure "racial purity" and the cleanliness of racial categories in the mountains. Ironically, the bodies of women who cleaned clothes for a living bore the brunt of such strategies. Around the turn of the last century, black women were the South's washerwomen.[65] Appalachia was no exception, as taking in laundry for wage earning seems to have been the job of black women whenever financially possible. Campbell's, Nickum's, and Stone and Pettit's collections all have photograph collections attached to their archival texts. Rather startlingly, *all* of the collections include pictures of the *same* three African American washerwomen. Although Campbell, Stone and Pettit were acquaintances, they do not acknowledge any cross-references concerning these women and in fact imply that the pictures are original to each of them; only Nickum admits purchasing her pictures from a studio.

The descriptions Nickum, Campbell, and Stone and Pettit write of the pictures highlight the racial anxiety inherent in the literature of the social crusader. Of the picture with a single figure, Nickum says: "A king might envy her content." The contentment that Nickum romantically assigns to the woman is challenged by the traditional low wages and hard work of laundering and by internal evidence of the picture—it portrays the difficulty of the work (with, for example, the washboard and long drop to the creek), the age of the woman, and the pile of work remaining to be done. Although the woman may have felt content with her life and labor, such a conclusion could only be justified from talking with her—something Nickum has not done. In a letter, Nickum explains: "I took the negro views especially for Mother. There are any number of old Mammies like the one washing here." Speaking more to social expectations than evidence in the picture, Nickum describes the women as "old Mammies" despite the fact that only one of the three adult women seems older; the other two look quite young, especially as they are posing with their children, the eldest of whom looks only eight or nine. Nickum treats the images as generic—as a representation that can stand in for any African Americans around Berea. She neither names the women, nor does she name the "old Mammies" whom she or the college might have hired to help with her own clothes.[66]

Campbell speaks as if she knows particular details of the washerwomen's lives. In one of the Campbells' photograph albums, all three pictures are grouped on to a single page. The accompanying caption is one of the longest and most detailed in the album: "There are some Negroes in the mountains—this is wash day near Manchester, Kentucky, which because of its salt works was settled by bluegrass families who brought their slaves with them."[67] The Campbells seem anxious to explain away African American mountain residents as anomalies; the lengthy and detailed caption suggests their nervousness that the images might trouble funding agencies' confidence in the pure whiteness of mountain work. By making sure readers know that the black people were transplanted from elsewhere (i.e., Kentucky's bluegrass region), outsiders' beliefs in the mountains' whiteness are never challenged.

Finally, Stone and Pettit mention at length the various African American washerwomen they employ. They say, for instance, "A colored woman came early to do the washing under Miss McCartney's directions and it was a picturesque scene by the creek between the house and Comfort Nook. There was a great fire under the kettle heating the water and the merry sound of the battling of the clothes echoed from mountain to mountain." The entry continues: "I spent part of the morning out on the loom house step writing and showing the colored woman how to do the ironing." On another day, they write, "Miss McCartney made bread this morning and showed the washwoman how to make it. She gave her the first lesson in reading." And later, Stone and Pettit claim that "Sarah Lizabeth, a sixteen year old negro girl, came to wash for us. Miss Pettit stayed by her all day teaching her to wash by kitchen garden rules."[68] The teaching involved in hiring each woman makes it unclear whether they had never taken in washing before or whether they had never encountered the activists' "kitchen garden rules" before—although one suspects the latter. Even when it comes to work like scrubbing clothes in a creek, the social crusaders believe in a single, essentialist, best way to perform the work.

Nickum, Campbell, Stone and Pettit use the same three photographs to reinforce their own whiteness and the socially constructed "superiority" that accompanies it. It may be no coincidence that no African American men appear in the photograph albums. In order to show people who challenge Appalachia's pure whiteness, other axes of power are carefully controlled. Thus, black women are not shown with men, because such a portrayal might imply the potential of population growth, as an implied healthy African American family is a more powerful image than a partial one. Similarly, the black women are only shown in the most primitive of locations doing one of the most difficult of jobs; in this way, there is no implication of burgeoning class power in the hands of African American Appalachians. More subtly, the women are not named—even by Stone, Pettit, and Campbell who otherwise suggest they might have met them. The one African American girl who is named, Sarah Lizabeth, is young enough at age sixteen to wield very little power. In Stone and Pettit's writing, the women are denied even their own knowledge of their profession; they must be taught how to wash and iron properly.[69] The hint in Nickum's letters that the pictures are, in fact, generic—in other words, available for purchase—further disenfranchises these particular women as owners of their own image. In other words, by having their image so commodified, the women become not *some* African Americans in Appalachia, but *the* African Americans in Appalachia.

The mainstream, middle-class values encoded in definitions of social hierarchies and class positions within those hierarchies met resistance by local mountain residents. The social crusaders' emphasis on cleanliness became a target of that resistance. Emma Bell Miles suggests in *The Spirit of the Mountains* that the focus on the surface—the equation of certain fashions and standards of cleanliness with goodness and morality—erases cultural practices developed to cope with the difficulty of life in the mountains; she also argues that the activists absolve themselves from any complicity stemming from their participation in the country's class privileges by their single-minded attention to the surface of mountain bodies and culture.[70] In other words, because activists do not address the macrolevel forces creating the pool of mountain residents in poverty and need, the details of dirt, dust, and fleas are all that can be seen in and around people in Appalachia.

The added irony, of course, of social crusaders' reactions to dirt, dust, and fleas is that just as social crusaders were escaping the confines of domesticity in their home communities by coming to the mountain work, they were teaching mountain women to embrace those confinements. Some mountain women might have had more personal freedom and mobility before they learned new, upper-class standards of cleanliness or propriety that were often predicated on household help, restrictive fashion, or one-size-fits-all family arrangements. Some may have had more class mobility in mountain communities before being categorized as "types." And some may have worn more practical clothes, used more sustainable, less expensive, and less time-consuming products to put food on their tables and clothes on their children—and worked for each other in cooperative childrearing situations that benefited several generations of women.

Conclusion: Sarah Barnwell Elliott's Reluctant Social Crusading

"It is ruination," Cartright said, "to lower that 'wild child of the forest' to civilization."

"On the contrary," Agnes answered, "she is being elevated."

"She looks cast down," Max rejoined.

"Of course; she is now realizing that she is not the highest; but that is necessary. We must see the heights before we can scale them."

"Are you sure civilization is a height?"

"Yes, Mr. Dudley, and I say, Rise at any cost. The girl is a different creature already. . . ."

They were on their way to a mission Sunday school, where, twice during the week, Agnes went to impart secular knowledge. As Max looked back now, there was a lack of spirit in the girl's whole bearing that was pathetic.[71]

Author and future president of the Tennessee Equal Suffrage Association, Sarah Barnwell Elliott felt some responsibility to her new community around the University of the South in Sewanee, Tennessee, but she also had reservations about the work of "elevating" mountain residents. Accordingly, her 1898 novel, *The Durket Sperret,* is ambivalent about the effect of social crusading on its main character, Hannah Warren. Over the course of the novel, Hannah faces emotional, physical, environmental, and economic abuse—from mountain residents but also from social crusaders like Agnes, who demands Hannah "Rise at any cost." Hannah's struggles reflect Elliott's intellectual questions about social crusading in Appalachia. Despite her reluctance, in the novel Elliott explores the personal freedom and mobility Appalachian nature can give women; categorizes Appalachian people, as well as places; judges mountain residents' moral worth on the basis of surface cleanliness; and places the responsibility for environmental damage on individual mountain residents rather than structural forces (152–53).

When the novel opens, Hannah lives in Lost Cove, just down the valley from Sewanee, with her two grandparents. The Warrens thought they were "well-to-do," which Elliott defines as "making at home almost everything they need" (5), but they never really interacted with the outside world. Since the University of the South has recently opened, the Warrens are no longer so geographically isolated from the United States or its values. Concurrently, the family now faces a crisis because its men are effectively absent: Hannah's father has been killed by a tree (39) and her grandfather is helpless with rheumatism (5). Hannah has sole responsibility for the farm and her grandparents' care; she plows and cooks, or as she puts it, "Since dawn she had worked like a man—now she must work like a woman" (126). The plot hinges on "an outlet from all this. [Hannah] could marry her cousin Si Durket" (6), who is full of the title's Durket spirit. Her grandmother, whose maiden name is Durket, along with Si, champions the family spirit (her husband says she "never knows the blossoms is a-blowin,' ner she never hears the rain a-talkin'; she never b'lieves in no sperret 'ceppen the Durket sperret" [148]) even though it turns out to be very bad for the family's women. Should Hannah embrace the domesticity and middle-class values of marriage, or should she struggle to remain a single, working woman supporting her extended family?

Hannah rejects the thought of marrying Si immediately, noting that "[s]he would rather cut wood all day! And the axe swung into the air with an ease and swiftness scarcely to be looked for in a woman" (6). She enjoys working outside; she has personal mobility and adventures as she shoulders the responsibility formerly carried by her father. Four pages later, readers discover—in a blunt and clear statement—why Hannah's reaction against marriage is so strong, despite the fact that Si is a middle-class landowner and educated: "A man who could strike his mother and curse his old father was not to be desired" (10). The reason is unambiguous—and it is repeated at several points in the text. Si's Durket spirit is violent; this marriage proposal exaggerates the threat of middle-class domesticity to a woman's personal freedoms. Desperate for a way out of having to accept Si, Hannah decides to defy her grandmother and "peddle"; she sells food to the university populations at Sewanee. She exults over the "fruits of the earth and the beasts of the field" that "had become her protectors against Si Durket" (34). The decision to enter the world of Sewanee brings Hannah into the realm of social crusaders, and in the process categorizes her as inescapably Appalachian and hence lower on the Sewanee social hierarchy.

When peddling is no longer an option, Hannah feels her only recourse is to enter the capitalist economy and "hire out" as a servant in a university household. Liberal, Progressive Agnes for whom Hannah works erases the distinctions Hannah sees between mountain residents by insisting that all white, mountain people are of the same—lower—class. Agnes's future husband, who is also a university resident, compares Hannah to an animal and, like writer and social crusader Frances Louisa Goodrich, removes even her ownership of her body: "Cartright met the eyes of the girl as she held the door open, 'like a dumb animal,' he thought, and hurried past." Hannah realizes that to Cartright and Agnes she is "only a thing. . . . A stick or a stone 'thout no feelin's" (165). When Si carries through his threat to ruin Hannah's reputation by gossiping that she has had "improper relations" with a different university man, she is fired because her employer feels embarrassed (even as Agnes assures Hannah that she does not believe the rumors). Hannah finds there is no protection in her new class category; she is treated as a stick or a stone and thrown away.

Although Elliott does not make mountain homes explicitly dirtier, dustier, or full of fleas, she does use dirt metaphorically to explain what has happened to Hannah. "Hannah Warren's name is in the dirt" (166), the community believes after Si gossips. Her grandfather, believing it is also "*my* name in the dirt," advises her to accept Si's subsequent marriage offer because "Thar's mighty few'd be willin' to pick a gal up outen the mud" (169). In addition, the university social crusaders worry throughout the book about mountain women who have "unnaturally" transcended their proper class positions by copying mainstream fashion from careless teachers. Such women end up with "frizzed bangs and a great love for chewing gum"; when the university residents ask each other about Hannah, "Shall we civilize her?" they are at pains to do the job right—to enforce proper ideas of class while teaching her how to cook, clean, and serve according to their middle-class values (73).

Elliott uses and condemns ecological attacks against Hannah by Si with Grandmother Warren's approval. Si takes Hannah's experiences with the land away from her because her increased freedom and mobility are threatening to ruin plans for the marriage (threatening by enabling Hannah to assume self-sufficient, more active gender roles). Si plows up graveyards, poisons animals, artificially increases the number of rabbits and other predators in gardens, and sabotages Hannah's ability to farm. Si is environmentally savvy, but he applies that knowledge in a damaging way. Si is the villain in the book, and his techniques are subsequently condemned by Elliott and the other characters. Larger threats to land in eastern Tennessee around 1898, run-off from textile mills, unplanned development, and timbering, threats that would demand structural criticisms, never appear in *The Durket Sperret*. What environmental criticism there is remains on the individual level of the novel.

Perhaps because of her ambivalence about social crusading, Elliott retreats into a sentimental conclusion. The gender roles resolve (no more working or swinging an axe like a man) and the music practically swells.

When Grandmother Warren drops dead and not one but two other (nonviolent) marriage proposals present themselves to Hannah, Elliott's interesting explorations in the literature of the social crusader come to an end. Elliott's story has a happy ending—but it is of questionable utility for actual mountain contemporaries of and readers about the fictional Hannah Warren (all abused women should find it so easy to get out of abusive situations). Hannah marries a mountain resident, she stays at home, the social crusaders go back to the university, and the status quo that reigned at the beginning of the novel returns.

Many similar endings occur in the literature of the social crusaders. Bertha Daisy Nickum did not return to Berea College; Daisy Gertrude Dame left Oneida Baptist Institute after a year and her letters end; Eleanor Marsh Frost stayed at Berea while her husband remained president. Katherine Pettit, May Stone, Olive Campbell, Lucy Furman, Frances Goodrich, and Mary Martin all stayed in Appalachia for the rest of their lives. Most continued with their social crusades, although they changed missions or alliances over the years.

For most, mainstream definitions of communities with only human members, unshaken beliefs in progress and capitalism, loyalty to essentialist ideas of womanhood and Progressive status quo domesticity continued. In practice, the same us-*versus*-them thinking so central in the literatures of the tourist and voyeur also drives the literature of the social crusader. Once again, Appalachians remain inferior to American "civilization" in the literature of the social crusader. Yet, out of the literature of the social crusader, surrounded by the literatures of the voyeur and the tourist, the roots of ecological feminism were ready to emerge. Mary Noailles Murfree and Effie Waller Smith helped take the first steps. Grace MacGowan Cooke and Emma Bell Miles took up the challenge and laid the theoretical groundwork for Appalachia's early ecological feminism.

CHAPTER FOUR

Mary Noailles Murfree and Effie Waller Smith

Ecological Feminism's Roots, Part 1

As a transcript of peculiar scenery in its many phases through the whole round of the sylvan year, the volume [by Mary Noailles Murfree] has more than a local value, adding as it does one more to the number which illustrate "Nature in American Literature."
—Anonymous review, *Literary World*

[In Murfree's writing,] the length and breadth of the land are finding speech.
—Katherine Lee Bates, *American Literature*

> TO EFFIE WALLER
> Far up among the mountains,
> Where rivers leave their fountains,
> And happy birds send forth their merry thrills;
> There dwells a little poet,
> Though few there be who know it,
> Whose voice is an echo from the hills.
>
> You may not like her station,
> For she is not Caucasian,
> Yet God with music touched the singer's heart;
> And thoughts in liquid measure,
> Doth flow out like a treasure,
> To charm us with the poet's mystic art.
>
> —Reverend Peter Clay, in Effie Waller Smith's *Songs of the Months*

As a young girl, Mary Noailles Murfree may have dreamed of contributing to "American Literature," but how she would do it—writing about the Appalachian mountains and their residents—surprised many. Growing up in Murfreesboro, Tennessee, in the flatter piedmont, Murfree was a tourist in Appalachia on family vacations; somewhere along the way, she had the idea that would shape the rest of her career. Murfree had her first pseudonymous publication in 1874 and quickly became a fixture in the era's magazines, publishing almost continuously from 1878 to 1921. "The Star in the Valley," *In the Tennessee Mountains, The Young Mountaineers,* and "Over on T'other Mounting"—her titles reflect her mission of writing about the people she met in and around Beersheba Springs, the resort community she and her family visited.[1]

Although she first achieved success with magazine sketches and short stories, Murfree also successfully published novels. Around 1885, she revealed to critics and the public that the virile, daring mountain stories by Charles Egbert Craddock were actually written by a shy, physically disabled woman (a detail of much interest to her contemporaries). Her stories remained enormously popular, and although the peak of her writing career was before the turn of the last century, she continued to write and publish until her death in 1922. Murfree never married and remained in Murfreesboro for most of her life. The genre of fiction about Appalachia was, in part, defined by Murfree's stories; then and now, reaction to her is rarely moderate. She has been deemed both forgettable and central to the history of American literature. She has been called a role model for women's capabilities, as well as a conservative spokesperson celebrating passivity for local women. Some have held her singly responsible for the worst, most damaging stereotypes about Appalachia; others find in her a sympathetic regionalist challenging structures of power that demean Appalachians.[2]

Murfree was twenty-nine years old when Effie Waller Smith, who was "not Caucasian," but whose voice Peter Clay called "an echo from the hills," was born in 1879 in Pikeville, Kentucky, in the Appalachian part of the state. There is no evidence Smith and Murfree ever met, although the social prominence and relative economic independence of Smith's African American family meant that Smith traveled and was trained in Tennessee as well as Kentucky—not a common occurrence for African American Appalachians from that part of Kentucky at the turn of the century. Smith, "the singing poet of the Cumberland," was a teacher who published her poems and stories in mainstream magazines, such as *Putnam's,* and in collected volumes.[3]

Before she died in 1960, Smith experienced both marriage and divorce, adopted a daughter, and eventually left the South and its racial politics behind. Writing from within a blossoming tradition of African American women's writing, Smith contributed stories and poems about Appalachia. Much like Frances Ellen Watkins Harper or Amelia E. Johnson, African American writers who were her contemporaries, Smith chose to downplay overt racial markers in her fiction; like Harper, Smith does discuss race in some of her poetry. Smith appeared only a handful of times in the national press; much of her writing remained unpublished until long after her death. Nonetheless, during her lifetime, Smith was hailed as an up-and-coming writer and was compared by critics with Paul Laurence Dunbar, the pre-eminent African American poet of the day. Despite the differences between them, the transitions, decisions, and experiences faced by both Murfree and Smith were dilemmas for many women in turn-of-the-century America; for Smith and Murfree, their viewpoints were filtered through their association with Appalachia.[4]

As an Appalachian reader, I thought I did not like the writings of Mary Noailles Murfree. I had heard too many arguments about how damaging her ideas were for Appalachians even today. I strongly dislike discussions about Appalachia that assume the whole region is isolated, poor, uneducated, all white, and starkly divided in its gender roles with patriarchal, active men and passive, unambitious women. Some individual characters in Murfree's works are isolated, poor, and uneducated. The world of her fiction is almost all white, and some of the local men about whom she writes are—or try to be—patriarchs of their extended families. But I have come to believe that what I actually dislike about Murfree is how her writings have been used—taken as fact by her contemporaries and later scholars, generalized to apply to all of Appalachia, and reduced to one or two repeatedly anthologized stories. As controversial as Murfree has been, relatively few scholarly works have read her novels carefully. I find, as I have begun to do just that, that the way Murfree writes about women is subtle and complex and that the outsiders in her stories are as fallible as the local mountain characters—and treated with equal suspicion by the narrator. I also find that the mountains are not the only dialect in her stories and that I am drawn into Murfree's interest in whether communication is possible and what it might look like between diverse community members.

My experience of Appalachia is of a place much more racially diverse than the canonical texts would lead one to believe. I was motivated to trace a history of Appalachian texts that better reflects Appalachia itself. Effie Waller Smith exemplifies the diversity that had to be erased in order to portray Appalachia as "pure white." Smith writes from within Appalachia but also from within the tradition of African American women writers. The work of scholar David Deskins, along with the Schomburg Library of Nineteenth-Century Black Women Writers, has brought Smith back into print and has begun to explore her life and work as an Appalachian African American female poet and writer. It is important not only that Smith is a black Appalachian writing about that experience, but also that Smith is an early writer from Appalachia who celebrates her love for Appalachia—its mountains, people, and quality of life. Other writers in the lineage of ecological feminism, such as Emma Bell Miles and Grace MacGowan Cooke, also claim Appalachia as a positive place and an Appalachian identity as having value. Yet, both sometimes distance themselves from Appalachian identities. Smith is unapologetic about what the mountains have meant to her. She truly misses them when she travels, and she claims outsiders are to be pitied for not having grown up among the Kentucky mountains. After finding so many dismissals of Appalachians and Appalachia itself in the literatures of the tourist, voyeur, and social crusader, reading Smith makes me breathe easier. That she also wrote poems celebrating women's independence, achievement, and feminism seems almost too good to be true. I find myself quoting Smith to friends, rereading her poetry in spare minutes, and always wishing she had written more.

I explored in the previous chapters how the women writing about and working in Appalachia participated in feminist movements at the turn of the twentieth century. In their writings, Appalachian nature could be personally moving and transformative for women. At the same time, they relied on essentialist discourses of Woman, arguing, for instance, that there is only one way to be a woman and that all who differ (like Tanis or the "defective" women photographed)[5] are freakish, pitiable, or dismissed. Similar essentialist ideas of Nature meant that Appalachian nature was always out there, in the picturesque background, and available to be controlled (as the dirt, dust, and fleas), transcended, or conquered. Such essentialist discourses led to the mutual exploitation of Appalachian women and Appalachian nature. They strengthened hierarchies based on status quo structures of power. Ideas about Appalachia and Appalachian women worked, in the literature of the social crusaders especially, to justify the presence of activists, to judge the success of the work, and to separate social crusaders from the people and places in which they worked. The literatures of the tourist, voyeur, and social crusader surround the roots of ecological feminism in Appalachia and had to be explored before the tangles could be unknotted and distinguished.

Mary Noailles Murfree, with her contribution to "Nature in American Literature," and Effie Waller Smith, "[w]hose voice is an echo from the hills," are the first two of four authors whose works are the roots of ecological feminism. Both wrote literature (neither, as far as I know, wrote theoretical essays or were political activists), but their literature starts to outline an alternative philosophy for living sustainably in diverse communities that marks early ecological feminism. Finding some of the roots in the writings of Murfree and Smith may be, I recognize, counterintuitive to some. However, the intuitive—social crusaders devoted to Appalachia, tourists visiting because of the scenic views, authors who were educated in hotbeds of early feminism—failed under close reading.

Unlike any author examined up to this point, Murfree dismantles the hierarchy of (outsider) subject over (Appalachian) objects. In addition, she brings animals, meteorology, and geology into her writing as autonomous, fully participating subjects. Elements of nature cease to be simply passive background set pieces and become active characters playing crucial roles in the community. Murfree introduces self-another relationships in Appalachia; as she does so, she criticizes the practices of U.S. corporate culture in terms of social and environmental justice issues. Unlike any author examined up to this point, Smith introduces fully realized African American characters who claim membership in and love for Appalachia. Smith actively places a particular African American feminism in Appalachia at the turn of the past century and demands that it be accorded a place at the table as well. Celebrating women's physical capabilities, Smith uses them to champion explicitly women's rights. Smith and Murfree contribute transformative definitions of diversity in human and nonhuman communities.

Mary Noailles Murfree and Nature's "Awesome Voice"

It was a great property, reckoned by metes and bounds. A day's journey might hardly suffice to traverse the whole of his domain. Yet there was no commensurate money value attaching to these leagues of mountain wilderness, that bore indeed a merely nominal price, and Kenneth Kenniston's was hardly the temperament to experience in aesthetic gratulation that his were those majestic domes which touched the clouds and withstood the lightnings and lifted up an awesome voice to answer the thunder, or that his title-deeds called for all the vast slopes thence down to the unimagined abysses of the abandoned mine in the depths of the gorge. It was the spirit of speculation that informed his glance with a certain respect for them, as he turned his eye upon the mountains and bethought himself how these austere craggy splendors were calculated to impress the shallow gaze of the wandering human swallow. He even appraised, in the interest of possible summer sojourners, the rare, pure, soft air with which his lungs expanded. Science was presently set a-prying about the margins of rocky springs, hitherto undiscovered and unnoticed save by oread or deer; a few blasts of dynamite, a great outgushing of exhaustless mineral waters, a triumphant chemical analysis ensued, and an infusion of enthusiasm began to pervade his consciousness. Such resources—infinitely smaller resources—elsewhere in the world meant a fortune; why not here?[6]

The first phrase of the first paragraph of *His Vanished Star* suggests Murfree's deep attention to place in the novel. It *is* a great property, however one measures it, and one way to summarize the book is as a struggle over who gets to tell the property's story, live with and on it, and be aided by it. The first paragraph, quoted in full here, deserves to be lingered upon, because not only does it set up the conventional perspective on subjects and objects, progress and development, science and reason, but also it foreshadows what will counter that perspective in the novel—the property itself, its voice, resources, and, later, its community and their actions.

As his "domain" extends beyond sight and stamina, Kenneth Kenniston truly believes that he is lord of all he surveys. He is, to his mind, the only subject in this story. It is his great property, which he is free to appraise, reckon, turn his eye, and literally survey—measure the land surveyor's "metes and bounds" or boundary lines, once and for all.[7] Because his is "hardly the temperament" to think otherwise, the domes, slopes, gorge, crags, air, oreads (a classical word for nymphs who live specifically in mountains and hills), deer, and springs are completely inanimate objects to him. He owns them, he exploits them, and he can afford to view them with only "the spirit of speculation." The mountain residents find that even in chance meetings in the depths of the woods, Kenniston has "a cigar in his mouth, a memorandum in his hand of the boundaries of his land" (Murfree, *Vanished Star,* 80). Murfree says of her architect, "the aspect of the world seemed to him parceled out in available sites" (2). Nothing can shake Kenniston's belief that Science, progress, development, and reason will prevail over

Appalachia and all Appalachians who stand in his way. It is with deep irony, then, that Kenniston and his perspective (so similar to the tourists and voyeurs) will lose their stranglehold on Appalachia through the actions of the "objects" in the first paragraph. In the end, Kenniston receives in reply to his initial question "Why not here?" the resounding answer: "Because we are here and you failed to see or hear us."

The first paragraph also introduces one of Murfree's more subtle strategies to change the hierarchy of outsider subjects and Appalachian objects in her novel. She retains the popular practice of rendering Appalachian characters' speech in dialect; and she also writes Kenniston's voice in educated, grammatically correct, uninflected English—strategies that enforce the distance between insiders and outsiders, subjects and objects. However, Murfree introduces a third voice in her story as well: to describe the nonhuman elements of the great property.[8] Sometimes romantic, often classical, frequently breathless, these are the "majestic domes," "awesome voice," and "austere craggy splendors" (Murfree, *Vanished Star,* 1). When describing the processioning of the land surveyor, Murfree frames the discussion as a conflict between Science, represented by Kenniston, and "the freedom of the wilds," with the human mountain residents somewhere in the middle.

Murfree describes Kenniston standing "with his riding-whip in his hand beside the surveyor . . . conscious of sustaining the curious attention of the chain-bearers," a prosaic description of the outsider that nevertheless introduces both his body and state of mind. The mountain residents are "two stalwart young fellows arrayed in brown jeans and heavy boots, amply competent for the task of carrying the chain through that rugged wilderness," a practical description emphasizing their physical capacities. The shift in language comes when Murfree turns to the nonhuman observers of the scene: "It might seem that all the oreads of the Great Smoky were set to flight by this invasion of their sylvan haunts, so many a flitting white robe fluttered elusive among the dense shadows of the trees, gone ere you could look again; so often a glistening white arm was upflung in the deepest green jungle of the laurel" (205–7). Whether Murfree really believes that oreads exist in Appalachia is less important than her belief that many elements of the community should have distinct voices to tell that community's story. Including a language for something other than outsiders and local residents starts to dislodge the automatic superiority inherent in the literatures of the voyeur, tourist, and social crusader.

If Kenniston were to finish his tourist resort, he might arrange the landscape and the buildings so that visitors felt they had discovered abstracted,

silent nature—beautiful, mysterious, and picturesque. He wants to sell vacations to the tourists and voyeurs; advertisements for his resort might appear
in the same magazines in which Murfree's stories appeared. He is fluent in the
language of the tourist and voyeur: speaking of nature study, for instance,
he says, "Every sylvan detail of the scene pleased his artistic and receptive
sense, as he stood on the great natural terrace." For those interested in
botanizing, he finds that "one could study its chasms and abysses, its jun-
gles of laurel and vast forests." For those in search of the picturesque, he
celebrates the view as "a wonderful fantasy painted in every gradation of
blue" and identifies "an open space [where] some scattered sheep were
feeding,—the effect pastoral and pictorial" (4–5). At the outset, it is hard to
see why Kenniston, an architect and developer, working with money from
investors in Bretonville, the nearest city, will not succeed in creating compe-
tition for Georgia's Tallulah Falls, West Virginia's Greenbriar, North Carolina's Grove Park Inn, or Tennessee's own Beersheba Springs.

Murfree, however, is interested in the story *before* the tourists, voyeurs,
and social crusaders arrive. *His Vanished Star* begins well before the artfully
constructed picturesque wilderness is in place, and the strategy allows
Murfree to explore the tensions around development in turn-of-the-century
Appalachia. Contrary to Kenniston's future propaganda, Murfree argues that
the great property is not untouched, nor does it exist out of modern times.
Rather, the property is a historically specific place, with a complicated
human and nonhuman community living on and in it. Although many of
Murfree's stories are set in "pioneer days" or an unspecified land out of time,
this particular novel was published in 1894, and it circles around contemporary people and their struggles. With the novel, Murfree explores how
the mountains are being sold to absent landowners, how a community
might resist development it does not want, who defines what is beautiful in
a community, and how much negotiation goes into creating a picturesque
wilderness for tourists to view.

The story begins with the arrival of Kenneth Kenniston and his plans
to build a resort hotel on one of the "majestic domes," but the resulting events
are only some of the many events in the novel. To make visible Murfree's
role in the roots of ecological feminism, it helps also to linger on stories of
community members other than Kenniston, for it is in their resistance that
alternatives to status quo structures of power emerge. For instance, the
prospect of an influx of tourists connects Kenniston to a group of moonshiners operating in the "unimagined abysses of the abandoned mine in the
depths of the gorge" (1); they wish desperately to stop the development. In

the course of the story, the building site of the hotel burns. A rigged land survey causes Kenniston to lose most of his land. The mine floods. A supernova (the star of the title) appears in the night sky and propels one of the moonshiners to a daring rescue of a rival in the now-flooded mine. Marriages are proposed, engagements broken, and new alliances formed. Whole households are disrupted by the arrival or exit of their women caretakers. Most events in the story are keyed to nature—fire, flood, earthquake, astronomical explosions—and within its 394 pages, a lot happens.

Yet *His Vanished Star* does not have a plot in the conventional sense. There is not one or even a couple of stories that propel the reader through the novel. The title star does not appear until page 156, and, when it does, it shows itself to a relatively minor character. Kenniston drops out of the book for long stretches, and his story largely wraps up one hundred pages before the end. All the novel's events are, in fact, secondary to the characters whose stories Murfree traces. Along with Kenniston, the characters include Cornelia Taft, a young girl raised by her grandmother to be "a spectacle of perfect precocity and prim perfection" (39), who now must live with her rough, desperately selfish father, Lorenzo Taft, the head of the moonshiners. The novel also traces the young Jack Espey, who has shot a man in a neighboring community and has fled in confusion; the widow Sabrina Larrabee, who takes in anything and anyone needing help because an anonymous woman once did the same for her dying son; two cousins, Julia and Adelicia Tems, with very different attitudes toward women's work and responsibilities, who consider marriage to Jack (in the end, Julia does); an old patriarch, so beautiful in his youth his name was changed from Luther to Lucy Tems, whose sense of honor and justice are severely challenged over the course of the novel; the deputy sheriff Rudolphus Reed, who combines the worst of city and country; and animals, mists, stars, mountains, and rain that take active roles in the unfolding of the characters' stories. The "his" in the title belongs to Jasper Larrabee, the widow's son, struggling to understand why a celestial vision (the supernova) seems to have come to him alone. It is Jasper who performs the rescue of Jack—which eventually results in Lorenzo Taft running off, Cornelia inheriting and running a local store, and Jasper marrying Adelicia.

Scholar Judith Fetterley suggests that "literary regionalism occurs primarily in the form of the sketch or short story"—forms similarly downplaying plot—"because this form made it possible to tell stories about elderly women with bristling chins, about women for whom the eventful means something other than marriage, about women in relation to each other, about women who take care of themselves." In *His Vanished Star,* the stories are not exclusively about women, but they do focus on characters frequently marginalized in literature at the turn of the twentieth century. The reader learns why a young man might turn to moonshining, how a young girl who has lived her whole life in the company of women will struggle when forced to move in with father and brother, why a family with little money might choose to take a stand on land to which they have only recently moved, and how a woman can be so silenced by her family that it takes a stranger's question for anyone to remember she can speak. Underneath Murfree's concessions to the form of Appalachian stories—dialect, conventional descriptions of mountain men and women, and *de rigueur* story devices such as the moonshining—she "represents in narrative a sense of place that reflects a gap between dominant ideological and aesthetic interests and the interests and stories of persons who reside in the locale," what Marjorie Pryse calls "writing out of the gap."[9]

What Murfree adds to the lineage of literary regionalism is her commitment to including the "interests and stories" of the meteorological, animal, and spiritual beings who live in and around the property; she lingers over the life stories of bears, foxes, deer, oreads, and mists. Leslie Marmon Silko suggests such life stories are crucial, because "[a] rock has being or spirit, although we may not understand it. The spirit may differ from the spirit we know in animals or plants or in ourselves. In the end we all originate from the depths of the earth." Similarly, Gary Snyder calls for honoring the watching and listening world; in 1894, Murfree gave nonhuman beings in her fictional community a language and acknowledged the active role they could play in Appalachia.[10]

Pryse argues place is entirely a human construction in texts of literary regionalism, that nature is constructed by the human author to serve or reflect particular "cultural, economic, geographical, and political 'position[s],'" which is certainly part of what "Appalachia" is in *His Vanished Star.* In Murfree's novel, however, place—and the nonhuman inhabitants of the place—are as integral to the story, as real and as important as the human characters. Murfree claims that for the long-term sustainability of a community the nonhuman must be acknowledged, nurtured, and respected. As I suggested in the beginning of this project, conceiving of nature, the nonhuman community, as subjects and not objects is one way modern scholars distinguish between nature as ecology and nature as environment. Greta Gaard and Patrick D. Murphy argue: "Ecology is not a study of the 'external' environment we enter—some big outside that we go to. Ecology is a study of interrelationship, with its bedrock being the recognition of the distinction between things-in-themselves and things-for-us." In other words, making the shift from an environmental perspective to an ecological one involves a theoretical move away from seeing place as in the background (i.e., as "the environment," full of passive objects), separate from humans, into viewing place and humans as inextricably entwined (i.e., as all being active subjects and elements of the "ecology"). Murfree's choice to bring the nonhuman community into her novel—and give them active parts to play in the story—puts her in the lineage of ecological, rather than environmental, thinkers.[11]

Her commitment to telling frequently marginalized stories further locates her in the history of feminism. Because there are so many characters in this novel and because Murfree gives most of them equal time, readers lose track of who is supposed to be the subject and who the objects are, further separating her from much of women's writing about Appalachia at the time. Her strategy, along with her language, irreparably fractures the dualism of subjects and objects into a collection of subjects. In other words, no one story is clearly more important than another, so no one kind of person is more important than another. The result is a definition of community that resists hierarchies based on gender, educational opportunity, social or economic class, or region.

Kenniston's Blindness: Science-versus-Community

Murfree begins, however, with Kenneth Kenniston and his perspective, a worldview familiar to readers of much literature about Appalachia written by women. *His Vanished Star* opens as if it is the literature of the voyeur or tourist but then startles the reader by turning the tables. Suddenly the viewer, the subject, and, by extension, the reader, are being looked back at. The objects in the novel look critically at the subject, the viewer; thus, the spectacle becomes not the exotic Appalachian but the out-of-place developer.[12] Being viewed makes Kenneth Kenniston profoundly uncomfortable. It is one of his first signs that the Appalachian community is not going to behave, that his belief in the primacy of his subject position may be flawed. For instance, when along for the survey of his land, Kenniston finds his "correct equestrian garb [was] sufficiently dissimilar to give him that air of peculiarity and modishness that somehow seems so unworthy and flippant . . . it made him a trifle ill at ease, and he had a sense of being out of his sphere" (Murfree, *Vanished Star*, 205). The switch is literal when the burning hotel and Kenniston's frustration are witnessed by many of the mountain residents who make special trips to view what "might be accounted a spectacle in some sort" (169). As the story unfolds, readers find the spectacle is, for the mountain residents, a chance to celebrate by witnessing, by viewing, the end of an unwanted incursion into their community—an incursion that would have resulted in them becoming objects for Americans to pay to view.

With her character Kenneth Kenniston, Murfree illustrates Patrick Murphy's discussion of the "continuing refusal to recognize reciprocity as a ubiquitous natural/cultural process." Kenniston is the symbol of mainstream, hierarchical philosophy—that which positions the self as an isolated, independent subject, always alienated from the Other, the object (whether that Other is human or nonhuman). In *Literature, Nature, and Other: Ecofeminist Critiques*, Murphy asks, "What if instead of alienation we posited *relation* as the primary mode of human-human and human-nature interaction? . . . What if we worked from a concept of relational difference and *anotherness* rather than Otherness?" Thinking about the world as a collection of self-another relations who reciprocally help each other is startlingly similar to Murfree's discussion of how the local characters process the Appalachian world around them. Defining community as self-another defeats Kenniston's proposed development. Murphy argues that the problem with a self-Other worldview (such as that of Kenniston) is that "Otherness isolated from anotherness suppresses knowledge of the ecological processes of interdependency—the ways in which humans and other entities survive, change, and learn by continuously mutually influencing each other—and denies any ethics of responsibility."[13] These processes of ecological interdependency, in Murfree's fictional imagining, lead to the effective stopping of Kenniston's nonconsensual, undiscussed development by a community without the law, money, or demographics on its side.

Much earlier in the story, when Kenniston is still at the planning stages of his development, he recognizes some of the human obstacles he faces: "The whole scene, with its blended solemnity and beauty and dignity, would well accord with the castellated edifice his fancy had set in its midst . . . were it not for a section of the foreground immediately below the cliffs of the terrace." The problem is that "there stood, bare and open and unsheltered, a primitive log cabin, a stretch of cornfields, a horse-lot, a pig-pen, and all the accessories of most modern and unimpressive American poverty and ignorance." This is the farm owned by the Tems family, which Kenniston plans on buying or, failing that, acquiring by intimidation. Initially,

Murfree describes the farm as Kenniston sees it, saying, "Being near, and bearing human significance, the prosaic little home seemed the most salient point, in its incongruity, in the whole magnificent landscape" (Murfree, *Vanished Star,* 5). Kenniston seems unaware of the irony in his statement: if he is successful, more human presence than ever before will be introduced to the scene, thus "solving" the incongruity of one sign of human life in the scene by installing teeming human life throughout the scene.[14] To Kenniston, however, an Appalachian family is just a group of objects to be moved at will.

The members of the Tems household do not behave as objects that can be easily moved. They insist on being subjects in the community in and around the great property. As Lorenzo Taft sums it up, "Ye want yer *home,* an' the company wants yer *hut*" (Murfree, *Vanished Star,* 17). The local residents in Murfree's mountain community recognize a broader connection to place than mere land ownership; as it would for most people, the idea of home reaches beyond the monetary value of the physical structure. But Murfree has even more in mind than this. Even though Luther Tems has argued "there he meant to stay, as his father and his grandfather had before him to a great age" (7), the family has been on the particular piece of land only five years (18). Yet, the mountain residents resist Kenniston because they have lived in the community—defined as on the mountain—for hundreds of years (19–20). For the Tems family, although they participate in the legalities of land ownership, *selling* land—any of the great property—for mere profit or the sake of vacationers' ease violates principles established by years of living with the land.

Kenniston's Defeat: The Agency of Bears and Fire

From the hotel's inception, all members of the mountain community—including those that are meteorological, animal, spiritual, as well as human—are involved in considering the resort, even though Kenniston never consults any of them. As construction begins, "the unfamiliar mists" are "shifting through it and drifting along corridor and ball-room and scaling the tower." Mountain storms "assailed" the new structure, testing its mettle. Murfree writes that "from far and near the mountaineers visited the unfinished structure." She describes how the mountain residents investigate all of the building, offer advice to the workers in charge of constructing the hotel, and ask questions about the structure. In addition, she gives examples of other elements of the community who visit the site. First, "a red fox was glimpsed early one morning, with brush in air, speeding along the joists

of the ball-room." Then, "a deer, doubtless a familiar of the springs, was visible once, leaping wildly down the rocks" to the construction area. And,
speaking of other, less recognizable—that is, more spiritual—familiars, she
says, "Others, too, of the ancient owners of the soil came on more prosaic
quest, but in the dead hour of darkness or the light of the midnight moon."
One of these was "a young bear." The bear is looking for food: "Perhaps it
was this alone that led him about the angles and turns of the building."
However, Murfree comments, he "seemed as censorious a critic" as any of
the human visitors were as he expressed his "sarcastic, snarling contempt"
of this "hotel, an outline of modern frivolity and summer pleasuring and
flimsy vastness" (165–67).

Although the humans—who by now have decided that they do not want
the development in their community—have their hands essentially tied,
other community members intervene. A reviewer in the *Critic* (of a different Murfree novel) suggested that the landscape "plays an almost human
part" in Murfree's stories and that she has "the power of making us feel the
life that is in inanimate objects"—essentially what happens here.[15] The same
young bear who wandered around the frame of the building is the agent of
the tourist resort's demise: "The wind could never have turned over the low
apparatus [a portable forge] set in the hollow of the ledges, but the bear
could, and did"—the charcoal combusts and the wood frame of the building catches on fire. This action is done entirely by the animal in the story,
as Murfree says, "save the impassive, neutral night, the event had no other
witness" except the bear (Murfree, *Vanished Star*, 168). In the passage, the
bear's actions are not anthropomorphized; in other words, the bear does not
consciously plan on turning over the forge in order to set the building on
fire. In fact, it flees once the flames catch hold. Yet, according the Murfree,
"the fact of the Bruin's agency was relegated to the state of things not
revealed, which we denominate mystery" (308). In other words, although not
the same as human agency (animal spirits are different from human, in
Silko's terms), and not easy to explain rationally, the bear does act as a subject in the story. The hotel is completely destroyed; the consensus decision
of the community is effectively enacted.

By the end of the novel, Kenniston leaves to focus on "plans for a great
public edifice in Bretonville" and the mountain resort is "definitely abandoned" (391). Fittingly, Kenniston ends up building monuments to humans
in the city—reminders of humans in a place built by and for human use;
he never escapes from his human-bound definitions of community. Kenniston's definition of nature as passive, inanimate, and without agency makes

him underestimate the resources of the community he is fighting. His initial defeat by the intervention of animals and fire is succeeded by a final blow engineered by a human but aimed at Kenniston's reliance on Science. Because Kenniston believes so strongly in the infallibility of Science, he accepts a flawed survey that gives most of the great property over to his nemesis, Lucy Tems. Although readers learn that the cornerstone, a gigantic boulder, has been moved by a well-placed charge of dynamite, Kenniston clings to his belief that rocks simply do not just get up and move—and accepts the survey (217).[16] The mountain residents' alternate definition of community as a interdependent web of relationships—with humans as one of many elements—has more resources to address a threat to it.

Gender, Class, and Race: Hidden Strengths and Limitations

The primary intermediaries between nonhuman and human community members are the novel's women. They live, for the most part, in a parallel women's community that is unseen by most of the men, including Kenniston. The community appears in several places in the novel, from Cornelia Taft's attempts to re-create the woman-only space she shared with her grandmother; to Sabrina Larrabee's caretaking of injured animals, women, men, and children because of the connection she feels to the woman who did the same for Larrabee's dying son; to the hard work (recognized by only one male character) done by Adelicia Tems to keep her uncle's household running; to Julia Tems's interior world, which is fulfilling enough that she rarely speaks to the men around her. Women's invisible labor and their private community are often connected implicitly to the nonhuman community: Julia's desire is made visible by the flowers she finds; Sabrina's baby turkey represents her kindness; Cornelia's reminiscences of her former home indirectly stop the moonshiners' abuses of nature; and Adelicia finds peace only when wandering in the woods. Murfree implies that the connections between women and Appalachia are profound and reciprocal, but she chooses not to explain them to unsympathetic readers or characters, perhaps to protect or preserve the women from unsympathetic viewers.

Although Kenniston cannot accept his defeat rationally or even see the power of the women around him, Murfree writes a scene in which he glimpses both metaphorically. In a dream sequence, an alliance of a woman and an animal counters Kenniston's human-only worldview. Kenniston dreams on a stormy night as he sleeps in the Tems house (taking advantage of their hospitality while simultaneously trying to convince them to sell).

At first, he is "processioning those wild acres of mountain fastnesses" (Murfree, *Vanished Star,* 36), which is the survey that will signal his final exit from the community, but which he thinks will force the Tems family to move. In the dream, "the serpentine lengths of the surveyor's chain seemed alive as the chain-bearers dragged it writhing through the grass" (38). Spiritual images of a serpent foreshadow Kenniston's experiences processioning the land; Murfree repeats the image months later during the actual surveying, when Kenniston watches as "the chain writhed through the grass between them like some living sinuous thing" (206). As the surveying results in Kenniston's "owning" less land than he thought (in fact not even owning the site for the hotel), the snake in the grass signals his own exile from Paradise, his inability to live on the great property.

The second half of the dream counters Kenniston's belief in Science and rationality. As he attempts to dismantle the Tems family's physical house, two startling figures appear in the dream before him: "[S]uddenly Julia [Tems] appeared, with a strange face, subtle and insidious and sinister, leading the panther which he had heard filling the night with terror" (38). Although it is a bear and not a panther that destroys Kenniston's development, the symbolism is obvious. In 1978, Susan Griffin named the power that comes from such alliances of women and animals, "the roaring inside her" and called for unleashing it in the service of social and planetary, rather than "objective," justice. Listen to Griffin's description of the man who listens only to measurements: "But for him this dialogue [between humans and nature] is over. He says he is not part of this world, that he was set on this world as a stranger. He sets himself apart from women and nature." Griffin continues her description, writing: "[I]deas [enter] his head on certain nights in the shapes of dreams. . . . And into these first moments of waking crept this doubt . . . creating an unnatural space between his soul and his flesh, this doubt of the justice of things after all."[17] More than eighty years earlier, Murfree created a portrait of such a man and wrote a book suggesting the fallibility of such a position. Kenniston, Murfree says, "was frightened, and awoke" (Murfree, *Vanished Star,* 38). Perhaps he has seen his defeat and the strength of the community against him for the first (and only) time. The alliance between humans and animals is exactly that which profoundly frightens Kenniston—and that by which his plans for developing the land without discussing it with the community are stopped.

Does Murfree mean that all development, all Progress, is bad for Appalachia? Critic Durwood Dunn argues she does, when he says Murfree's "Tennessee mountaineer could only survive by eschewing any encroachment into his domain of modern industrial America." Understandably, Dunn finds such a conclusion to be both paternalistic and untenable for actual Appalachians.[18] Rejecting Kenniston's resort hotel could be read as rejecting progress. Yet, despite living in a rural community, Murfree's mountain residents themselves are neither isolated nor primitive when Kenniston arrives. Characters like Jack Espey, the Larrabees, and Rudolphus Reed move in and out of the community, aware of and participating in both country, town, and, in the case of Sabrina Larrabee's son, nation (as he was a war casualty). Additionally, the "American poverty" (Murfree, *Vanished Star*, 5) of the Tems family is, after all, connected to and caused in part by larger national practices and economic trends. At least in *His Vanished Star*, Murfree's answer is more complicated than simply arguing that all progress is bad.

More directly, the novel suggests the mountain residents are not rejecting progress wholesale, just the kind that does not take into account the health of the whole community. Along with the resort hotel, the mountain residents also reject that quintessential symbol of "primitive" Appalachia, moonshining—because it too is unhealthy for the long-term community. As symbols of lawless, precivilized times, the moonshiners operate symbolically as anti-Progress. But Murfree claims the violence, economics, and rebellion fostered by moonshining is as out of line with the wider human and nonhuman community as the hotel was. Of the support beams in the walls of the moonshiners' operation, located in the abandoned mine, she writes: "[W]hat sordid translation from the noble forests without, where the unstricken of their kindred still towered toward the stars, and sang with the winds, and received glad gifts from the seasons in springing sap and spreading leaf, in acorn and cone, and kept a covenant with time registering the years in mystic rings in their inmost hearts!" (56). Trees are not meant to be bent to the moonshiner's will. Lorenzo Taft, the ringleader, is just as misguided as Kenniston was in thinking he can create and maintain an isolated human community in Appalachia.[19] In the end of *His Vanished Star*, the moonshiners' cave is destroyed when Taft sets charges to destroy evidence of the still. These explosions cause a flood that prevents the cave from ever being used again for moonshining (Murfree, *Vanished Star*, 382). Thus, as with the hotel, the nonhuman community assists less in simply rejecting Progress and more in ending an unnatural use of resources to restore balance to the community.

Lost in the literature of the tourist, voyeur, and social crusader, what appears in Mary Noailles Murfree's *His Vanished Star* are effective interventions by an Appalachian community into unwanted development—whose importance it is hard to overstate. For the first time in all the literature discussed here, an Appalachian community steps in and makes a change based on the consensus of local human and nonhuman community members.

Yet Murfree's vision is not a perfect one. Hers is a selective vision of Appalachia itself. What she does not do in this novel is incorporate the diversity of the turn-of-the-century Appalachian communities on which she modeled her fictional world. According to William H. Turner, approximately 14 percent of the population in southern Appalachia was African American between 1890 and 1910. Lenwood Davis in *The Black Heritage of Western North Carolina* finds that, in 1887, an urban center like Asheville, North Carolina, had a population of 2,607 African Americans and 4,561 white Americans. By 1890, the African American population in Asheville had grown to 3,567 African Americans. During the time period of *His Vanished Star,* other writers were gathering information about Appalachia's African Americans. George S. Dickerman, writing in the *Southern Workman,* argued in 1905 that the counties of eastern Tennessee—in and around Murfree's Beersheba Springs—had "one Negro to nine white people."[20]

Although the 1838 violent removal, the infamous "Trail of Tears," devastated southern Appalachia's Native American population, especially the Cherokee peoples, Appalachia at the turn of the century still had a significant Native American constituency as well. Emily K. Herron argued in 1900 in the *Southern Workman* that "over a thousand [Cherokees] who loved their homes too ardently to leave sought refuge in the mountains until their right to retain a portion of their lands in North Carolina was established. In 1889 this remnant of the tribe was incorporated by the General Assembly of the State." By 1906 the Eastern Band of the Cherokees had enough of a political presence in the region to win a case before the U.S. Supreme Court, which led to the appointment of Indian Inspector Frank Churchill. He was hired to create a survey of all the eligible tribe members in the Appalachian region and found many even with his rigorous (and disturbing) racial standards. Along with Cherokees were members of other tribes, such as Creeks, Choctaws, and Chickasaws, inhabiting the Appalachians about which Murfree wrote.[21] Although Murfree's stories can be read for their ecological theoretical insights she explores through fiction, given the mountains' racial diversity, it is misguided at best, racist at worst, to read them as somehow "true" to the "real" Appalachia. Fortunately, writers such as Effie Waller Smith were exploring how full participation of nonwhite residents would further redefine community in Appalachia.

Figure 8. Effie Waller Smith upon her graduation from Kentucky Normal School, Frankfort, Kentucky. From the collection of Mr. David E. Deskins.

EFFIE WALLER SMITH RHYMING
FROM AND FOR THE CUMBERLANDS

ANSWER TO VERSES ADDRESSED TO ME BY PETER CLAY
Backward down the stream of time
My wandering mind now floats,
When I a hoyden country lass,
In homespun petticoats

That reached down to my ankles bare,
Ankles bare and brown, too;
Not browned by summer suns, for birth
Had giv'n to them that hue.

I think now of those days when hills
And vales with music rang,
Of which in crude, uneven,
Yet rhythmic, words, I sang.

And I'm thinking, poet friend,
How you have, oftentimes,
Admired with pure unselfishness
Those simple, homely rhymes.

For 'tis the genius of the soul
(Though underneath a skin
Of dusky hue its fire may burn)
Your unfeigned praises win.

Oh that earth had more of beings
With generous minds like yours,
Who alike, true worth and honor
To the black and white secures.

Accept, dear poet, then, my thanks
For your glowing words of praise,
For the simple, homely, faulty rhymes
Of my early girlhood days.[22]

Effie Waller Smith expands the meaning of the terms "woman" and
"Appalachian" at the turn of the past century, by insisting on a complex
and dynamic interplay between African American, Appalachian, and woman

writer. Her poetry and short stories about Appalachia, as well as her exploration of one woman's artistic consciousness—her self-named "genius of the
soul / (Though underneath a skin / Of dusky hue its fire may burn)"—suggest that she wished readers to acknowledge her and her characters as
inseparably Appalachian, black, and gendered.[23] Whether discussing grief,
women's independence, feminism, racism, or the importance of nature in
individual lives, Smith almost always spoke as a voice from the hills. Doing
so transforms the definition of community in Appalachia to include still
more of its diverse community members and pushes readers to reconsider
and perhaps reject hierarchies of race, class, gender, and place.

Smith's poem, "On Receiving a Souvenir Postcard,"[24] from 1909, begins
"On the little desk before me, / A pictured post-card lies." In the following stanza, Smith establishes that "It was sent from Kentucky, where / My
childhood's home used to be." The poem, which could be mistaken for a
sentimental poem simplistically celebrating Appalachian nature, certainly
lingers over cherished outdoor activities, such as fishing, daydreaming, and
keeping track of the river and its traffic:

> There's the winding Sandy river
> And the "Big Rocks" by its side,
> Where together we've sat fishing,
> Or looking across the tide.
>
> Have wondered at the steamboats
> Painted in colors gay
> On the other side of the river
> Smoking and puffing away.
>
> Or at the town in the distant
> Sometimes we'd sit and gaze
> And dream bright dreams of the future—
> Air castles of childhood days.

Along with observing natural events, Smith describes specific human events
in her poem—lovers who "fall out and quarrel" but then make up, for
instance. Finally, she steps back from the particular to describe in abstract
a life's major emotions—love, anger, and joy—metaphorically as natural
phenomena: "darkened valleys," "mountain's height," "cloud-hung heav-
ens," and "sunshine bright." Humans and Appalachia are deeply, significantly entwined in Smith's poem.

Yet, the poem does more than simply celebrate interconnections between people and Appalachian places. Smith introduces the idea that, unlike in the literature of the tourist, voyeur, and social crusader, her first priority is not to explain Appalachia to people unfamiliar with it. Instead, "On Receiving a Souvenir Postcard" is a poem for insiders, relying on shared experience. Readers who do not understand how important Appalachia can be to a person from Appalachia are not Smith's concern: "The rustic scene in black and white, / . . . / Might not interest you at all." She continues:

> You may not care to look at it,
> What matter if you don't;
> Your not having any interest, for
> This pictured post-card won't. [sic]
> Make less for me the memories
> . . . .
> And which to-day entwine.

In other words, Smith's preferred audience stands in something like the "self-another" relationship Patrick Murphy discussed—with reciprocity between insiders, the poet, and Appalachia. Others can, of course, read the poem; but by not explaining Appalachia and the relationship between the poet, the place, and her lover, Smith expects unfamiliar readers to find their own knowledge, to find their own way into Appalachia. A reader like Kenneth Kenniston might not understand "On Receiving a Souvenir Postcard," but Sabrina Larrabee and Adelicia Tems could have recognized in Smith's poem their own private relationships with nonhuman Appalachia.

Unlike Murfree's writing, the poem's "rustic scene in black and white" is further complicated by Smith's discussions of what it was like to be African American at the turn of the past century. The play on words, in which "black and white" refers both to photography and to Appalachia's African American and European residents, emphasizes the diversity Smith remembers around the Sandy River. In her "Answer to Verses Addressed to Me by Peter Clay," quoted in full at the beginning of this section, Smith wishes that other white Americans could give "true worth and honor" to both "black and white" in Kentucky. In "Answer," Smith also writes as an artist to an artist, describing Clay as "pure unselfishness" for admiring her rhymes; in so doing, Smith emphasizes not only the racial diversity present but also the artistic insight that comes from giving voice to diverse community members. "On Receiving a Souvenir Postcard" is an example of such artistic insight, as its rustic scene is available to any person united with the place through a love of the Sandy River.

The Comfort and Strength of Mountains

In other poems, Smith hints at the racism and classism that make in- cluding diverse voices in Appalachian communities—black and white— difficult. "A Mountain Graveyard,"[25] also published in 1909, describes the practice of scattering glass and shells on graves, a mourning ritual of some African American communities. Smith again splits her potential audience into people who will understand and people who will not, and again her sympathy lies with those who will. She directly challenges visitors to the gravesite and her readers who may be hostile, dismissive, or think them- selves superior to the mourners:

> Smile not, ye who pass them by,
> For the love that placed them there
> Deemed that they were things most fair.

Smith acknowledges that some viewers—perhaps more urban, more wealthy, or not from a racial and cultural group that would decorate graves in such a way—will smile, or, by extension, dismiss and ridicule the people who spread the shells and glass. In so doing, she argues at the least that several communities exist simultaneously in Appalachia. Furthermore, she hints that tension underlies communication between the communities. By defend- ing the ritual, Smith hints that she and those for whom she speaks in this poem will work to preserve cultural practices—and that such work has "true worth and honor."

More importantly, however, "A Mountain Graveyard" is a poem about the death of subsistence farmers, people whose life was made difficult by "The unending strife for bread / That has stunted heart and head." The men buried in this graveyard are remembered by human and nonhuman alike as the wind sounds "Sobs of immemorial grief" and the trees lift limbs to the sky "Like wild arms . . . mad with loss, / And with human hearts did share / Grief's long protest and despair." Not only are the human community members remembering the nonhuman (as they do in "On Receiving A Sou- venir Postcard"), but the nonhuman beings also mark the passing of humans. Within the sparse poetic form, Smith makes visible multiple Appalachian communities, nods to potential conflict between them, and then presents

African American Appalachians as fully rounded characters whose lives have been shaped by America's larger economic and social hierarchies that keep certain people in difficult careers such as subsistence farming. For readers who understand, the poem argues that not having the money to erect "tall marbles, gleaming white" (88–89) does not mean the graves are any less dignified, nor the deaths any less important. Grief, in this poem, gives way to the comfort that Appalachian nature, cultural ritual, and faith in a life after death provide to poet and insider reader.

Writing in and about her roots in Pikeville, Kentucky, Smith goes beyond presenting nature as a gentle comfort for residents. Smith wants that comfort to extend to times and situations that defy expectations about women's and African American's roles and capabilities. In "A Meadow Brook" and "The Hills," Smith argues that love, joy, and comfort from the nonhuman world should not be limited to people of a particular skin color or bank account. A nostalgic, shorter poem, "A Meadow Brook"[26] gives Smith the opportunity to self-identify as a "nature-loving soul" and explore how such a person finds solace in nature:

> How often there from perplexing care
> Listening to the brooklet's flow,
> Have I laid at rest on the grassy breast
> Of Mother Earth long ago.

The "cool retreat" she describes seems to be for body and soul, but reading Smith's poems, I am often struck by her sense of physical safety and freedom for women and, more particularly, African American women, in Appalachia. "To the Reader"[27] extends the relaxation in the outdoors of "A Meadow Brook" to nighttime sojourns in the same wilderness. "To the Reader" says:

> There musing oft at night
> When clear and soft the light
> Fell from the stars so bright,
> I've wandered solitary,
> When Nature seemed at ease,
> When soft and low the cooing gales
> Whispered among the trees.

Writing in the first decade of 1900, when lynch mob violence was rampant, Smith claims women can be safe outside by themselves. With her poetry, then, she enacts a vision of how safe the world should be in the face of how dangerous it often was. One of the communities in which Smith surely must have participated, given her family's emphasis on education and middle-class resources, was in the readership of black-owned newspapers. Reading both local and national papers, Smith would have known of Ida B. Wells-Barnett from nearby Memphis, Tennessee, who was actively documenting violence by white Americans against African Americans. Wells-Barnett began her work documenting and analyzing American violence after being forced by race rioting and threats out of her home and her part ownership and editorship of the black-owned newspaper, the *Memphis Free Speech*. When Wells-Barnett argues, "The negro has suffered far more from the commission of [assaults] against the women of his race by white men than the white race has ever suffered through *his* crimes,"[28] the stakes are raised on Smith wandering alone by herself in the woods.

Within Appalachia, the anonymous article, "Girls in the Open Air," printed in Chattanooga's *Justice* in 1887, argued: "Out of door exercise is essential to vigor of body, and vigor of body is essential to youthfulness of appearance. . . . It is as natural for girls to romp and play in the open air as it is for colts to do . . . [yet their health is] impaired by the hot house bringing up which the girls have to undergo."[29] Smith's call for girls' unfettered access to the outdoors echoes the African American Appalachian editors of the *Justice*. Given the evidence collected by Wells-Barnett, both "To the Reader" and "Girls in the Open Air" become politicized statements involving social justice and societal change, because neither are givens for many girls in their audiences. Instead, violence or efforts taken daily to avoid violence, were more likely shared experiences. Finally, Smith herself had firsthand knowledge of the dangers faced by African American men and women, not only in her role as a schoolteacher, but also through the unsolved murder of her husband, a deputy sheriff.[30] The post-Reconstruction South was a difficult place for any African American to be in the open air. Nevertheless, Smith claims the freedom for women to walk, to muse, to "wander solitary," and to be at ease in the mountains of Appalachia.

Claiming Her Place: Smith as a Female Athlete

"The Hills"[31] extends the images of women alone in the wilderness found in "A Meadow Brook" and "To the Reader." Much like the literature of the social crusader, this poem calls for women to explore, adventure, and form independent identities from the breadth of the mountains; however, the stakes are higher when races other than the social crusader's white Euro-peans are included. In other words, Smith is no longer content with pock-ets of safety, "cool retreats"; she now wants expanded and extended safe spaces for active, athletic women wanderers. The first space to open, how-ever, is a mental one; "The Hills" begins with a gesture to displace typical criticisms of Appalachia and Appalachian identities that so limited moun-tain residents' agency in the literatures of the tourist, voyeur, and social cru-sader. Smith says:

> He is not destitute of lore,—
> Far, far from it is he,—
> Who doth the mighty hills adore,
> And love them reverently.

Value, depth of culture, and sophistication, the stanza claims, can emerge from a deep and thoughtful identification with the mountains themselves. Rather than marking ignorance or noble savagery, loving the hills with delib-eration (i.e., reverence) brings shared cultural identity, history, and authen-ticity. The rest of the poem makes clear that Smith is not content with her opening stanza's subtle critique of city people and their patronizing of Appalachian people. In a later stanza, she addresses the city reader directly:

> Tho' sweet your city life may be,
> Yet sweeter, sweeter still
> Is my quiet country life to me.

She equalizes city and country, rejecting any hierarchy of urban over rural. Out of the now-authentic mountain culture, the poet speaks.

As she addresses the reader, Smith shifts away from the generic male pronoun of the poem's beginning to the poet's female voice, and by so doing strengthens the poem's force and persuasion. The poem, as it develops, also undermines its initial claim about Appalachia's "quiet country life." But first, Smith says:

> Far from the city's strife and care
> I live a life obscure;
> I breathe the sweet health-giving ai[r]
> And drink the water pure.

Calling upon the first-person, female "I" makes the poem a journey of discovery for Appalachian women. It moves Smith beyond generic criticisms of Appalachia (or the rural) in American society to the strengths Appalachia contains for individual women.

The stanza does more than simply claim the poet's voice; it also brings the surrounding ecology into the poem. Smith identifies human and non-human strengths of mountain life: less stress and worries on the human psyche, as well as better, cleaner water and air for all community members. Yet, as ecologically significant as the indictment of cities' unhealthiness and impurities may be, the poem at this point retains fairly passive or typical roles for women. Breathing and drinking do not especially challenge the reader's expectations of femininity. But Smith in the poem does not actually settle for living "a life obscure" and quiet (although the historical erasure of this ambitious author lends the line increased poignancy). Instead, the female figure slowly reveals her active, self-defined, and athletic life. She roams the vales and "views their summits high," presumably after hiking or riding to the mountain peaks. As it was for the social crusaders, Appalachia is personally liberating and freeing for the poem's female voice. Also, as with the social crusaders, lessons and challenges emerge from women's botanizing or nature study:

> The rugged, rocky peaks I climb,
> Which bold and peerless stand,
> Majestic, mighty, huge, sublime,
> So beautiful and grand!
>
> The wondrous works of God I view
> In every dell and nook;
> And daily learn some lesson new,
> From Nature's open book.

Smith's experiences, her celebration of the joy and education that comes from exploring Appalachian nature, are reflected by other articles in the African American Appalachian press during the era. For instance, newspapers and magazines include articles about not-to-be-missed natural sites, birds, and trees. They also promote the virtues of nature study in school. Smith chooses to speak on a personal level about the transformative power of "Nature's open book." The newspaper articles suggest that in some African American Appalachians she would find a willing audience.[32]

However, unlike the social crusaders, Smith's personal growth and development is not predicated on the diminishment of Appalachian women. In another poem, "Apple Sauce and Chicken Fried,"[33] Smith explicitly counters outside visitors who devalue local women's knowledge, by saying,

> You may talk about the knowledge
> Which our farmers' girls have gained
> From cooking-schools and cook-books[.]

With the rest of the poem, Smith instead celebrates food cooked in the traditional way by her mother. Furthermore, the poem implies, learning her mother's knowledge is more difficult than copying recipes from books (Smith herself has tried "in vain"). Finally, "Apple Sauce and Chicken Fried" does something that the fancy "Chicken a la Française, / And also fricassee" cannot: it binds together communities—mothers, daughters, preachers, and families. No one is diminished, and many are included, in Smith's definition of community.

Although community is essential to Smith, she also represents her own artistic development in "The Hills." For Smith, such growth does not have to be built on status quo social hierarchies and is available by extension to any female reader of her poems. Smith does not address but, equally importantly, does not preclude, other women's agency developing out of Appalachian and African American experiences. Instead she models her agency and independence by musing about how Appalachian nature inspires and challenges her artistic gifts:

> Here calm and wooded glens afford
> The noblest, purest kind
> Of inspiration for the bard's
> Dreamy and gifted mind.
>
> And here is music never still,
> Not tiresome, weird or dull;
> And here are scenes for artist's eye,
> Lovely and beautiful.

Smith's final gesture in the poem is to claim these summits and "majestic, mighty, huge, sublime" peaks as home—her home, where she hopes to "live and die!" "The Hills" is a poem about women loving mountains, women exploring alone, and local women defining themselves as full, participating members of human and nonhuman mountain communities.

Smith's Black Feminist Voice

Between the discussions of personal and community identity, Smith's poetry also creates space for explicit feminist statements. "The 'Bachelor Girl'"[34] demonstrates Smith's knowledge of and engagement with feminism in women's lives. Although not written in first person as were some of the previously discussed poems, "The 'Bachelor Girl'" brings Smith into close conversation with turn-of-the-century "Woman's Rights." Because the poet's sympathy clearly lies with the "self-supporting" girl, the poem argues without having to state explicitly that black women have their own feminism, that their feminism helps to change the world, and that the feminism emerging from black women fits comfortably into Smith's definition of Appalachia and home.

Over the course of the poem, Smith outlines many myths about feminists current in her time. For instance, they are old maids who have simply been unsuccessful finding husbands. They suffer from nervous conditions, such as the diseases outlined by the new generation of sexologists with their various cures for women. Feminists are humorless, cross, and inexplicably angry. They have no common sense, being instead full of impractical, misguided ideas. However, acknowledging these myths is not the same as accepting them; in fact, Smith introduces the stereotypes so as to counter their truths with what she says the bachelor girl actually is.

In addition to defying expectations about feminists, Smith outlines the specific characteristics of stereotypical femininity that the bachelor girl rejects. She is not fulfilled simply by having a "Mrs." in front of her name. She rejects the time, effort, and effect of mainstream fashion. Cute things—puppies, kittens, children's clothes—do not hold her attention. She does not define her self-worth by the number of children she has. She is not impressed by love stories and purely sentimental poems (neither is Smith, for that matter), opting instead for a gender-neutral, far-reaching education. Finally, the bachelor girl is not willing to be dependent on parents until the perfect husband comes along to take over her support. As soon as she raises each possibility, Smith counters the myths to claim that "bachelor girls" are not these stereotypes.

Perhaps not surprisingly, some of the best features of the bachelor girl are those Smith has celebrated in her other poems. She feels free to go outdoors alone. Like the woman in "To the Reader," the bachelor girl wanders by herself at night—with the added protection (for threatening humans, not animals) of a side arm. Comfortable in nature, the bachelor girl is not scared of animals (even the typical mouse). As the speaker in "The Hills" would have to be to see the summits and majestic mountains, the bachelor girl is athletic. Even without the first-person pronoun, the overlap of desirable attributes across Smith's poetry brings the bachelor girl and the "I" in her other poems quite close together.

Yet, one senses, the bachelor girl solves what the poetic persona in "A Meadow Brook" or "The Hills" could only implicitly counter. The bachelor girl remains healthy and centered while escaping the "life obscure." In this poem, Smith celebrates both city and country: along with her time outdoors, this character is comfortable in the "fast hustling whirl," the "hurry and the flurry" of the urban world. Rather than turning inward to the artistic mind, and inviting others along only insofar as they too can identify as artists, the bachelor girl is an activist; she understands, speaks about, and participates in the larger world to help other disenfranchised women and men. Her strong opinions on politics, international history and biography, and the latest political strategies culminate in the poem's penultimate stanza. Above all, the bachelor girl embraces and promotes the cause of "Woman's Rights." Smith's women loving mountains, finding independent agency, and promoting a diverse definition of Appalachia to include African Americans and all women, also turn out to be feminist poets with concern and devotion to Appalachian communities. Like Effie Waller Smith, above all, the bachelor girl is self-supporting, and, as Smith should be, she is "here to stay." Here is the poem in full:

THE "BACHELOR GIRL"
She's no "old maid," she's not afraid
To let you know she's her own "boss,"
She's easy pleased, she's not diseased,
She is not nervous, is not cross.

She's no desire whatever for
Mrs. to precede her name,
The blessedness of singleness
She all her life will proudly claim.

She does not sit around and knit
On baby caps and mittens,

She does not play her time away
With puggy dogs and kittens.

And if a mouse about the house
She sees, she will not jump and scream;
Of handsome beaux and billet doux
The "bachelor girl" does never dream.

She does not puff and frizz and fluff
Her hair, nor squeeze and pad her form.
With painted face, affected grace,
The "bachelor girl" ne'er seeks to charm.

She reads history, biography,
Tales of adventure far and near,
On sea or land, but poetry and
Love stories rarely interest her.

She's lots of wit, and uses it,
Of "horse sense," too, she has a store;
The latest news she always knows,
She scans the daily papers o'er.

Of politics and all the tricks
And schemes that politicians use,
She knows full well and she can tell
With eloquence of them her views.

An athlete that's hard to beat
The "bachelor girl" surely is,
When playing games she makes good aims
And always strictly minds her "biz."

Amid the hurry and the flurry
Of this life she goes alone,
No matter where you see her
She seldom has a chaperon.

But when you meet her on the street
At night she has a "32,"
And she can shoot you, bet your boots,
When necessity demands her to.

Her heart is kind and you will find
Her often scattering sunshine bright
Among the poor, and she is sure
To always advocate the right.

On her *pater* and her *mater*
For her support she does not lean,
She talks and writes of "Woman's Rights"
In language forceful and clean.

She does not shirk, but does her work,
Amid the world's fast hustling whirl,
And come what may, she's here to stay,
The self-supporting "bachelor girl."

It may, on the surface, seem unexpected to find black feminism in an Appalachian voice at the turn of the twentieth century. Yet, scholar Beverly Guy-Sheftall has traced black U.S. feminism going back to the early nineteenth century and significantly predating Effie Waller Smith. Defining black feminism as "the emancipatory vision and acts of resistance among a diverse group of African American women," Guy-Sheftall finds in black feminist texts struggles for "self-definition, the liberation of black people, and gender equality," all of which are also Smith's concerns. Deborah Gray White explains why, even among scholars searching for them, black feminists like Smith have been hard to find in historical sources, writing that "in part a manifestation of the black woman's perennial concern with image, a justifiable concern born of centuries of vilification[, b]lack women's reluctance to donate personal papers also stems from the adversarial nature of the relationship that countless black women have had with many public institutions and the resultant suspicion of anyone seeking private information."[35] Smith herself stopped publishing after 1917, although she lived until 1960. Black feminists in Appalachia may especially have had cause to be cautious, given the turn-of-the-century political climate that sought actively to construct Appalachia as "pure white."

At the end of Reconstruction in the United States, the desire for national reconciliation at any cost grew among its white citizens. At the same time, activism for white Appalachians was growing, as activism for southern African Americans was shrinking. Acknowledging African Americans who were native to the region threatened the neatness and "safety" of Appalachian activism and led to what Edward J. Cabbell named "black invisibility" in writings about Appalachia. Sometimes the effort to erase nonwhite community members leads to humorously convoluted passages, as when social crusader Grace Funk Myers writes: "Never having worked among the colored people at any time, and not wishing to engage in both lines of work— the colored and the white—and with my hands and mind fully occupied, I had failed to give any attention whatever to a thrifty class of colored people located a short distance from our headquarters."[36] Yet writers such as Effie Waller Smith and characters such as her bachelor girl lived and wrote in Appalachia. The diversity they bring to definitions of Appalachian communities proves transformative in the roots of ecological feminism.

If I could stand on Pack Square in Asheville, North Carolina, on a spring day in 1909, I would find an Appalachia that is quite different from that portrayed in the literature of the tourist, the voyeur, or the social crusader. I might find traces of their Appalachia—if, for instance, I walked to the downtown offices that Olive and John Campbell secured as a home base for their research trips. Or if I went down to Biltmore Village for tea with the Vanderbilt women and their friends. Along with our delicate sandwiches on yeast bread and fruits (so different from the local corn bread and greens), we might well enjoy someone reading aloud from a Mary Noailles Murfree novel. The more sophisticated in taste around the parlor might suggest that Murfree's insistence on describing nature over and over again is no longer in fashion. Literary realism, exposés, adventure stories of the Wild West, those are all the rage in New York literary circles these days. Yet we all would agree that Miss Murfree still knows how to tell a story.

From Pack Square, I could also walk over to the meeting rooms at the Young Men's Institute Building,[37] one of the central gathering places for African American citizens of Asheville. There I might attend a meeting of the literary organization; we could discuss short stories or poetry written by Effie Waller Smith. Black readers in Asheville could have found her writing and recognized the racial markers embedded therein; living among the North Carolina mountains, they also may have appreciated her genuine love for the mountains of her home. More than that, however, at the Young Men's Institute Building, we would probably discuss the progress of students in the schools for black men and women, job opportunities, and newspapers reporting on the community's concerns. As understood within the institute's walls, Appalachia never was "pure white," but the persistent myth that it was restricted possible social change in mountain communities like Asheville. My day in Asheville could end at an evening meeting of a chapter of the

North Carolina Federation of Women's Clubs. Providing coffee for prisoners, establishing a public library, building better roads, and improving housing for the growing city all could be on the agenda. Gathering in the home of one of Asheville's leading women, the campaign for safe city drinking water would be planned; later, I could go along with Rosanna Frances Chapman, one of the younger members of the club, when she, "along with a half-dozen other girls, was asked to follow up creeks and coves and report the positions of pig pens, privies and other outbuildings"[38] in order to fight typhoid in Asheville. As Chapman and I met the town's citizenry, we would come into contact with women in the fairly new communities of Greek Orthodox immigrants and their plans for food drives for even more recently arriving residents.

At the general store owned by Chapman's father in nearby Leicester, where tourists rarely found their way, top prices would still be offered for wildcrafted ginseng, snakeroot, and other herbs, but customers also might want to discuss rumors of efforts to found a national park in the Great Smoky Mountains. Some of the more concerned residents might voice their worries that certain animals have not yet been spotted this year in their traditional haunts, that the ginseng is getting harder and harder to find since the new resorts have been built, or that the children of the mountain residents who have left for South Carolina to work in the mills never get to go outside anymore.

If this project does nothing else, I hope that it will, with all the recent scholarship with which it is in conversation, finally put to rest the idea that Appalachia was a monolithic, primitive community, full of stereotypical white mountaineers who did not know or care about the larger world. Appalachia contained, at the turn of the previous century, theorists who included the nonhuman world in the definition of community and who discussed the self-another, reciprocal relationships they had. It held feminists, aware of the latest developments in women's rights, working for social justice and criticizing the practices of U.S. corporate culture. And Appalachia always contained overlapping communities of different races, classes, genders, and species, who were fully autonomous subjects, many of whom embraced mountain identities. Forming the roots of ecological feminism in Appalachia, theorists recognizing Appalachia's communities' diversity, of whom, in different ways, Smith and Murfree were just two, spoke eloquently about the region's strengths and weaknesses. In the writings of Emma Bell Miles and Grace MacGowan Cooke, the roots of ecological feminism show their fullest expression.

CHAPTER FIVE

Emma Bell Miles and Grace MacGowan Cooke

Ecological Feminism's Roots, Part 2

I know there are writers and even a few thinkers in this part of the country, but they never get together. Miss Murfree, who writes novels of the
mountaineers lives somewhere on our blue horizon. . . . The MacGowan
sisters—they write for Harpers Monthly a good deal—are warm friends
of mine but have now left the country.

—Emma Bell Miles to Anna Ricketson, March 9, 1907

Residents of Chattanooga, Tennessee, Emma Bell Miles and Grace Mac-
Gowan Cooke were acquaintances and sometime collaborators. In 1905,
Miles published *The Spirit of the Mountains*, a genre-blurring, semiautobiographical work that analyzes gender roles in Tennessee mountain society
and foretells the effect of industrial and tourist capitalism on Appalachian
human and nonhuman communities. Five years later, Cooke published *The
Power and the Glory*, a novel specifically addressing mountain women's experiences in the new, environmentally damaging cotton mills. Both authors
criticize misguided social crusading, superficial tourist accounts, and voy-
eurism about mountain residents. Both outline regional women's issues
obscured in much women's writing about Appalachia. Cooke writes explicitly about the activism women can engage in to improve all life in the mountains; Miles's implicit discussion of activism is coupled with her public role
as a naturalist and suffragist. Both give women agency, responsibility, and

support emerging from and answerable to whole communities. Together they bring the roots of ecological feminism into full bloom at the beginning of the twentieth century.[1]

Grace MacGowan Cooke belonged to a prominent Chattanooga family; her father was the editor of the town's newspaper for more than thirty years. She lived in Appalachia from age two until forty-three. Cooke began publishing at age twenty-five in 1888 and continued until her death in 1944; as Miles said, Grace and her sister, Alice MacGowan, did indeed "write for Harpers Monthly a good deal." In her later career, Cooke produced novels, screenplays, and stage scripts as well. She had connections to many writers of the turn of the past century, extending beyond Appalachian authors such as Alice and Miles. Beginning with her decision to leave her husband in 1906, she entered the circles of national literary figures. Grace and Alice lived for several months at Upton Sinclair's utopian experiment, Helicon Hall. Later they moved to the new writer's colony at Carmel-by-the-Sea, where Cooke and her sister financially supported themselves and their children comfortably from their writing. The group at Carmel-by-the-Sea eventually included authors such as Sinclair Lewis, Jack London, and Mary Austin. Cooke mentored the younger Lewis, even letting him live for a while on her property. Cooke's writing shares with Sinclair's the willingness to expose factory conditions; with Austin's, ecological values and respect for Native American cultures; with Helicon Hall's suffragists, feminism and belief in women's abilities; and with London's, adventurous storytelling. *The Power and the Glory* was written in California and informed by the contacts she developed there, but it is set in Chattanooga and reflects her deep connections to Appalachia.[2]

Neither Cooke nor Miles was born in Appalachia. Emma Bell began life in Indiana in 1879. From age nine until her death at age thirty-nine in 1919, she lived in the mountains around Tennessee and Kentucky. More than Cooke, Miles self-identifies as a mountain woman, at one point writing that "it is often hard for me to notice points of difference between our way of life and civilization, I am so used to the backwoods." Whether the community accepted her mountain identity is a different question; certainly not everyone would agree it is in contrast to "civilization." In her book, Miles takes off and puts on her identity as a mountain woman as befits the argument she is making; she herself complicates the backwoods-*versus*-civilization dichotomy. Early in her life, wealthy patrons recognized artistic talent in Miles; with their help, she studied for two winters at the St. Louis School of Design. However, suffering homesickness, she wrote: "I wanted to go back to the mountains and reality, and back I went, almost at once. That summer I spent in the woods, trying to 'find myself' and decided that the city was not the place for me." Upon returning to Walden's Ridge, she married Frank Miles, a man whose family had helped settle the ridge for European Americans.[3]

From her marriage until her death, the family struggled economically. Miles avidly loved the writings of Henry David Thoreau (she and Frank read him together, and she corresponded for many years with Anna Ricketson, who used to be in Thoreau's inner circle, after Miles wrote a poem celebrating the great nature lover). Miles was also a proponent of women's rights living with a chronically underemployed husband. Rather than being the stereotypical middle-class woman reformer, Miles occasionally had to live with her family in a tent because that was the only housing they could afford. Emma and Frank had five children together, and she had at least four miscarriages. She wrote in her diary about hiding their economic need from the children: "I had only cornbread and wild greens, with a very little potted ham; but we used big green leaves for plates, leaving them in the hollows of our left hands, and the children enjoyed it." In addition, their life was characterized by a series of separations, talks of divorce, and reconciliation. Miles's letters and diaries reveal a deeply conflicted and often sad woman who also truly loved her husband and children. To her friend Ricketson, Miles described herself as "fortunate as a wife, as a mother, and as a lover of outdoors."[4]

Despite the family's struggles, Miles continued to paint and publish her writings; as is the case with many artists, the money became a powerful incentive for her family while her art became increasingly important to her personally. She was a painter who had to decorate tourist postcards in order to obtain art supplies; she was a writer who had to correspond in pencil both because "there's not a pen in the house!" and because the only time she could find to write was while nursing an infant, making pen and ink too challenging. Her early death was caused by tuberculosis, a common, slow, and painful disease. She wrote and painted until the very end of her life, with her final book appearing posthumously. *The Spirit of the Mountains* was her first book-length text, but she had already published poems, essays, and short stories by the time it appeared. Along with writing, Miles painted commissioned artwork for city residents and lectured to women's groups around the area on environmental, social, and literary topics. Although she strongly criticized short-term tourists in Appalachia in 1905, by 1908 Miles was under such great economic pressure that she accepted an invitation from "a new hotel to be opened on the Ridge next summer" to lecture "several times for the hotel and summer people" on the mountains and the mountain people.[5]

Miles may not have been able to address the political challenges facing mountain residents in her resort-hotel lectures, but by 1914 she landed a job writing a regular column for a Chattanooga newspaper in which she could restate the political arguments about Appalachia she had begun in *The Spirit of the Mountains*. Her articles explicitly support suffrage and feminism and join Cooke's published support for women's political participation. Miles in her journal and Cooke in her fiction explore socialism and whether it might be the key to women's liberation. Both are very interested in modern inventions that free women from drudgery; Miles describes the solar cooker she has modified from a magazine article to finish her dinners for her so that she can go outside. Several of Cooke's novels feature automobiles; they are metaphors, among other things, for women's increased physical mobility.[6]

Both *The Spirit of the Mountains* and *The Power and the Glory* borrow from the literatures of the tourist, voyeur, and social crusader with their vignettes of mountain life and stories in dialect, but their conclusions differ radically from those of the other literatures. That women in Appalachia belong to the modern world is a given for both of these authors. Cooke and Miles find it useful at times to be outsiders to Appalachia; but both can also legitimately write from an insider's perspective. As a result, the novels do not inherently separate subject and object, because self and another are entwined in their authors' identities. The question becomes one of emphasis rather than hierarchy. Together, Cooke and Miles redefine mainstream environmentalism to suggest that it should support the long-term health of all community members, human and nonhuman. Like Effie Waller Smith, both authors understand turn-of-the-century feminism and have the confidence to criticize and modify it for Appalachia. In the process, Miles's and Cooke's writings provide the fullest expressions of the roots of ecological feminism in Appalachia.

The Spirit of the Mountains:
Practicing Feminism on Walden's Ridge

Solitude is deep water, and small boats do not ride well in it. Only a superficial observer could fail to understand that the mountain people really love their wilderness—love it for its beauty, for its freedom. Their intimacy with it dates from a babyhood when the thrill of clean wet sand was good to little feet; when "frog houses" were built, and little tracks were printed in rows all over the shore of the creek; when the beginnings of aesthetic feeling found expression in necklaces of scarlet haws and headdresses pinned and braided together of oak leaves, cardinal flowers and fern; when beargrass in spring, "services" and berries in summer and muscadines in autumn were first sought after and prized most for the "wild flavor," the peculiar tang of the woods which they contain.

I once rode up the Side with a grandmother from Sawyers' Springs, who cried out, as the overhanging curve of the bluff, crowned with pines, came into view: "Now, ain't that finer than any picter you ever seed in your life?—and they call us pore mountaineers! We git more out o' life than anybody."[7]

The Spirit of the Mountains has ten chapters with titles such as "The Log Church School," "Grandmothers and Sons," "Supernatural," and "Some Real American Music." To accompany her text, Miles provided original paintings that complement the chapters and bring to life her written descriptions of Appalachian life. Some chapters are narrative, telling the story of a day at the school, or the conversations that happen as women gather together to set up a loom. Other chapters are anthropological, detailing songs or rhymes that ought to be preserved from Appalachia's musical and literary culture. Only the narrator's voice connects the chapters to each other. Yet in some way, in every chapter, Miles repeats her claim that "the mountain people really love their wilderness." Opening the book, the frontispiece, painted by Miles and labeled "King's Creek," shows a wide creek; the whole view is of plants, water, earth, and sky. The water runs toward the viewer, and its sources recede into the mountain in the background. There are no people here, only nature. In other words, Miles argues that community in Appalachia includes wilderness before the text even begins.

The mountains in which Miles grounds her text are more than geographically specific; they are also historically specific. Writing ten years after Murfree's *His Vanished Star*,[8] Miles has seen resort hotels built on "great property" that have not been stopped by communities. She is witnessing an influx of new mills and factories around Chattanooga. Aware that urban communities are growing and wilderness areas are shrinking across Appalachia, Miles picked up her pen to write a manifesto on mountain society because outside influences were exploiting the region she loved. When in her final chapter Miles writes: "My people, everywhere on the borders of the mountain country, are being laid hold of and swept away by the oncoming tide of civilization" (Miles, *Spirit of the Mountains,* 190), she points to the already present cotton mills, tourist resorts, large-scale sawmills, and factories. As Murfree does, Miles also concludes that unchecked development is most often a dangerous one-way colonialism supplanting any potential for healthy exchange. Miles's book steps into a dynamic historical moment affecting Appalachia and Appalachians; Miles's narrator, unlike Murfree's, joins the mountain residents in loving the mountain communities.

Moreover, in almost every chapter Miles makes women's voices the strongest advocates for the mountains. Whereas the literatures of the tourist, voyeur, and social crusader did not imagine Appalachian women's culture at all, and whereas Murfree imagined it but did not or could not give the women voices, Miles makes the culture of Appalachian women explicitly political and vocal. In Miles's text, the parade of heretofore mostly silent Appalachian women, such as Murfree's Sabrina Larrabee or Julia Tems, speak out about their communities. Sharing the trait with Effie Waller Smith's female narrators who love the Kentucky wilderness, women in Miles's book treasure and love the nonhuman in their communities. In other words, they love Tennessee's mountains. The many grandmothers in *The Spirit of the Mountains* agree that, although life is frequently difficult for women, female survivors in Appalachia do indeed "git more out o' life than anybody." Wilderness and women's voices become the "spirit[s] of the mountains" in the text. Miles's strategy of giving women the lead in speaking for communities hints at her ecological feminism and her belief that women should take action to preserve the human and nonhuman communities in which they live. But Miles is never naive or simplistic about the difficulty of creating ecological and feminist social justice in Appalachia.

Because she believes the problems facing Appalachia and "sweeping away" Appalachians are complex, Miles creates an equally complex narrator who lives in the community, and, perhaps more importantly, has been there since childhood. Although the narrator begins the text speaking in the third person, she soon changes. A story that objectively describes the mountain residents on King's Creek shifts when the narrator admits, "I was a child" attending the Log Church school. In a single story about the school, the narrator moves from teacher-observer to student-resident, as "a number of us, on the heels of some prank, once hid in [the fireplace] from the wrath of the teacher" (4). Later in the text, the narrator admits: "I am accustomed to handling yarn and carpet spun-truck, too" (51), which describes her continued participation in the culture. Miles combines subjective knowledge with objective distance and thus adds persuasive force to her observations. The narrator-teacher has been a student in the school; she is of the mountains; she has roots on the spot. Self and Other combine in the body of the narrator, preventing absolute separation.

At the same time, Miles does not stay with the first-person voice of a community member once she shifts to it. Throughout the text, she constantly changes pronouns and perspectives. Moving between first and third person can be frustrating for a reader; sometimes Miles seems patronizing about mountain residents, sometimes she seems defensive about her own identity. She calls mountain residents "primitive," but she also argues that all of them (including herself) are sophisticated observers of tourists and social crusaders. The result is a "bicultural" narrator, who is not limited to a single perspective. Many scholars linger over Miles's (the author's) personal biculturalism—her experiences having lived both in and out of Appalachia. David Whisnant seems to have coined the term for her; with it he emphasizes her "keen" observations "of the complex interplay between mountain people's lives and life elsewhere." He suggests she moves between the Appalachian "culture of extraordinary and unexamined richness" and the "culture of the metropolitan northeast."[9]

Yet, as in her personal life, in which she regularly interacted with women such as the MacGowan sisters who also moved in and out of mountainous Tennessee, Miles's bicultural narrator is not unique within the book. Other mountain residents talk about feeling different from what isolated Appalachians are supposed to feel. For instance, the grandmother who exclaims that "they call us pore mountaineers! We git more out o' life than anybody" steps out of one identity into another and reflects on the difference between the two. The activism Miles ultimately advocates is modeled by her text; its goal is to find a language that moves between mountain and mainstream culture to value the former while addressing the realities of the latter—and to blur the differences between them. Not a land out of time, not simply a primitive culture, Appalachia (and its residents) influence and are influenced by the rest of the United States.

Because of the shifting perspectives and the emphasis on women and wilderness, critics struggle with the book. Should it be taken as autobiography (and thus its "facts" researched to see how faithfully she tells her own life story)? Should it be read as a novel (and its lack of coherence criticized)? Should it be judged as a comprehensive cultural study (and its fictionalized conversations dismissed as inappropriate)?[10] Because it crosses so many genres (fiction, anthropological case study, art, autobiography), critics often respond to it intuitively or personally. They talk about how Miles makes them feel, how she speaks to their own experiences of Appalachia, or what they wish she had done differently. I, too, respond to Miles by wanting to research her life, tell when I first read her, count how many friends I called to read portions of her book, and learn why I respond so passionately to her voice. These reactions are signs that Miles's book—far from being structurally unsound—succeeds. She so unsettles the reader (by eroding the distinction between subject and object, giving nature agency, criticizing capitalism and corporate notions of "Progress," and identifying gender hierarchies in daily life) that she forces self-reflection and self-examination on her readers. Patrick D. Murphy, in a discussion of contemporary writings, writes: "Environmental literature by women not only cuts across genres, but also creates new categories and redefines boundaries on the basis of thematics and sympathies rather than formal properties and prescriptive definitions."[11] *The Spirit of the Mountains* and its feminism often occupy the difficult space between genres, categories, and forms; as a result, its strategies are subtle, complex, and innovative. In short, the roots of ecological feminism are so well developed in Miles's text that they carry something like an ethical challenge to examine one's own philosophies.

On Windows, Moonshine, and Loving Appalachia

Miles's difficult text reflects the challenge she has set herself of providing accurate representations of Appalachians in order to supplant the fashionably inaccurate accounts of the tourists, voyeurs, and social crusaders. She argues that many who attempt to speak for Appalachians (including perhaps Murfree—"somewhere on our blue horizon")[12] misunderstand because "[s]olitude is deep water, and small boats do not ride well in it." Outside observers, those who would presume to know Appalachia from touring, looking voyeuristically, or entering Appalachia as social crusaders, are the "small boats" to the mountain culture's "deep water" in Miles's metaphor. When Miles concludes, "Only a superficial observer could fail to understand that the mountain people really love their wilderness," she does more than claim that mountain people should be subjects in their stories along with the outsiders. She temporarily puts outsider readers in the role of objects to mountain subjects. Instead of answering *what* the outsiders see, Miles shifts to question *why* they *cannot* see. Not only are viewers superficial, but mountain residents become harder to understand and so worthy of "deep" observation as well.

Instead of minimizing or denying Appalachian practices that have been stereotyped, Miles explores the logic behind them. For instance, viewers often completely misread windowless cabins in Appalachia. Miles explains that air and a good source of water are valued more than light or fashionable home construction: "Pure air is prized as highly as pure water, and a cabin door is always open," which makes "windows superfluous" (Miles, *Spirit of the Mountains*, 20). Cabins are windowless because windows have no value—not because mountain residents cannot afford them, are ignorant of them, or are too lazy to install them—but outsiders, in their small boats, do not understand. Against the stereotype that everyone drinks moonshine and no one eats well in Appalachia, Miles counters that imported, processed, and synthesized alternatives may be worse in the long run than mountain food and drink. She writes: "Civilization is not likely soon to remedy this evil since it substitutes drugged whiskey for their own moonshine" (24) and claims imported whiskey makes "the evil of drunkenness ten times worse" (194)—remarkable statements given the almost universal condemnation of moonshine at the turn of the last century. Adulterated, mass-marketed tobacco and cheap baking powders also provoke Miles's criticisms, and she concludes, "How different from the actual state of affairs is that widespread popular idea, fostered by newspaper stories, that no class of people in America is more lawless than the mountaineers!" (74). In Miles's book, "Civilization" is not automatically superior, and readers who participate in it are not automatically better; in fact, those readers may be most appropriately viewed as ignorant or lazy themselves if they rely on poor research about Appalachia. They must understand the culture of Appalachia that ties mountain residents to the nonhuman community.

Further, the love of wilderness celebrated by Miles develops in the bodies and minds of Appalachians over time. In the literature of the tourist and social crusader, the close connection between bodies, minds, and wilderness was only available to a select few—upper-class tourist Emily Wooten in Rebecca Harding Davis's "A Wayside Episode"[13] or certain social crusaders who were trained in nature study, for instance. In Miles's world, love of wilderness is most available to mountain people—regardless of class—who grow up in and with Appalachian nature. As Miles describes "clean wet sand" on "little feet," building "frog-houses," and playing in the creek, she connects "aesthetic feeling" to the place. Not only do mountain residents appreciate the mountains' beauty, but their very ideas of beauty are created by the mountains, for "the beginnings of aesthetic feeling found expression in necklaces of scarlet haws and headdresses pinned and braided together of oak leaves, cardinal flowers and fern." Connecting human and nonhuman nature, the scene brings human self and nonhuman Other, in Patrick Murphy's terminology, into reciprocal "self-another" relationships. The communion—taking in the wild through herbs, berries, and fruit—cements the relationship between community members. Later in the text, Miles writes: "We . . . are never at ease without the feel of the forest on every side—room to breathe, to expand, to develop, as well as to hunt and to wander at will" (Miles, *Spirit of the Mountains*, 73). Forest and mountain residents are necessary to each other and Miles provides examples from across the life cycle. Love of the "tang of the woods" and "intimacy" with the wilderness are not abandoned with maturity; not a phase to outgrow, they continue from "babyhood" to "grandmother."

Charting the life cycle of mountain residents in terms of interaction with and love of wilderness, Miles explains why mountain people stay in Appalachia. Claiming they know they could leave and that life elsewhere might be easier, Miles suggests mountain people choose to stay in the mountains (and those who leave mark time until they can return): "All alike cling to the ungracious acres they have so patiently and hardly won, because of the wild world that lies outside their puny fences, because of the dream-vistas, blue and violet, that lead their eyes afar among the hills" (19). Mountain residents, in other words, stay not because of human society or human values but because of the mountains themselves. This land is not conquered or passive Other; it is "ungracious" and "hardly won"; fences on it are "puny." As a part of the community, the land has a say in the decisions made by other—human—community members. Mountain people do not look out at the hills or over the hills; their eyes are led (perhaps by the mountains themselves) "among" them. Decisions about whether to stay take into account not only human factors but nonhuman as well. The preposition in Miles's phrase "lead their eyes afar among the hills" signals equality, rather than hierarchy, and introduces dialogue between human and nonhuman in the community. Less graphically but no less significantly than in Murfree's novel, the land in *The Spirit of the Mountains* has agency.

From the beginning, Miles explores how humans are not separate from the environment. She introduces a more ecological definition of humans and nonhumans together in the first scene of the book, when she writes: "On King's Creek there is a log house of one large pen that is schoolhouse, church and townhall, all in one, and thus easily the most important building in the district" (1). The school "stands in the forest" (3) and is one with the living forest: "Woodpeckers drum on its roof in the daytime and whippoorwills sing there at night. Acorns drop upon it in October with resounding taps that startle all the little ones within." Animals join humans in seeing no distinction between building and forest. The building has been created out of the forest: "Its walls are laid of heavy pine timbers squared roughly and well notched together, the cracks chinked with chips driven in slantwise and daubed with native clay" (4). Its name reflects the partnership between humans and nature. The "Log Church School" acknowledges the interconnected forest ("log") and people ("church school") in the King's Creek community.

With a schoolteacher-narrator, Miles does something not seen in Murfree's or Smith's texts: Miles explores how humans in whole communities *learn* about their connection to the nonhuman world. Examining what education might look like if human and nonhuman are included together, she writes: "The path to the school door is one that few care to tread, with the boundless forest to choose from." At first, Miles ambivalently acknowledges that school "may or may not be about what one really wants to know" (3). Her ambivalence suggests there may be more than one important kind of knowledge in the world—that of the school and that of the "boundless forest." As Whisnant suggests, the book "neither romanticizes nor condescends, and . . . does not depend for its analysis upon the unconscious acceptance of middle-class mainstream values."[14] Privileging neither book learning nor forest play demonstrates that the narrator of this text questions, considers, and judges traditional interpretations of issues and also raises counterproposals.

Miles does not reject school or book knowledge out of hand. Maintaining her bicultural viewpoint, she describes in detail the lessons she teaches, including reading, arithmetic, spelling, grammar, and geography. At the same time, she includes and values participation of nonhuman community members in education. Thus, mixed in with traditional lessons are local games and crafts to teach similar lessons: "hull-gull, hand-full, how many?" for arithmetic, and drawing lessons to design "blocks of patchwork," a lesson that would presumably involve geometry too (Miles, *Spirit of the Mountains,* 7). She begins by writing that "we often spend the hot afternoons of September outside, with our books—old McGuffey readers, blue-back spellers, Testaments or whatever comes to hand, scattered about on the ground." Do leaves, nuts, insects, and rocks join the readers, spellers and Testaments at the log church school? Miles suggests they do by saying, "If the young minds wander afield with the scampering and flitting of little brothers of tree-top and burrow, what matter? Perhaps they learn at such times something not to be found between the covers of Webster" (5).[15] At such moments, her students learn from the natural world around them. Their minds are *literally* afield, their teachers are the animals in the field, and the lessons combine cultural lore with that of the forest and field of the school. With a female teacher-narrator outlining lessons applicable for both girls and boys and incorporating the nonhuman community, Miles begins to build her ecological feminism.

Along with lessons that can be learned in or near the school, Miles suggests that connections between human and nonhuman are so profound that searches for human wisdom and subsequent feminist activism ought to—and, in Walden's Ridge, do—begin with literal journeys into the woods. Thus, the narrator describes her walk to and from school in great detail (Miles, *Spirit of the Mountains,* 14–16). When she sets out to learn from an older woman in the community (about, it turns out, the gendered division of work and daily life in the mountains), the narrator shuts her "cabin door" and "[takes her] way down the mountain." She walks alone in the forest from early morning to noon and finds that "[r]ain had fallen in the night, and the trees stood immersed in a lake of thin mist, bluish, and shot with sunbeams." The forest interacts with the narrator as, for instance, "[c]ool wet leaves slapped softly together at my face and hands" and "[t]he little sensitive-plant caught at my skirt now and again" (38–39). As Smith did, Miles asserts that humans, and especially women, need to hike alone in the woods.

Women's Wisdom: Listening to the "Old Prophetesses"

In *The Spirit of the Mountains,* hiking is not simply for adventure's sake; the narrator's journey has a destination. It leads her to the home of Aunt Genevy, the teacher's teacher. Miles claims that a community's older women are important sources of wisdom. She calls them "old prophetesses" and writes: "The range of their experience is wonderful; they are, moreover, repositories of tribal lore—tradition and song, medical and religious learning. They are the nurses, the teachers of practical arts, the priestesses, and their wisdom commands the respect of all" (37). Even in old age, these prophetesses remain vital and dynamic; they are "yet able to toil almost as severely as ever"; and thus they possess a "strength and endurance [that] are beyond imagination to women of the sheltered life." Mountain women, Miles says, escape the fate of women elsewhere in the United States, who eventually become "lace-capped and felt-shod pets of the household" (54).

Nonmountain women could learn from mountain women, but differences in class and region often prevent the cultural exchange from happening.

Fittingly, then, communication at Aunt Genevy's centers around women's shared labor on a quintessential "Appalachian" task. When the narrator arrives on Aunt Genevy's porch, Miles receives Aunt Genevy's "pleasant, quiet welcome" (39)—and is almost immediately put to work. Visiting on the porch, helping Aunt Genevy to set up her loom and weave, provides the opportunity for a scene with three women of varying ages. Miles uses the scene to outline both women's oppression and sources of strength available to them in the community:

> "Law, I know all about children, Mary, and work, too. Mine was never more'n two year apart. Don't you lose heart, Mary; there's better days a-comin' for ye whenever this is over."
>
> She meant, as I discovered later, more than she said in the last sentence. It was known in the neighborhood that Gideon Burns, although not a pronounced drunkard or villain, was cruel to his wife beyond what is usual to mountain men. He never struck her, or, if he did, it was not known; and Mary rarely complained. But the sympathy of the neighbor women was with her, and the more experienced hoped that the coming of the child would work a change. (42–43)

Miles's subtext is that feminism gains strength and balance when it draws from and benefits women of all ages. The women in this scene are the narrator, Aunt Genevy, and a neighbor, Mary Burns, who is pregnant and poor, a "bare-footed woman, clad in a single faded calico garment" (40). Miles leaves open the possibility that if Mary survives her youth she may become like Aunt Genevy, and, instead of letting her stand apart, she places the narrator on a continuum between Genevy and Mary.

After detailing the work each woman does in a day, Miles lingers over the help Aunt Genevy provides Mary to withstand her abusive husband. She details the food Aunt Genevy's household gives Mary, the personal sacrifices Aunt Genevy makes during Mary's childbirth, and the important, nonjudgmental conversations that happen as women work together on Aunt Genevy's porch. That Miles is willing to discuss the emotional, economic, and possible physical violence against women in mountain culture demonstrates her commitment to criticize mountain culture when appropriate, not simply to romanticize it. Her phrasing, that Gideon Burns is "not a pronounced drunkard or villain" but is "cruel to his wife beyond what is usual to mountain men," keeps him from being a walking stereotype—he is not a drunken moonshiner or a villainous hillbilly. Yet even as the narrator rejects popular critiques of her culture, she does not resort to glorifying or whitewashing it. Hence, the narrator says of Mary: "I knew better than to interfere by so much as a word, or I should have advised the poor child to make her way back to her father's house, where, by all the traditions of the land, she should have been well and tactfully received. But I do not think she would have wished to go" (56). The narrator acknowledges and publicly lists possible solutions while recognizing the individuals involved.

Miles has not written her way out of the problem—her text is not feminist prescription or utopia. Miles's narrator observes a scene about violence in the mountains from a feminist perspective but leaves it to her readers to formulate proper approaches to the issues presented—while warning of "the continual failure of well-meant efforts to bridge the gulf fixed by the mountaineers between woman and man" (64). Unlike the social crusaders' photograph albums, which supposed that once mountain men and women could be posed in a traditional family arrangement the work was done, Miles dares to dream of emotional, physical, and social equality between men and women in Appalachia.

Miles carefully outlines unhelpful, albeit well-meaning, activisms. First, she lists the unequal division of labor between most women and men on King's Creek: women, she says, not only meet "all the ordinary care of the household," but they also perform a list of additional tasks comparable to men's. About women's extra work, Miles concludes that "it is a very fortunate wife, indeed, who does not carry a considerable burden of duties properly supposed to belong to masculine shoulders, such as bringing wood and water, milking, and raising garden" (21). Mary Burns certainly would benefit from activism to address the turn-of-the-century, mountain "second shift" that leaves women to do their husbands' full day's work after completing their own.[16] But, Miles says wryly, the general response from outsiders such as the social crusaders focuses on the dirt, dust, and fleas they see or imagine. The prescription women like Mary Burns often receive is to follow the latest hygiene and clean themselves up. But, "[O]h, dear! how *can* she comb her hair every day?" (Miles, *Spirit of the Mountains*, 21), says Miles, her sarcasm dismantling both a feminine insistence on beauty and fashion and, perhaps more importantly, the social crusaders' model of feminist uplift. Rejecting the facile notion that combed hair and neat clothing in and of themselves improve women's lives, Miles critiques upper-class feminism while simultaneously celebrating and supporting women's hard work.

In her personal diary, Miles expands the book's analysis of society's expectations of women. It is an issue she and many married women face:

> In effect, a man says to his chosen: "I love you because you are a little finer than others. . . . If you love me, come and spend the best years of your life in the kitchen, which I shall precariously provide for you, doing the drudgery for which otherwise I should have to hire a negro. Your hours will be from 5 A.M. to 5 A.M., your recompense will be the right to bear my name, and board rather poorer than that in the cheapest houses, and the cheapest clothes you can find. Be very humble now, and very grateful indeed; for without a man's name to yours you can have no love under the law. And in any case remember that the reward of love is mortal peril." . . . I wonder what exactly the Socialists propose? I believe they alone have fairly faced this question. Why do I think of these things? Because of my daughters, perhaps. However it coarsens them, I mean to send them into life with open eyes, that they may not suffer as I have.[17]

Miles's own struggles with pregnancy and women's work (at one point in her diary she discusses resuming all her house and field work only nine days after giving birth) give added weight to her sarcasm in *The Spirit of the Mountains*. How *can* she comb her hair every day—and will it really make a difference if she does?

In place of an idealistic but impractical solution, Miles gives readers a discussion of a source of strength for women against the violence and oppression they may face—one that acknowledges and relies on their awareness of nonhuman community members. The narrator claims a mountain woman "has heard the stories of everything in the house, from the brown and cracked old cups and bowls to the roof-beams themselves, until they have become her literature." When the narrator says of old furniture: "They are friendly, too," and claims: "They stand about her with the sympathy of like experience in times of distress and grief," she is outlining a system of support (Miles, *Spirit of the Mountains,* 67). In other words, the items around humans, many of which are literally made out of plants, animals, and land of the forest and mountains, communicate with and support those humans. Facing violence, women can turn for support to other women and to the nonhuman in their community. As a reader, I wish Mary would get out of her abusive marriage, but Miles provides a practical, if partial, answer to a complex problem. As she does, she displays feminist and ecological sensibilities and sets the stage for her final chapter.

Limitations of Miles's "White Mountaineer"

Despite groundbreaking analysis that rigorously includes women and women's voices in portraits of Appalachia, Miles is still a product of her times. Her inclusive vision, much like Mary Murfree's, does not extend to nonwhite Appalachians. The roots of ecological feminism in her work are limited by her creation of a "mountaineer race" that is in contrast to the "Negro race." Miles makes all Appalachians white without explicitly saying so. In "Some Real American Music," she claims that, although Dvořák and others have explored "negro themes" and "aboriginal Indian music," the real American music is Appalachian (146–47). Similarly, when judging dialect and literature of groups in America in her chapter "The Literature of a Wolf-Race," she finds most forms—like "French-English, Mexican-English, negro-English"—are "corrupted from Standard English or are bastard forms arising from a mixture with some other language." She concludes that there is "not one which possesses a true literary value, unless it be the speech of the mountaineers" (173). Rather than including all human community members, Miles uses the perceived whiteness of Appalachians to lobby for a larger share when a finite pool of resources is distributed among economically or socially oppressed "racial" groups in the United States. Although she argues against systems of unjust economic privilege, rather than challenging structures of racial privilege that benefit white people over everyone else, Miles tries to get that racial privilege extended to white Appalachians.

When she discusses the relationship of white, mountain residents to Cherokee people, Miles is less stereotypical in her discussion; yet, she is still of her times. Her portrait of Cherokees is complicated, occasionally contradictory, but often surprisingly appreciative. Miles admits the skills and knowledge for which the white settlers owe a great debt to the Cherokees: "Their woodcraft is Indian—the thousand contrivances of the naked man cast on his own resources in the forest. The savage had reduced the art of living and traveling in the wilderness to an exact science. . . . And with all his knowledge the white man could not better so finished a product, could only borrow it outright and in detail" (86). Miles manages to be both racist and respectful in the same paragraph; phrases such as "borrow it outright" erase the white violence that accompanied the establishment of a "mountaineer race." And yet, Miles acknowledges the superior knowledge of displaced

Cherokees by calling their skills "art" and "science" and admitting that the "white man could not better" those skills. Cherokees exist in a faded historical past in *The Spirit of the Mountains;* neither Native American men and women nor mixed-race residents live in Miles's Appalachia. Yet despite her racial essentialism, Miles creates a framework in her final chapter that is attentive to class and gender as well as the nonhuman community and that works for broadly defined social and environmental justice in Appalachia.

"My People": Miles's Ecological Feminist Manifesto

Miles's final chapter criticizes capitalism, tourism, development, and mainstream activism and feminism in the mountains. More explicitly than did Smith or Murfree, Miles draws upon language similar to today's ecological feminism by identifying economic and social privilege as systems keeping women apart. It begins:

> My people, everywhere on the borders of the mountain country, are being laid hold of and swept away by the oncoming tide of civilization, that drowns as many as it uplifts. And in this way:
> One day a hotel is built, a summer settlement begun, in some fastness of the mountains hitherto secluded from the outer world. The pure air, the mineral waters, are advertised abroad, and the summer people begin to come in. Good roads are built in place of the old creek-beds and trails, and rubber-tired carriages whirl past the plodding oxen and mule teams. Handsome cottages are erected in contrast to the cabins, and sunbonnets turn aside in wonder at bright creations of roses and chiffon. The mountain people come in groups to look on, some from homes so deep in the woods that the children take fright at the approach of even a home-made "tar-grinder" wagon. They are easily bewildered, of course, and cannot at once respond to the need of a new standard of values. Perhaps instead of a hotel it is a factory or a mill of some kind that presents the thin edge of the wedge, but the results are as certain to follow. (190–91)

Although still shifting, the narrative voice in this chapter passionately advocates for the mountains and mountain people as it criticizes "civilization" and "uplift." Miles chooses resort hotels and their "summer people" as her case study and focuses on changes to roads, housing, and the economy that they bring. Although I could find no evidence that Miles read *His Vanished*

Star, the resemblance between Murfree's first paragraph, when Kenniston is dreaming of advertising his rare, pure air, and Miles's description of how resort developers think about things like pure air stands as testimony to how common the practice was. But, Miles carefully notes, the development might just as well be a "factory or mill of some kind that presents the thin edge of the wedge, but the results are as certain to follow." Five years later, when Cooke publishes *The Power and the Glory,* she takes as her starting point the "thin edge of the wedge" of Chattanooga's factories. These three women's stories, combined with Smith's call for (bachelor) women to participate in economics and politics, speak a coherent message about Appalachia. Miles focuses on two major problems mountain residents face when the wedge appears.[18]

First, Miles targets the short-term rewards of working for the tourists. Watching mountain people move quickly into this instant, booming market, Miles does not claim mountain people have existed outside of capitalism entirely. Rather, she finds the unstable and temporary introduction of the hotel's outsider-driven market disturbing. The problem, as she outlines it, is that the prosperity is only temporary. In particular, winter underscores the effect of the tourists' departure since the local "folk [are] huddled round their fires in cheap store calicoes . . . [and are] buying meal by the half-peck to eat with the invariable white gravy." Miles recognizes the well-meant charity of summer women who leave gifts behind for local people they have employed. Yet, visiting women (and "city people" in general) ask: "Have we not built roads for a people too lazy to build for themselves? . . . Have we not served them in many ways? Are not church, school, and newspaper a true benefit, a light in their ignorance?" Miles summarizes this position (again, with sarcasm) as *"haven't we paid them well?"* Miles finds the visiting women's solutions too general and condemns the social crusaders for not staying in the communities they "serve": "They do not understand that the semblance of prosperity is only a temporary illusion that vanishes with [their] departure" (Miles, *Spirit of the Mountains,* 193–96). Miles wants authentic community building; she sets her vision against activists who commodify their services and make activism a zero-sum game.

Contrary to the prevailing myths of "civilization," that it "acts as a useful precipitant in thus sending the dregs to the bottom," Miles writes that "it is only the shrewder and more determined, not the truly fit, that survive in this struggle." Further, the narrator-teacher worries, "The value of money, the false importance of riches, is evident to [mountain people's] minds before the need of education." Miles concludes the temporary boom is not "so well proportioned to the sacrifice, after all," when mountain people find they have sold their "birthright for a mess of pottage" (193–97). Although the narrative voice can sound distant from the mountain residents here, it may be because the situation is too personal for Miles; her letters and diary show her own family spending many winters in similar conditions. Even better-educated mountain people, who realize the dangers of the new economy, have few resources with which to resist.

Second, according to Miles, the capitalist boom misuses the talents of the local people. Mountain people "are constantly made to feel themselves inferior to the newcomers" (194). In particular, Miles grieves that women, who are highly skilled at design, weaving, and sewing, are under the "wedge" of development "breaking health and spirit over a thankless tub of suds" (198). Even worse, because hotel work is full time while it lasts, "the old pursuits are abandoned" (191). Skills that formerly helped people through hard times are vanishing. Thus, hotels erode self-sufficiency of individuals and cultures. Miles does not find them to be sustainable or good for the long-term health of the community.

As an alternative, Miles suggests, "Let us be given work that will make us better mountaineers, instead of turning us into poor imitation city people." In other words, Miles wants solutions tailored specifically to whole communities. A metaphor from nature subtly recalls the nonhuman members of the community: "In the mountains the need is for development not foreign to our natures, cultivation of talents already in blossom" (198). Here again, the voice shifts from "their" to "our," and a powerful speaker for Appalachian women emerges. Also, Miles subtly shifts the meaning of "development"—no longer is it capitalist development involving changes to the community (cutting trees, building roads, locating factories)—instead, personal, educational development builds citizens responsible to the human and nonhuman community.

Work that values the Appalachians as people can support the following philosophical leap Miles finds ultimately necessary for the healthy survival of people on King's Creek: "the mountaineers must awaken to consciousness of themselves as a people" (200). Her turn-of-the-century consciousness-raising, then, is Miles's complicated answer to the complicated problems facing Appalachia. She does not see perfectly and does not predict the outcome. Miles does not describe what a mountain identity might look like or exactly what effect it will have. But The Spirit of the Mountains itself stands as a hopeful step in its creation.

Given her emphasis on gender in the text, it is not surprising that the other solution proposed by Miles is women's activism. She writes: "Several such settlements have been established already, where the industries encouraged are those crafts in which the mountaineers excel—weaving, woodwork, basketmaking, and quilting" (199). Although it is ironic that Miles brings back an innovation of the social crusaders after criticizing them so, she cannot deny the potential of settlement houses. Cooke will come to the same conclusion. Neither Miles nor Cooke is willing to give up the quintessential form of women's activism in Appalachia. Both find such strengths in the idea of women living and working together in Appalachia that they ultimately decide to modify the basic model. For both, the settlement house must be organized around early ecological feminist principles: valuing human and nonhuman community members, giving the nonhuman community agency in decision making for the whole community, addressing environmental as well as social justice issues, and recognizing the particular effects on and roles for women in activism. Miles's book makes space for mountain cultural knowledge, forest knowledge, and national (or book) knowledge. Her position in the history of ecological feminism is different from Cooke's. Discussing the dangers of development, Miles does not explicitly link, for instance, capitalist development with poisoning streams or air quality with human quality of life. Yet what Miles does in decentering humans, emphasizing women's knowledge, telling complicated stories, and insisting on local solutions is build a philosophy to make feminist and ecological principles the bases of social change. *The Spirit of the Mountains* provides one model for how women and their societies can survive with the help of the roots of ecological feminism.

The Power and the Glory: Appalachian, Ecological, and Feminist Activism

Cottonville bordered a creek, a starveling, wet-weather stream which offered the sole suggestion of sewerage.

• • •

"Do you reckon the water's unhealthy down here in Cottonville?"[19]

The Power and the Glory explores mountain women's experiences in the new cotton mills in Appalachia. Grace MacGowan Cooke's novel deals with the aftereffects of the "thin edge of the wedge" of development Miles predicted. The novel's main character, Johnnie Consadine, has left her home deep in Tennessee's Unaka Mountains to take a job in a mill on the

Tennessee-Georgia border. Johnnie sends most of her wages back to her mother on the mountain; in the meantime, she joins the Uplift Club (a women's progressive organization), is disturbed by women's exclusion from unions, falls in love, and, in the end, founds a new grassroots settlement house, utopian mine, and mill village to help other women like herself. The novel takes a long look at the new cotton-mill culture, includes automobiles and mountain residents who are familiar with them, and even discusses the merits of U.S. socialism and chiropractic medicine. Cooke's mountain residents read the popular magazines, are educated (even the antagonists), invent and patent improvements to industrial machinery (even the women), debate women's rights and different forms of patriarchy, and face corporate environmental poisoning. Through Johnnie, Cooke criticizes labor practices at the turn of the twentieth century; she examines and modifies feminist benevolent activism to make it work better in the mountains.

Cooke's real achievement in *The Power and the Glory* is to outline the roots of ecological feminism while writing a truly fun novel. Romance, lost treasure, scheming villains, guns, automobiles, caves, and true love all make appearances in the book. Johnnie, embarrassed by her family's reputation for "borrowing" rather than working, leaves her mountain home to work in a cotton mill in a Chattanooga suburb. Helped by an old school friend, Shade Buckheath, to get a job, she meets Gray Stoddard before she even starts working. Gray lives in Cottonville because he has inherited stock in cotton mills from his rich family in the Northeast and has decided to work in a mill to see what he really owns. His socialist leanings place him outside the upper-class society in Cottonville, but his wealth puts him back at its center. Despite the fact that Gray owns mills and Johnnie works in them, they court over exchanged books (including, like Emma Bell and Frank Miles, Thoreau), love of flowers, and interest in mechanical things, including Gray's automobile. But many people and social pressures stand in the way of their romance.

Lydia Sessions, unmarried sister-in-law of the wealthiest mill owner, is one obstacle. She wants to marry Gray herself and comes to dislike Johnnie strongly; Lydia does whatever she can to hurt Johnnie in the community. Shade Buckheath decides he should marry Johnnie (although it is not clear Johnnie has any interest in marriage to anyone, for much of the book). Because of her repeated refusals of him, he also tries to injure Johnnie's reputation, spreading rumors about her behavior with Stoddard, stealing and then attempting to patent her invention to make the machines safer for women and children, and ultimately kidnapping Gray. He forms an alliance with Pap Himes, the owner of the boardinghouse in which Johnnie stays. Shade and Pap Himes conspire not only on the invention but also over a reputed silver mine for which Johnnie's uncle has spent most of his life searching. Pap, a widower, tricks Johnnie's mother into marrying him in order to, he hopes, secure the fortune of the lost mine, should Uncle Pros ever find it. Pap insists that Johnnie's younger sisters and brothers must also go to work in the mills.

Despite all the people working against her, Johnnie rises in the mill structure, gaining promotions and added responsibility (although not much extra money). She continues her education, reading the books Gray Stoddard shares with her (and replying to the notes he tucks inside the books). Mandy Meacham, Johnnie's roommate in the boardinghouse, and Mavity Bence, a daughter of Pap Himes and the midwife who birthed Johnnie, also look out for Johnnie's best interests. When Uncle Pros finally locates the mine, Pap Himes and Shade Buckheath attack him, causing him to lose his memory and sense; but it is Mavity who comes forward to help Johnnie and her uncle. As Johnnie, with poor Uncle Pros in tow, sets off to rescue Gray from the kidnappers, a final advocate materializes. A wandering chiropractor finds Johnnie and her uncle by the side of the road. Diagnosing Uncle Pros's misaligned atlas vertebrae, the chiropractor performs an impromptu adjustment that restores Uncle Pros's memory and intelligence. Nevertheless, the heroics of rescuing Gray fall to Johnnie. Escaping a shoot-out, with a shackled Gray in the back of the car, Johnnie drives all three of them to safety. The silver mine turns out to be nickel instead, which assures Johnnie of steady riches; her patent comes through in her name; and Johnnie and Gray suddenly belong to the same social class. The novel ends with Gray trying to convince the girl from the Unaka Mountains to marry him.

Remarkably, Cooke manages her complex plot without relying on stereotypes to develop character or setting. Rather than using Miles's strategy of explaining the local logic in practices outsiders make into stereotypes, Cooke carefully links stereotypes in the mountains to national and international ideas. For instance, male dominance among the mountain residents is supported by current philosophical thought; Pap Himes, a character who rules the women in his life with a controlling hand, shares "Schopenhauer's distaste for 'the low-statured, wide-hipped, narrow-shouldered sex'" (42). In this way, Appalachian problems are American problems. Readers are, by extension, connected to these characters; they cannot separate from nor imagine themselves as automatically superior to Appalachians in the novel's American family. Cooke's hopeful corollary is that Appalachian strengths are

American strengths. She wants readers to judge all Cottonville community members on their own merits.

Lydia Sessions and the "Upliftin' Business"

Lydia Sessions embodies all that can go wrong with a feminist activism that stereotypes, ignores the effects of capitalism, and tries to apply Band-Aids to systemic problems. Lydia receives Cooke's harshest criticisms. Because Lydia wants to marry Gray Stoddard, she has studied his unconventional political ideas (although she has thoroughly misread them). In order to attract him, Lydia decides to make "her devoir to these by engaging zealously in semi-charitable enterprises among the mill girls" (58). One of the mill girls explains:

> "Miss Lyddy she ain't as young as she once was, and the boys has quit hangin' 'round her as much as they used to; so now she has took up with good works," the girl on the bed explained with a directness which Miss Sessions would not perhaps have appreciated. "Her and some other of the nobby folks has started what they call a Uplift club amongst the mill girls. Thar's a big room whar you dance—if you can—and whar they give little suppers for us with not much to eat; and thar's a place where they sorter preach to ye— lecture she calls it. I don't know what-all Miss Lyddy hain't got for her club. But you jist go, and listen, and say how much obliged you are, an she'll do a lot for you, besides payin' your wages to get you out of the mill any day she wants you for the Upliftin' business." (47–48)

While the fictional Lydia is set apart from many benevolent workers in the mountains by her egregiously selfish motives, their shared use of the vocabulary of the benevolent movement puts her on a continuum with Appalachia's social crusaders.

Although, in the poverty and desperate living conditions of the mill town, a supper with enough to eat might be helpful to the mill workers, the Uplift Club follows the whims of Lydia Sessions and its board of upper-class women volunteers. Lydia is not exactly a social crusader, but she pretends to be one when convenient. For instance, the narrator notes sarcastically that it seems "people do not need uplifting so much in hot weather" (116). Instead of helping orphans, providing coal to families, or distributing winter clothing, Lydia proclaims that "their souls must be fed too ... and who can reach the souls of these young girls so well as we who are near their own age, and who have had time for culture and spiritual growth?" (96). There is no evidence that anyone else in the town helps abandoned children, provides fuel, or donates clothing to people in need.

The same mill worker who sees through Lydia Sessions to comment on her age and aspirations to marriage is considered by Lydia to be her biggest success—and Lydia does not hesitate, in the narrator's words, to "exploit" the "poor and helpless" Mandy Meacham's story (100). However, Mandy possesses sophisticated strategies to interact with Lydia Sessions, and she shares them with her roommate, Johnnie. Although Johnnie adopts different strategies, Mandy effectively counters the dehumanizing effects of Lydia Sessions's charity. Besides suggesting that "you jist go, and listen, and say how much obliged you are" (48), Mandy continues, "If she takes a shine to you it'll be money in your pocket" (59). Further, Mandy says you should take the books Lydia occasionally offers to the mill women—"but you don't have to read 'em ... you take 'em home, and after so long a time you take 'em back sayin' how much good they done you" (48). Mandy's grasp of class dynamics in the Uplift Club extends even to dress: "Ef you fix up like that ... you're bound to look too nice to suit Miss Lyddy.... I'm goin' to wear my workin' dress and tell her I hadn't nary minute nor nary cent to do other." In fact, she says of Lydia Sessions and the board, "They'll attend to all the fine lookin' theirselves. What they want is to know how bad off you air, an' to have you say how much what they have did or give has helped you" (97). Mandy effectively subverts an otherwise demeaning system of charity by insisting on a clear division between who she is and the face she presents to the Uplift Club, thus reaping material benefits without revealing her own vulnerabilities. Lydia's middle-class solutions exploit working-class Mandy, but Mandy intelligently manipulates Lydia in return.

As the relationship between Lydia and Mandy shows, Cooke does not presume an automatic, essentialist sisterhood between women in Cottonville: class, race, and other structures of power divide women. At the same time, Cooke holds on to the idea that women (and men) can work together for social change. Such alliances, she suggests, must be based on political coalition and respectful, reciprocal relationships. Thus, Cooke also does not categorize the mountain residents into one undistinguished, lower-class group. Although many mill women are (like Mary Burns was, in *The Spirit of the Mountains*) poor, pregnant, and uneducated, Johnnie, for instance, has had the benefit of some schooling (16); she is single, not a mother, and so has time to read on her own. It makes sense, of course, for the protagonist of a novel to be outstanding; accordingly, Johnnie's natural dignity and sophistication strikes everyone she meets. Yet, she is not so exceptional as to be the *token* different mountain character; other women have the potential to be like Johnnie (such as her mother, her siblings, Mandy, and even the midwife who birthed her). Cooke's mountain residents form a fully realized, complex society.

Lydia's dislike of Johnnie stems from her growing realization that Gray is her best hope for marriage. Her attacks on Johnnie escalate from the general patronizing and dehumanizing of the Uplift Club to specifically targeted strategies to make Johnnie less of a woman.[20] Throughout the novel, Lydia consistently alters Johnnie's name to call her "John." Presumably, this less feminine John does not wield the sexual power over Gray that Mandy suggests Lydia has lost. A questioner concerned about Johnnie's ability to work overtime in the mills and support her young brothers and sisters hears from Johnnie, "I'm a mighty big, stout, healthy somebody and I aim to keep so." But with Johnnie out of sight, Lydia turns the intent of the exchange (with its subtext of dangerous mill conditions) into a parallel attack on Johnnie's femininity and humanity: "Yes, John Consadine is quite a marked type of the mountaineer. She is, as she said to you, a stout healthy creature, and I understand, very industrious. I approve of John" (100). Although Johnnie thinks of herself as a "somebody," Lydia would much prefer her to be an unmarryable "creature"—an exploitable other, with little or no agency, but with a useful story for her "devoir" to Gray.

Johnnie's first uplift lecture exposes the fundamental hypocrisy of Lydia and, by extension, other insensitive feminists. A guest speaker from London lectures the mill women on "aspiration," a speech that has been successful before many women's clubs. The speech overflows with generalizations and empty promises: "You struggle and climb and strive ... when, if you only knew it, you have wings. And what are the wings of the soul? The wings of the soul are aspiration. Oh, that we would spread them and fly to the heights our longing eyes behold." When Johnnie suggests the argument is too general, not sufficiently attentive to Appalachia or Cottonville, by asking (gently, but sarcastically) if Lydia's "dress-body" is an appropriate thing for which to "aspire," Lydia's vision is shown to be vague and empty. Lydia can only stutter that "it would be a gross, material idea to aspire after blouses and such-like, when the poor child needs—er—other things so much more" (102–6). When pushed, Lydia is shown to be completely unaware of the needs of the women she pretends to serve.

Early in the novel, Mandy refers to Lydia's work as "the Upliftin' business" (48). Given that the club's token support for women greatly benefits the business of the mills, Mandy's is a trenchant comment. The Uplift Club is a public relations gesture that does not challenge the status quo; as such, Lydia's complicity with the very things making the mill women in need of uplift is significant and profound. At times, she speaks as a mouthpiece for the mill owners: "The work is very light—you know that. Young people work a great deal harder racing about in their play room than at anything they have to do in a spooling room." In case any confusion remains, the narrator breaks in to say: "Individuals who work in cotton mills, and are not adults, are never alluded to as children. . . . They are always spoken of—even those scarcely more than three feet high—as 'young people'" (212–13). For Cooke, a southern writer, to speak so emphatically against child labor and against the hypocritical rhetoric of mill owners signals her radical courage. Instead of the middle-class Lydia Sessions, Johnnie Consadine emerges as the voice of authority on feminism in the community, providing an actual list of the needs and obstacles to mountain residents' aspirations: "I'm mighty near as barefoot as a rabbit and the little'uns back home has to have every cent I can save" (106–7). Collapsed into the sentence are pressing feminist problems of food, clothing, and economic exploitation of the working-class mill women. Cooke continues outlining the effect of the mills on women and children—but she expands to discuss their effect on the nonhuman community. Environmental poisoning condoned by "the Company" takes center stage.

Environmental Justice: Danger in Air, Water, and Fire

Just as in Miles's text, a scene between three women serves to initiate Johnnie, who is still new to the mills, and readers into the expanded range of women's issues in Cooke's fictional mill town. Mandy, who is increasingly physically ill from mill work, and Mavity, who now juggles work in the mills and the boardinghouse, join Johnnie in conversation. These women are of varying ages, work experience, and education, but they all provide astute observations of the mill community:

> Most of the yards were unfenced, and here and there a row of shanties would be crowded so close together that speech in one could be heard in the other.
> "And then if any ketchin' disease does break out, like the dipthery

did last year," Mavity Bence said one evening as she walked home with Johnnie, "hit's sartin shore to go through 'em like it would go through a family."

Johnnie looked curiously at the dirty yards with their débris of lard buckets and tin cans. Space—air, earth and sky—was cheap and plentiful in the mountains. It seemed strange to be sparing of it, down here where people were so rich.

"What makes 'em build so close, Aunt Mavity?" she asked.

"Hit's the Company," returned Mrs. Bence lifelessly. "They don't want to spend any more than they have to for land. Besides they want everything to be nigh to the mill. Lord—hit don't make no differ. Only when a fire starts in a row of 'em hit cleans up the Company's property same as it does the plunder of the folks that lives in 'em. You just got to be thankful if there don't chance to be one or more baby children locked up in the houses and burned along with the other stuff. I've knowed that to happen more than oncet."

Johnnie's face whitened.

"Miss Lydia says she's going to persuade her brother-in-law to furnish a kindergarten and a day nursery for the Hardwick Mill," she offered hastily. "They have one at some other mill down in Georgia, and she says it's fine the way they take care of the children while the mothers are at work in the factory."

"Uh-uh," put in Mandy Meacham slowly, speaking over the shoulders of the two, "but I'd a heap ruther take care of my own child—ef I had one. An' ef the mills can afford to pay for it the one way, they can afford to pay for it t'other way. Miss Liddy's schemes is all for the showin' off of the swells and the rich folks. I reckon that, with her, hit'll end in talk, anyhow—hit always does."

"Aunt Mavity," pursued Johnnie timidly, "do you reckon the water's unhealthy down here in Cottonville?" (112–14)

Not only are houses built too close together, causing noise pollution and disease epidemics, but periodic fires are encouraged to "clean" the town— at the cost of the babies who invariably burn to death in those fires. Women are paid too little to provide childcare, yet they know the dangers of the mill's plan to warehouse children (the children who are currently locked in poor housing during shifts): no fresh air, no education, and dangerous health care. The mills are particularly unsafe and unhealthy for children and the frail. Although Mavity dismisses Johnnie's concerns about the water, instead blaming the air and working hours children face in the mills, Cooke clearly raises the connection between the health of women and children and polluted water. Elsewhere Cooke mentions that women are expected to insulate their own houses against winter (219) on their meager paychecks and even scarcer free time. Cooke even suggests that the mills negatively affect the workers' mental health—Mavity's daughter has committed suicide out of despair from the mill work (40). Women and children work the worst shifts for the least pay and suffer the resulting ill-health.

In fact, Cooke explicitly compares life in the mills with life in jail; for both, humans are cut off from the nonhuman community. Of the mill, Cooke writes that "the suggestion was dangerously apt of a penitentiary, with its high wooden barrier, around all the building." High, sealed windows, unhealthy air, and a walled-in, barren employee yard complete the metaphor. But for Cooke, the issue of worker health centers not only on what is in the building, but also on what is kept out—plants, animals, water, and air of the mountain world. Shown in relief by the "little grassy square of its own, tree-shadowed, with proud walks and flower beds" (55) that the mill managers have built for their private use, an interaction with nonhuman nature at the workplace is missing for the workers.

Furthermore, Cooke indicts the mills for affecting the ecology of the mountains. In other words, they do not merely take the mountain people they employ out of their natural world, but the mills negatively affect that natural world as well. As Johnnie says, "Space—air, earth and sky—was cheap and plentiful in the mountains," yet the mill owners were "sparing of it, down here where people were so rich." At first, Cooke gently foreshadows the point. On Johnnie's first view of the mill town, it is "shrouded with rosy mist, which she did not identify as transmuted coal smoke" (25). Also, Cooke says, "Cottonville bordered a creek, a starveling, wet-weather stream which offered the sole suggestion of sewerage" (36) and had added pollutants as it "flowed from tank to tank among the factories" (26). By the time Johnnie asks, at the end of the passage quoted above, "do you reckon the water's unsafe down here in Cottonville?" (113–14), the connections between stream conditions, air, built spaces, and a society's health are explicit. What has changed is Johnnie's political consciousness to be able to see and criticize these ecological problems. By the end of the novel, Johnnie acts for environmental and social justice. Taken as a whole, then, the novel makes a strong ecological statement *against* environmental poisoning and capitalism supporting it and *for* healthy communities.

Race, Class, and Gender in Cottonville

Cooke does not stop at investigating how unjust economic structures affect women and their environment; she also examines unjust oppression based explicitly on gender. The influx of capital from outside the region has certainly accelerated ecological crises in the mountains. Cooke suggests, however, that traditions and structures of male-dominated hierarchies, with their own economic oppression and violence, have supported the corporate practices outlined by Mavity, Mandy, and Johnnie. Women experience the negative effects of a power structure that benefits (white) men in the structural mechanisms of the mill and the mill town economy. What was previously only implied by the pivotal conversation between women now becomes concrete: not only does *The Power and the Glory* call for ecological activism, but it also argues that feminism is the crucial tool to bring change.

Early on, Johnnie observes the experiences of work had by men, women, and children at the mills and notices the extra free time enjoyed by men, who are better paid and unionized. For instance, she says of male-only "loom-fixers and mechanics": "It was a significant point for any student of economic conditions to note these strapping young males sitting at ease upon the porches of their homes or boarding houses, when the sweating, fagged women weavers and childish spinners trooped across the bridges an hour after" (123). Mill owners, then, are not the only enforcers of these hierarchies; Cooke establishes that local men directly benefit from and thus fight to preserve gender inequalities.

The division of labor instituted by mills and unions on women is doubled by local inequalities, as women have to relinquish their already reduced paychecks to the men in their lives. Pap Himes expects Johnnie's pay when he marries her mother; he forces Johnnie's much younger brothers and sisters into work to earn their keep (228). Despite being a skilled mechanic, Pap lives off women's labor: Mavity's (who runs "his" boardinghouse and works in the mills), his new wife's family, and the mill women who board under his roof. In fact, Cooke has explained: "In the mountains a woman works, of course, and earns her board and keep. She is a valuable industrial possession or chattel to the man, who may profit by her labour; never a luxury—a bill of expense" (32). As Miles argued in *The Spirit of the Mountains* (54), women in Appalachian communities are not "lace-capped and felt-shod pets of the household." Cooke, using the modern term, "industrial," and the premodern one, "chattel," signals that both "tradition" and cutting-edge "civilization" support the oppression of mountain women. Thus, it is no surprise that the experiences women have in their traditionally organized families also privilege men by limiting women's options. Johnnie objects to the expected subservience of women by saying, "I ain't aimin' to wed any man, fixed like I am. Mother and the children have to be looked after, and I can't ask a man to do for 'em, so I have to do it myself" (132). Women and children (like Johnnie's relatives) who are "expenses" are in jeopardy of falling through the cracks in a male-privileging system—at the mills, in the town, in their own homes.

In addition, racial hierarchies in Appalachia keep labor coalitions from forming. An intriguing conversation between an African American woman and Johnnie hints at the possibility of alliance on the basis of class, without regard to race, in the mountains. In the scene, Johnnie is at her lowest point, with her brothers and sisters forced to work in the mills, her uncle ill, her friends desperate for housing and work, and Gray at the greatest distance from her. Desperate for help, she turns to Lydia but is shut outside looking in at one of Lydia's parties. She is found there by the "yellow waitress" who is head servant. Cassy and Johnnie know each other—they speak familiarly, with Johnnie asking Cassy for a favor and Cassy deciding to help because "everybody liked Johnnie." Although Cassy's job is a traditional one for black women in the South, she holds unusual power in the scene—with the rather surprising result that Cassy decides to hire Johnnie for the evening so that Johnnie can get close to Lydia. Cassy says: "I couldn't disturb her whilst she's got company—without you want to put on this here cap and apron and come he'p me sarve the refreshments," which Johnnie does (232–33). Cooke gives Cassy some stereotypical comic substitutions, "disappearance" for "appearance" and "resist" for "assist," which undermine her agency. However, because the scene hints at ongoing relationships across the races that are not employer-employee, the potential for radical, multirace labor coalition at least exists.[21]

As well as interracial alliances, Cooke suggests that male-female alliances are important to the long-term health of the mountain community. Yet, after outlining the ways men are complicit in unfair structures of power, she must outline what kind of man is fit for coalition work. Thus, Cooke carefully cites Gray's activist pedigree: "Upon his mother's side he was the grandson of one of the great antislavery agitators. The sister of this man, Gray's great-aunt, had stood beside him on the platform when there was danger in it; and after the Negro was freed and enfranchised, she had devoted a long life to the cause of woman suffrage" (58). Aligning Gray with feminist and antiracist activism makes possible his coalition with Johnnie to enact social and environmental justice in Appalachia.[22]

"The Lives of All Three Depended on Her Cool Head": The Rescue

Gray plays a crucial role as Johnnie's ally, but it is Johnnie who becomes the dynamic hero, reversing gender roles, saving Gray, and discovering the key to her own financial independence. When Shade Buckheath and some of the other mountain residents capture, manacle, and imprison Gray, they hide him in a cave on the mountain that the women in Johnnie's family have used for at least four generations. Johnnie's uncle describes it as "the one whar my mammy kept her milk and butter" (Cooke, *Power and Glory,* 361). The female imagery of the shape of caves, combined with the women's fertility symbols of milk and butter, and the fetuslike helplessness of the shackled Gray all make for a scene in which he is reborn as Johnnie rescues him from the kidnappers. He has "dreamed about [Johnnie] here in the dark" and is "pale, disheveled, with a long mark of black leaf-mould across his cheek" (342). The only clue Gray has been able to drop for Johnnie to find is a pink moccasin flower they bonded over when they first met (338). His rebirth connects him to the nonhuman community and gives him the courage to ignore the differences between humans—specifically the class differences between Johnnie and himself—and propose marriage to Johnnie.

The final key to their egalitarian relationship is found at the end of the same cave. Johnnie's Uncle Pros says: "Somehow, I never did think about goin' to the end of that. Looked like it was too near home to have a silver mine in it" (361)—and when the silver turns out to be nickel, Johnnie's fortune is secure. By the time the novel concludes, Johnnie and her family are independently wealthy, crucial because the economic poverty of the women and children in her extended family, and her own sense of responsibility to them, have kept Johnnie from marrying up until this point. With their new wealth, Johnnie can decide to marry without a sense of indebtedness or dependence on Gray. In other words, Cooke can conclude her sentimental story on a note of true love rather than practical expedience.

But first Gray must be rescued from the cave:

> She leaped into the car. Would her memory serve her? Would she forget some detail that she must know? There were two levers under the steering-wheel. She advanced her spark and partly opened the throttle. From the steady, comfortable purr which had undertoned

all sounds in the tiny glen, the machine burst at once into a deep-toned roar. The narrow depression vibrated with its joyous clamour. . . .

Johnnie worked over her machine wildly. Gray had told her of the foot-brake only; but her hand encountering the lever of the emergency brake, she grasped it at a hazard and shoved it forward, as the god of luck had ordered, just short of a zigzag in the steep mountain road which, at the speed they had been making would have piled them, a mass of wreckage, beneath the cliff.

The sudden, violent check—shooting along at the speed they were, it amounted almost to a stoppage—gave the girl a sense of power. If she could do that, they were fairly safe. With the relief, her brain cleared; she was able to study the machine with some calmness. Gray could not help her—out of the side of her eye she could see where he lay inert and senseless in Passmore's hold. The lives of all three depended on her cool head at this moment. . . .

"They've done got him—they've found him! Miss Johnnie Consadine's a'bringin' him down in his own cyar!" (343–51)

Johnnie's "sense of power" and "cool head" prevail. Modern machinery and Appalachia are not incompatible, when the machine is piloted by a woman who is of the community and aware of the human and nonhuman. Mountain women are capable, intelligent, able to assume nontraditional roles and succeed in them, and are not doomed to remain a "bill of expense" to men on whom they must depend. Johnnie stepping into the situation and assuming the hero's role so much that she rescues him in his own vehicle—"a'bringin' him down in his own cyar!"—demonstrates the lengths to which Cooke will go to establish her main character's value. The substitution is crucial because the resolution of Cooke's novel depends on absolute equality between Johnnie and Gray.

In the end it is a partnership between men and women that brings human and nonhuman communities into balance. Cooke's vision in 1910 is startlingly reminiscent of Carolyn Merchant's description in 1997 of a partnership ethic with the earth: "[B]oth women and men can enter into mutual relationships with each other and the planet independently of gender and [it] does not hold women alone responsible for 'cleaning up the mess' made by male-dominated science, technology, and capitalism."[23] With Johnnie and Gray as equal partners, able to assume each other's roles (and thus not relying on essentialist ideas about men and women's jobs), Appalachia's social and environmental injustices can be addressed.

At the very end of the novel, Johnnie and Gray make joint proposals of workable activism for the mill towns. Combining feminist and ecological concerns, they target women's lives both as sites of needed activism and as centers of authority and agency for that activism. All their suggestions are predicated on living in the place; Gray joins Johnnie in making a lifetime commitment to the mountains (Cooke, *Power and Glory*, 364). Thus, unlike Lydia's efforts, their programs are embedded in and responsible to the long-term mountain community. Among other things, Johnnie sets "about seeing that Mavity Bence and Mandy Meacham were comfortably provided for in the old boarding house, where ... they could do more good than many Uplift clubs." This boardinghouse restores women's access to nature with its "truck-patch up there, and a couple of cows and some chickens" (359). Johnnie's version of a settlement house provides women respite from the mills to recover their physical and emotional health without giving up their financial independence. They will be hired to perform light housework and help with the outdoor work of the garden. Cooke does not advocate an absolute rejection of progress or a "return" to isolation for mountain people. Instead, Gray proposes to build an ideal cotton mill village with his holdings, and Johnnie plans an ideal mining community with her newly dis- covered nickel mine (361). Cooke does not outline specifically how her two main protagonists will carry out these ambitious projects, but they symbol- ically reconcile mountain culture and values with the best of national life and progress.

In *The Power and the Glory*, happiness for Johnnie Consadine of the Unaka Mountains depends on the mountains. Intimate connections between humans and community, as seen through the figure of a strong, empowered woman, make the community function in sustainable ways that are both ecological and feminist. Cooke's vision is ecological because it is holistic in its consideration of connections among issues, varied community members, and structural institutions, and it is place specific in its discussion and potential solutions. It is feminist because of her strong criticism of gender hierarchies and her foundation of women's agency and responsibility against these structures. It stands, then, as an example from 1910 of the roots of eco- logical feminism.

Both Cooke's *The Power and the Glory* and Miles's *The Spirit of the Moun- tains* begin with a more ecological definition of the human and nonhuman community of Appalachia. They both identify women and feminist activism as crucial. Women have agency, responsibility, and support that emerges from and is answerable to whole communities, human and nonhuman. Both texts criticize inappropriate activism, especially inattentive feminism, as ultimately ineffective and even damaging for mountain women. A particular Appalachian feminism emerges that is effectively ecological.

What follows is a brief exploration of a text from halfway through the twentieth century. It is presented as an afterword to this project because it links the roots of ecological feminism in texts such as Murfree's *His Vanished Star,* Smith's poems, Cooke's *The Power and the Glory,* and Miles's *The Spirit of the Mountains* to the post-1970s sense of the movement. Wilma Dykeman's *The French Broad* displays much of the same emphasis on redefining communities to make them less essentialist, human-centered, and supportive of the status quo. She is in the legacy of authors at the turn of the past century and is a living ancestor of today's ecological feminist theorists. Her presence suggests that these earlier writers are not isolated incidents but are instead part of a movement throughout the century—a movement of women authors writing about gender and nature in Appalachia in such a way that ecological and feminist concerns are intimately interdependent.

Afterword

Mary Noailles Murfree's *His Vanished Star* ends with Cornelia Taft running the store her father has abandoned. Wanted by the law for his role in destroying the moonshining cave and sabotaging Kenniston's land survey, her father, Lorenzo, will not be seen in the community again. Adelicia mentors Cornelia from her new home, helping Cornelia find happiness as well as success. The women's community she lost when her grandmother died is thus restored at the novel's end. The young women are joined by the widow, Sabrina Larrabee, the woman who befriends hurt or lonely animals and humans who come to her doorstep. That Murfree ends her exploration of the dangers of undebated development with a portrait of women intimately involved in human and nonhuman community building means that a new kind of "progress" is possible in her mountain world.[1]

The last poem Effie Waller Smith published reached one of her largest audiences when it appeared in prestigious *Harper's* magazine in 1917. On the national stage, Smith still wrote about one woman's relationship with nonhuman Appalachian nature. Entitled "Autumn Winds," the poem reads in part:

> You bring to me no message of dismay,
> No tender sorrow for the year's decay;
> Rather you sing of giant trees that cast
> Their leaves aside to grapple with the blast,
> Strong and exultant for the stormy fray!

Smith ends the poem with the poet learning from the trees how to "stand forth free to struggle and endure" whatever the world brings. Smith's vision was sorely needed for the twentieth century in Appalachia. Through world wars, labor crises, and civil rights, the "stormy fray" certainly blew through the mountains. Yet, the vision of a woman standing "strong and exultant" hints at the joys to be found when communities come together.[2]

Emma Bell Miles occupied her last days in a tuberculosis sanitarium creating her final book, *Our Southern Birds*, which was published posthumously. Her years of observing and lecturing about the nonhuman world around Walden's Ridge prepared her well to create her bird book—all while lying outside on a cot in cold weather, taking the era's only treatment for her illness. To accompany her exploration of Appalachia's humans in *The Spirit of the Mountains*, she carefully portrayed with words and paintings the communities of birds in the Tennessee mountains. The two books together quietly testify to Miles's belief that humans always have lessons to learn from nonhuman Appalachia.[3]

Grace MacGowan Cooke's *The Power and the Glory* wraps up with Johnnie and Gray planning their future in Appalachia. Her extended family is healthy and happy; her friends are running the women's boardinghouse to help other mill workers; and Gray and Johnnie's ideal mill and mine villages are in the works. They have time to turn to the personal. He talks her out of going to Europe for a year, arguing that the Appalachian culture provides just as much education and depth as anything in England, France, or Italy.[4] Cooke ends her book with the message that a well-supported, healthy culture, wherever it occurs, contains wisdom and wealth. She reinforces her argument that Appalachian strengths should be cherished and celebrated.

In all four women's texts, humans are not separated from nonhumans in Appalachian communities. Nature has agency in their stories, which results in decision making that consults whole communities. Environmental and social justice issues are tackled by those whole communities, and structures of power that oppress, damage, and silence community members begin to be criticized. All four women highlight the particular effects on and roles for women in activism without erasing differences in power and privilege between humans. In other words, throughout their texts and even careers, Murfree, Smith, Miles, and Cooke nurture the roots of ecological feminism in Appalachia.

In 1955, another writer in whose works the roots of ecological feminism flourish published a book about an Appalachian river, *The French Broad.* Eight years before Rachel Carson's *Silent Spring,* a text often celebrated as one of the first to condemn the effects of environmental pollution, Wilma Dykeman's book similarly criticizes industrial poisoning of human and nonhuman communities. Through her novels, essays, and nonfiction books, Dykeman, a writer with roots in the North Carolina and Tennessee mountains, has celebrated and championed the Appalachian region. The concerns of *The French Broad* connect Dykeman to Murfree, Smith, Miles, and Cooke, as Dykeman analyzes the effects of undebated development, tells the story of African Americans, Native Americans, and European Americans who love Appalachia, writes her own manifesto for Appalachian people, and thinks about women's roles in cleaning up factory pollution. At the end of her text, Dykeman proposes a grassroots activism that empowers and makes responsible the women and men who live along the river. "Pollution is an ugly word. A sick word. A dead one," she says in no uncertain terms before suggesting that "the least that those who are fortunate enough to be dwellers of the French Broad country can do, out of humble thankfulness for nature's bounty to them, is make certain that their town, their city, and the industries around them at last shoulder this responsibility." She reiterates, "Filth is the price we pay for apathy."[5] Texts like Dykeman's suggest that the roots of ecological feminism did not die when Murfree, Smith, Miles, and Cooke stopped writing. Those roots continued to grow throughout the century in Appalachia.

The Appalachia I know continues to struggle with environmental and social justice issues. Many of us who are Appalachians still know the feeling of being subjected to the voyeur's gaze ("Could I record you? Your accent is so charming!"). Spring Break brings church groups, college classes, and high school clubs to "remote" Appalachia for a week's worth of social crusading. Each summer we wait with mixed feelings for the tourists to arrive. Factory workers in West Virginia's Chemical Valley share with Cooke's Cottonville mill workers concerns about air, water, and soil quality but also the economic need that makes activism difficult. Residents of western North Carolina who are being priced out of their towns by real estate buyers looking for vacation homes can empathize with Murfree's mountain community staring down Kenneth Kenniston and his resort. Women through-hikers on the Appalachian Trail join Smith in hoping that all women feel safe in the wilderness and will use that sense of empowerment to help their home communities. Residents throughout the mountains struggle just as Miles did to find a balance between valuing tradition and embracing social and cultural change that improves life in Appalachia. The philosophies and struggles of early ecological feminists from the turn of the previous century might just provide insights and inspiration for us, just three years into the twenty-first century. I hope women's texts like those of Murfree, Smith, Miles and Cooke will continue to be read because they need to be read and because they may offer possible solutions to ecological and feminist challenges—not only for Appalachia but for the rest of the United States as well.

At the end of *The French Broad,* Dykeman paraphrases Robert Frost: "I'm going out to clean the spring and wait for it to flow clear again. . . . Won't you come too?" She continues: "I'm going out to hear the slow talk of some stranger becoming friend as I listen to his life; to see the wide sweep of the river's silent power around a certain bend beneath the sycamores. I'm going out to smell fresh rain on summer dust and the prehistoric water odors of the old French Broad in flood. Won't you come too?"[6] Not only does Dykeman make space for Miles, Murfree, Smith, and Cooke to join her beside an Appalachian river, but she also invites all of us to come and sit with her beside the river and listen, carefully listen, to each other and to the world around us.

Notes

INTRODUCTION

1. Mary Noailles Murfree [Charles Egbert Craddock, pseud.], *His Vanished Star* (Boston: Houghton Mifflin, 1894), 1, 2.

2. Ellen Griffith Spears, *The Newtown Story: One Community's Fight for Environmental Justice* (Atlanta: Center for Democratic Renewal and Newtown Florist Club, 1998); Emma Bell Miles, *The Spirit of the Mountains* (1905; reprinted, with a foreword by Roger D. Abrahams and introduction by David E. Whisnant, Knoxville: University of Tennessee Press, 1975), 37.

3. Grace MacGowan Cooke, *The Power and the Glory: An Appalachian Novel* (1910; reprinted, with an introduction by Elizabeth S. D. Engelhardt, Boston: Northeastern University Press, 2003), 112.

4. Effie Waller Smith, "The Hills," in *Songs of the Months* (1904; reprinted in *The Collected Works of Effie Waller Smith*, with an introduction by David Deskins, Schomburg Library of Nineteenth-Century Black Women Writers, New York: Oxford University Press, 1991), 48.

5. Amelie Rives [Troubetzkoy], *Tanis, the Sang-Digger* (New York: Town Topics, 1893), 17; Maria Louise Pool, *In Buncombe County* (Chicago: Herbert S. Stone, 1896); Daisy Gertrude Dame to "My Dear," 24 July 1909, Daisy Gertrude Dame Papers, 4431, Southern Historical Collection, Wilson Library, University of North Carolina at Chapel Hill.

6. I have chosen to use "nonhuman world" or "nonhuman community" instead of "nature" or "Nature" because of the ideological and cultural baggage the concept of nature carries. I hope with the more unfamiliar term "nonhuman" to signal that, however we construct it, there are trees, clouds, mountains, and animals in the material world that are different from humans.

7. Patrick D. Murphy, *Literature, Nature, and Other: Ecofeminist Critiques* (Albany: State University of New York Press, 1995), 35. For longer discussions on the difference between the environment (out-there from humans) and the ecology (in which humans and nonhumans exist together in mutual interdependence), see Carolyn Merchant, *Earthcare: Women and the Environment* (New York: Routledge, 1995); Cheryll Glotfelty, "Introduction: Literary Studies in an Age of Environmental Crisis," in *Ecocriticism Reader: Landmarks in Literary Ecology*, ed. Cheryll Glotfelty and Harold Fromm (Athens: University of Georgia Press, 1996), xv–xxxvii. Chris J. Cuomo provides a helpful distinction between ecofeminism and ecological feminism in her *Feminism and Ecological Communities: An Ethic*

of Flourishing (London: Routledge, 1998). I am also indebted to Karen J. Warren's *Ecofeminist Philosophy: A Western Perspective on What It Is and Why It Matters* (Lanham, Md.: Rowman and Littlefield, 2000); Stacy Alaimo's *Undomesticated Ground: Recasting Nature as Feminist Space* (Ithaca: Cornell University Press, 2000); and Giovanna Di Chiro, "Nature as Community: The Convergence of Environment and Social Justice," in *Uncommon Ground: Rethinking the Human Place in Nature,* ed. William Cronon (New York: W. W. Norton, 1996), 298–320.

8. Leslie Marmon Silko, "Landscape, History, and the Pueblo Imagination," in *Ecocriticism Reader,* 264–75; Gary Snyder, *The Practice of the Wild* (New York: North Point Press, 1990), 20.

9. Smith, 48.

10. Miles, *Spirit of the Mountains,* 37; Cooke, *Power and Glory,* 112.

11. Ian Marshall, *Story Line: Exploring the Literature of the Appalachian Trail* (Charlottesville: University Press of Virginia, 1998), 3.

CHAPTER 1

1. Such books include Dwight Billings, Gurney Norman, and Katherine Ledford, eds., *Back Talk from Appalachia: Confronting Stereotypes* (Lexington: University Press of Kentucky, 2000); Danny L. Miller, "The Paradox of Appalachia and the Stereotype of the Mountain Woman," in his *Wingless Flights: Appalachian Women in Fiction* (Bowling Green, Oh.: Bowling Green State University Popular Press, 1996); Stephen L. Fisher, ed., *Fighting Back in Appalachia: Traditions of Resistance and Change* (Philadelphia: Temple University Press, 1993); David C. Hsiung, *Two Worlds in the Tennessee Mountains: Exploring the Origins of Appalachian Stereotypes* (Lexington: University Press of Kentucky, 1997); Barbara Ellen Smith, "'Beyond the Mountains': The Paradox of Women's Place in Appalachian History," *NWSA Journal* 11, no. 3 (fall 1999): 1–17.

2. Appalachian Regional Commission, "The Appalachian Region." Accessed 6 May 2002. Available from World Wide Web: <http://www.arc.gov/aboutarc/region/abtapreg.htm>.

3. For biographical information on Elliott's political life see Clara Childs MacKenzie, *Sarah Barnwell Elliott* (Boston: Twayne, 1980), 15–56; her equal rights manifesto is quoted in A. Elizabeth Taylor, *The Woman Suffrage Movement in Tennessee* (New York: Bookman, 1957), 71.

4. For a discussion of Tennessee's role in the national suffrage campaign, see Anne Firor Scott and Andrew MacKay Scott, *One Half the People: The Fight for Woman Suffrage* (Urbana: University of Illinois Press, 1982); and Taylor, *Woman Suffrage Movement in Tennessee;* on Wells-Barnett and the Alpha Suffrage Club, see Linda O. McMurry, *To Keep the Waters Troubled: The Life of Ida B. Wells* (New York: Oxford University Press, 1998), 305.

5. MacKenzie, 15–56. On Elliott's stories, see Gayle Gaskill, "Sarah Barnwell Elliott," in *American Women Writers: A Critical Reference Guide from Colonial Times to the Present,* ed. Lina Mainiero (New York: Frederick Ungar, 1979), 1: 588–90.

6. On Troubetzkoy's suffrage activities, see Lloyd C. Taylor Jr., "Amelie Louise Rives," in *Notable American Women, 1607–1950: A Biographical Dictionary,* ed. Edward T. James (Cambridge: Harvard University Press, Belknap Press, 1971), 3: 169–70; Miles's newspaper columns are discussed in Kay Baker Gaston, "Emma Bell Miles and the 'Fountain Square' Conversations," *Tennessee Historical Quarterly* 37, no. 4 (winter 1978): 416–29; a

typescript copy of Miles's diary is included in the Emma Bell Miles Papers, Hist. C. acc. 43, Chattanooga-Hamilton County Bicentennial Library, Chattanooga, Tennessee (hereafter cited as Miles Papers). Helen M. Lewis's activities are outlined in Margaret Supplee Smith and Emily Herring Wilson, *North Carolina Women: Making History* (Chapel Hill: University of North Carolina Press, 1999), 216.

7. Margaret W. Morley, *The Carolina Mountains* (Boston: Houghton Mifflin, 1913), 190.

8. See Goodrich, "Extracts from Letters," 20 Nov. 1892, vol. 3, Frances Louisa Goodrich Papers, Rare Book, Manuscript, and Special Collections Library, Duke University; [Miss] Matt Crim, "The Strike at Mr. Mobley's," *Century* 50 (July 1895): 379.

9. David E. Whisnant, *All That Is Native and Fine: The Politics of Culture in an American Region* (Chapel Hill: University of North Carolina Press, 1983), 88; Henry D. Shapiro makes a similar argument in his *Appalachia on Our Mind: The Southern Mountains and Mountaineers in the American Consciousness, 1870–1920* (Chapel Hill: University of North Carolina Press, 1978); Annelise Orleck, *Common Sense and a Little Fire: Women and Working-Class Politics in the United States, 1900–1965* (Chapel Hill: University of North Carolina Press, 1995), 54; Ella May Wiggins's most famous song is "A Mill Mother's Lament," and her life and murder are discussed in Smith and Wilson, 262–65; the statistic on women and children in the textile-mill work force also comes from Smith and Wilson, 167; Jacquelyn Dowd Hall researched the Elizabethton strike in "Disorderly Women: Gender and Labor Militancy in the Appalachian South," *Journal of American History* 73, no. 2 (Sept. 1986): 354–82.

10. Magazines and newspapers also attest to the presence and organization of non-white communities within Appalachia. Some publications also include short stories, poems, and serialized novels. Knoxville, Tennessee, could boast the *Weekly Negro World,* later known as the *Knoxville Negro World.* Nearby Chattanooga printed the *Justice;* Maryville, Tennessee, had the *Maryville Republican.* Jackson, Tennessee, published the *Jackson Headlight,* and Martinsburg, West Virginia, had the *Pioneer Press.* In border regions of the mountains, newspapers such as the *Richmond Planet* or the *Virginia Star* (both from Richmond, Virginia) appeared; these, too, occasionally report on African American life in Appalachia. I created this (surely incomplete) list from American Council of Learned Societies, Committee on Negro Studies, *Microfilm Series Negro Newspaper: Microform* (Washington, D.C.: Library of Congress for the Committee on Negro Studies of the American Council of Learned Societies, 1947). James Danky's *African-American Newspapers and Periodicals: A National Bibliography* (Cambridge: Harvard University Press, 1998) is also invaluable. *Talks and Thoughts* is discussed in Paulette Fairbanks Molin, "'Training the Hand, the Head, and the Heart': Indian Education at Hampton Institute," *Minnesota History* 51, no. 3 (fall 1988): 87. Unfortunately, I have been unable to locate extant copies of *The Mountain Gleaner.* It is discussed in I. Garland Penn, *Afro-American Press and Its Editors* (1891; reprinted, New York: Arno, 1969), 212.

11. Taylor, *Woman Suffrage Movement in Tennessee,* 71.

12. Rebecca Harding Davis's "The Yares of the Black Mountains" first appeared in 1875; she republished it in her collection of short stories, *Silhouettes of American Life* (New York: Charles Scribner's Sons, 1892); Lucy Furman, *The Glass Window: A Story of the Quare Women* (Boston: Little, Brown, and Co., 1925). For an overall introduction to nineteenth-century women's activism, see Carroll Smith-Rosenberg, *Disorderly Conduct: Visions of Gender in Victorian America* (New York: Alfred A. Knopf, 1985). For research showing the

activism of southern women, see Anne Firor Scott, *Making the Invisible Woman Visible* (Urbana: University of Illinois Press, 1984), 217. Beverly Guy-Sheftall's *Words of Fire: An Anthology of African-American Feminist Thought* (New York: New Press, 1995) contains primary source documents of the African American women who were "lifting as they climbed" in their women's club work.

13. Although only six settlement houses existed in the United States in 1891, there were one hundred across the country by 1900, and 400 by 1910, according to Whisnant, *All That Is Native and Fine*, 22. For a discussion of the Appalachian modifications, see Whisnant, *All That Is Native and Fine*, 17–102, and Shapiro, 133–56.

14. For biographical information on Pettit, see Jess Stoddart, introduction to *The Quare Women's Journals: May Stone and Katherine Pettit's Summers in the Kentucky Mountains and the Founding of the Hindman Settlement School*, by May Stone and Katherine Pettit, ed. Jess Stoddart (Ashland, Ky.: Jesse Stuart Foundation, 1997), 17–57; Whisnant, *All That Is Native and Fine*, 24–34; Elizabeth S. Peck, "Katherine Pettit," in *Notable American Women, 1607–1950*, 3:56–58.

15. *City Directory, Colored Section, Asheville, North Carolina, 1900–1901* (Pack Library, Archives, Buncombe County, Asheville, North Carolina). Information about early industrial schools in Asheville comes from Lenwood Davis, *The Black Heritage of Western North Carolina* (Asheville: University Graphics, University of North Carolina, Asheville, n.d.), 56. Research on the Young Men's Institute can be found in "Young Men's Institute Building, Nomination Form for National Register of Historic Places," 77.10.3.8, Black Highlander Collection, Ramsey Library, University of North Carolina–Asheville. William H. Turner, "The Demography of Black Appalachia: Past and Present," in *Blacks in Appalachia*, ed. William H. Turner and Edward J. Cabbell (Lexington: University of Kentucky Press, 1985), 237–61; Ancella R. Bickley and Lynda Ann Ewen, eds., *Memphis Tennessee Garrison: The Remarkable Story of a Black Appalachian Woman* (Athens: Ohio University Press, 2001); Deborah Weiner, "Jewish Women in the Central Appalachian Coal Fields, 1880–1960: From Breadwinners to Community Builders," *American Jewish Archives Journal* 52, nos. 1–2 (2000): Accessed 12 May 2002. Available from World Wide Web: <http://huc.edu/aja/00-1.htm>.

16. For biographical information on May Stone, see Stoddart, 17–57; Whisnant, *All That Is Native and Fine*, 34–37.

17. Anna D. McBain, "What It Means to Be a Teacher," *Berea Quarterly* (May 1901): 19. Almost all the research to recover Effie Waller Smith, including biographical work, has been done by David Deskins. See his introduction to *The Collected Works of Effie Waller Smith* (Schomburg Library of Nineteenth-Century Black Women Writers, New York: Oxford University Press, 1991), and his earlier "Effie Waller Smith: An Echo within the Hills," *Kentucky Review* 8, no. 3 (autumn 1988): 26–46.

18. Information on the region's historically black colleges comes from George S. Dickerman, "Ten Years' Changes in East Tennessee," *Southern Workman* 34, no. 5 (May 1905): 268. On Storer College, see Beth Jane Toren and Alisha Myers, "Storer College: A Photographic Exhibit of the First African American College in West Virginia." Accessed 12 May 2002. Available from World Wide Web: <http://www.libraries.wvu.edu/storer/>. Details about Cherokee students come from Smith and Wilson, 178–86, who also note resistance to white educational models from Cherokee elders; for a contemporary perspective, see Emily K. Herron, "Our Cherokee Neighbors," *Southern Workman* 29, no. 8 (August 1900): 469.

19. John Charles Campbell to Mrs. John Glenn, 15 May 1908, John Charles and Olive Dame Campbell Papers, 3800, Southern Historical Collection, Wilson Library, University of North Carolina at Chapel Hill (hereafter cited as Campbell Papers). Olive Dame Campbell, preface to *The Southern Highlander and His Homeland*, by John C. Campbell (New York: Russell Sage Foundation, 1921), xvi.

20. The miles Campbell covered and number of schools she visited are calculated in Smith and Wilson, 255.

21. On the shocking revelation about Murfree's gender, see Emily Satterwhite, "Such a Thing as 'Literary Material'": Unveiling the "Habitats and Habits of Charles Egbert Craddock," (draft) accessed 3 Feb. 2002. Available from World Wide Web: <http://www. etsu.edu/writing/apptravel/murfree.htm>. Biographical information on Troubetzkoy can be found in Taylor, "Amelie Rives," 170; also, see Welford Dunaway Taylor, *Amelie Rives (Princess Troubetzkoy)* (New York: Twayne, 1973). Troubetzkoy, 97.

22. Miles diary, 24 July 1914 and 23 Feb. 1915, Miles Papers.

23. For biographical information on Grace MacGowan Cooke, see Kay Baker Gaston, "The MacGowan Girls," *California History: The Magazine of the California Historical Society* 59, no. 2 (summer 1980): 124. Smith-Rosenberg discusses the friendships and relationships formed between women as combining "female bonding and traditional female familial concepts" to create new models of womanhood (255). Examples of being labeled "quare women" are in Furman's *Glass Window* and *The Quare Women: A Story of the Kentucky Mountains* (Boston: Atlantic Monthly Press, 1923); "fotched-on" women are discussed in David E. Whisnant, "Second-level Appalachian History: Another Look at Some Fotched-On Women," *Appalachian Journal* 9, nos. 2–3 (winter–spring 1982): 115–23.

24. Some of these connections are outlined in Whisnant, *All That Is Native and Fine,* 39, 43. On Dame, see Daisy Gertrude Dame Papers, 4331, Southern Historical Collection, Wilson Library, University of North Carolina at Chapel Hill (hereafter cited as Dame Papers).

25. For biographical information on Frost, see Deborah L. Blackwell, "Eleanor Marsh Frost and the Gender Dimensions of Appalachian Reform Efforts," *Register of the Kentucky Historical Society* 94, no. 3 (summer 1996): 225–46. Frost's April 20, 1901, visit to Washington is documented in her diary. See Eleanor Marsh Frost, correspondence, reports, and diary, the papers of William Goodell Frost, Berea College Archives, Hutchins Library, Berea, Kentucky (hereafter cited as Frost Papers). It is possible that Campbell met and discussed teaching with Emma Bell Miles. This is inconclusive, but after reporting on November 3, 1908, that they were climbing "Walden's Ridge," Miles's home community, Campbell says on November 9, 1908, that they "[w]ent to Beechams to dinner, where we met a Mrs. Miles from [unreadable word] and a Mrs. ? formerly a teacher." For her visits with Frost, Goodrich, and Pettit, see Campbell diary, 28 Nov. 1908; 6, 7, and 31 Dec. 1908; and 19 Feb. 1909, Campbell Papers. Mary R. Martin, *Mother Pioneered at Montreat (Her Letters 1898–1899)*, adapted by Emilie Miller Vaughan (Montreat, N.C.: Presbyterian Church [U.S.A.] Department of History and Records Management Services, 1996), 9, 14.

26. Miles diary, 15 Jan. 1913, Miles Papers; Gaston, "MacGowan Girls," 117–20.

27. Vera Norwood, *Made from This Earth: American Women and Nature* (Chapel Hill: University of North Carolina Press, 1993), 261; Carolyn Merchant, *Earthcare: Women and the Environment* (New York: Routledge, 1995), 109.

28. Information for this paragraph comes from Merchant, 111–21; Norwood, 127; Polly Welts Kaufman, *National Parks and the Woman's Voice: A History* (Albuquerque: University of New Mexico Press, 1996), 27–44; and Jennifer Price, *Flight Maps: Adventures with Nature in Modern America* (New York: Basic Books, 1999), 61. Merchant does not give and I have been unable to find Mrs. Lovell White's first name.

29. Albert E. Cowdrey, *This Land, This South: An Environmental History* (Lexington: University Press of Kentucky, 1983), 103–24. Henry Grady is quoted in C. Vann Woodward, *Origins of the New South, 1877–1913,* with a critical essay on recent works by Charles B. Dew (Baton Rouge: Louisiana State University Press, 1971), 166; Price, 96; Whisnant, *All That Is Native and Fine,* 24; Hall, 357.

30. Merchant, 132–35.

31. Morley, *Carolina Mountains,* 30. For information on the park, see Carlos C. Campbell, *Birth of a National Park in the Great Smoky Mountains,* 2d ed. (Knoxville: University of Tennessee Press, 1969); also, Michael Frome, *Strangers in High Places: The Story of the Great Smoky Mountains* (Knoxville: University of Tennessee Press, 1994), 182. The fact that Mrs. Davis's name is never recounted symbolizes how mythologized the story has become.

32. Price, 61, 97; and "Appeal for the Birds," *Richmond (Virginia) Planet,* 27 June 1903.

33. Whisnant, *All That Is Native and Fine,* 32, 73; Katherine Pettit, "Come One, Come All," flier, Katherine Pettit Papers, Southern Appalachian Archives, Hutchins Library, Berea College, Berea, Kentucky. For information on E. Lucy Braun and the logging of Lynn Fork, see Marcia Bonta, ed., *American Women Afield: Writings by Pioneering Women Naturalists* (College Station: Texas A & M University Press, 1995), 226.

34. Lucy Furman, "Katherine Pettit: A Pioneer Mountain Worker," *Mountain Life and Work* 12 (October 1936): 20.

35. Frost, "Mountain Trip 1914, Kentucky–North Carolina," Frost Papers.

36. Dame to "My Dear," 24 July 1909, Dame Papers. Laura Maria Miller Grout, undated, untitled speech that begins "A person taking a trip." Laura Maria Miller Grout was assistant principal of the Pleasant Hill Academy in Tennessee from 1890 to 1892. Many of her papers are texts of speeches. Those speeches have titles such as "Christian Work among the Mt. Whites of Tenn." (1894) and "Home Prayer Meeting" (1894). Her papers are at the Rare Book, Manuscript, and Special Collections Library, Duke University. Grace Funk Myers, *"Them Missionary Women"; or, Work in the Southern Mountains* (Hillsdale, Mich.: by the author, 1911); Martha S. Gielow, *Old Andy, the Moonshiner* (Washington, D.C.: W. F. Roberts, 1909); and Mrs. F. L. [Meta] Townsend, *In the Nantahalas* (Nashville: Publishing House M. E. Church, South, 1910). A little more than ten years later, my grandmother would enroll in the Brevard School, then known as the Brevard Institute; today it survives as Brevard College, a four-year school.

37. See Nickum to "Home Folks," 18 Nov. 1901, 17 Feb. and 12 Mar. 1902, Bertha Daisy Nickum Letters and Photographs, Record Group 8: Students, Berea College Archives, Hutchins Library, Berea, Kentucky.

38. Dame to "My Dear," 24 July 1909, and to family, 19 Jan. 1910, Dame Papers.

39. See inside back cover of Frost diary, March–September 1898, Frost Papers. Campbell diary, 22 Jan. 1909, Campbell Papers. I have been unable to find the author of "The Dark Corner" but see Dame to Billy [brother], 17 Aug. 1909, Dame Papers.

CHAPTER 2

1. Grace MacGowan Cooke, *The Power and the Glory: An Appalachian Novel* (1910; reprinted, with an introduction by Elizabeth S. D. Engelhardt, Boston: Northeastern University Press, 2003), 27; Mary P. Montague, "Little Kaintuck," *Atlantic Monthly* 105, no. 5 (May 1910): 609–16; Mary Noailles Murfree [Charles Egbert Craddock, pseud.], *In the Tennessee Mountains* (Boston: Houghton Mifflin, 1884); Alice MacGowan, "The Homecoming of Byrd Forebush: A Love Story of Little Turkey Track," *Munsey's Magazine* 30, no. 3 (Dec 1903): 397–404.

2. Researcher Sydney Saylor Farr counts 45 novels by women in her bibliography of Appalachian writing, *Appalachian Women: An Annotated Bibliography* (Lexington: University Press of Kentucky, 1981); working with a slightly different definition, Lorise C. Boger gives 103 works in *The Southern Mountaineer in Literature: An Annotated Bibliography* (Morgantown: West Virginia University Library, 1964). Carvel Collins lists approximately 59 Appalachian novels and short stories by women authors between 1890 and 1900, "The Literary Tradition of the Southern Mountaineer, 1824–1900," reprinted from *The Bulletin of Bibliography* 17, nos. 9–10 (September–December 1942; January–April 1943), North Carolina Collection, Wilson Library, University of North Carolina at Chapel Hill. Although I use "literary regionalism" to describe certain women's writings later in this project, I deliberately am not using Judith Fetterley and Marjorie Pryse's term for the literatures of the voyeur and tourist, *American Women Regionalists, 1850–1910* (New York: W. W. Norton, 1992), xi–xx. I agree with Fetterley's distinction that "regionalism ... models a subjectivity attained by standing up for others, not on them"; see Fetterley, "'Not in the Least American': Nineteenth-Century Literary Regionalism as UnAmerican Literature," in *Nineteenth-Century American Women Writers: A Critical Reader,* ed. Karen Kilcup (Oxford: Blackwell, 1998), 16. Nevertheless, a problem in naming remains—the terms "local color," "literary realism," "regionalist fiction," and even "regional realism" have all been variously employed for the body of texts about Appalachia. I have chosen to retain the awkward but descriptive "writings by women about Appalachia" in order to move the discussion away from genre and toward cultural, social, and ecological conversations in which the writings participated and by which they were shaped.

3. Louise R. Baker, *Cis Martin, Or, The Furriners in the Tennessee Mountains* (New York: Eaton and Mains, 1898), 71; Annie Maria Barnes, *The Ferry Maid of the Chattahoochee: A Story for Girls* (Philadelphia: Pennsylvania Publishing Co., 1899); Marie Van Vorst, *Amanda of the Mill* (New York: Dodd, Mead and Co., 1905). The limitations described here—stories set at and written during the turn of the twentieth century—were made to make more visible the contemporary cultural and social milieu out of which the stories emerge and which the stories reflect.

4. Henry D. Shapiro, *Appalachia on Our Mind: The Southern Mountains and Mountaineers in the American Consciousness, 1870–1920* (Chapel Hill: University of North Carolina Press, 1978), xi. I differ from Shapiro in that, although he, too, looks at the philosophical assumptions contained in writings about Appalachia (dating them from the 1870s and 1880s), Shapiro's focus does not lead him to discuss the specific constructions used by women writers. Nor does the environmental fit into his exploration of the idea of

Appalachia. Nevertheless, his work informs my own, especially in his discussion of male and gender-neutral travelers to Appalachia.

5. Amelie Rives [Troubetzkoy], *Tanis, the Sang-Digger* (New York: Town Topics, 1893), 8–9. Subsequent parenthetical references are to this edition.

6. On Troubetzkoy's experiences at home in Virginia, see Welford Dunaway Taylor, *Amelie Rives (Princess Troubetzkoy)* (New York: Twayne, 1973), 19–25.

7. Ibid., 40.

8. Van Vorst, 13; Mary Nelson Carter, *North Carolina Sketches: Phases of Life Where the Galax Grows* (Chicago: A. C. McClurg, 1900), 59–60.

9. Martha S. Gielow, *Old Andy, the Moonshiner* (Washington, D.C.: W. F. Roberts, 1909).

10. Albert E. Cowdrey, *This Land, This South: An Environmental History* (Lexington: University Press of Kentucky, 1983), 103–24.

11. Mary Noailles Murfree [Charles Egbert Craddock, pseud.], *His Vanished Star* (Boston: Houghton Mifflin, 1894), 8; Sarah Barnwell Elliott, *The Durket Sperret* (New York: Henry Holt, 1898), 5; Maria Louise Pool, *In Buncombe County* (Chicago: Herbert S. Stone, 1896).

12. Grace MacGowan Cooke, "The Capture of Andy Proudfoot," in *Southern Lights and Shadows*, ed. William Dean Howells and Henry Mills Alden (New York: Harper and Brothers, 1907), 8–10, 16, 17.

13. Rebecca Harding Davis, "The Yares of the Black Mountains," in *Silhouettes of American Life* (New York: Charles Scribner's Sons, 1892), 255 (subsequent references appear in parentheses in the text).

14. Ibid.; Pool, 3; Davis, "A Wayside Episode," in *Silhouettes of American Life,* 145–71; Alice MacGowan, *Judith of the Cumberlands* (New York: Putnam, 1908), v–vi. A good source on nineteenth-century tourism is John F. Sears, *Sacred Places: American Tourist Attractions in the Nineteenth Century* (New York: Oxford University Press, 1989), although I disagree with his assertion that tourism "was never gender identified" (8). For a discussion of gender and tourism, see Brigitte Georgi-Findlay, *The Frontiers of Women's Writing: Women's Narratives and the Rhetoric of Westward Expansion* (Tucson: University of Arizona Press, 1996). For a discussion of modern intersections of Appalachia and tourism, see Melinda Bollar Wagner et al. "Appalachia: A Tourist Attraction?" in *The Impact of Institutions in Appalachia: Proceedings of the Eighth Annual Appalachian Studies Conference,* ed. Jim Lloyd and Anne G. Campbell (Boone, N.C.: Appalachian Consortium Press, 1986), 73–87.

15. Alison Byerly, "The Uses of Landscape: The Picturesque Aesthetic and the National Park System," in *Ecocriticism Reader: Landmarks in Literary Ecology,* ed. Cheryll Glotfelty and Harold Fromm (Athens: University of Georgia Press, 1996), 53–55.

16. Nickum to "Folks at Home," 4 Nov. 1901, Bertha Daisy Nickum Letters and Photographs, Record Group 8: Students, Berea College Archives, Hutchins Library, Berea, Kentucky; Goodrich, "Extracts from Letters," 7 Nov. 1890, vol. 1, Frances Louisa Goodrich Papers, Rare Book, Manuscript, and Special Collections Library, Duke University; Campbell diary, 23 Nov. 1908, John Charles and Olive Dame Campbell Papers, 3800, Southern Historical Collection, Wilson Library, University of North Carolina at Chapel Hill (hereafter cited as Campbell Papers); May Stone and Katherine Pettit, *The Quare Women's Journals: May Stone and Katherine Pettit's Summers in the Kentucky Mountains and the Founding of the Hindman Settlement School,* ed. Jess Stoddart (Ashland, Ky.: Jesse Stuart Foundation, 1997), 175, 168.

17. Laura Maria Miller Grout, "Christian Work Among the Mt. Whites of Tenn." (1894), Papers, Rare Book, Manuscript, and Special Collections Library, Duke University; Byerly, 54; Dame to "Dear [Sweetest?] Dearest," 5 Apr. 1910, Daisy Gertrude Dame Papers, 4331, Southern Historical Collection, Wilson Library, University of North Carolina at Chapel Hill.

18. Annette Kolodny, *The Land Before Her: Fantasy and Experience of the American Frontiers, 1630–1860* (Chapel Hill: University of North Carolina Press, 1984), and *The Lay of the Land: Metaphor as Experience and History in American Life and Letters* (Chapel Hill: University of North Carolina Press, 1975), although Kolodny only extends her arguments until 1860, before most of the writers here were even born; Louise H. Westling, *The Green Breast of the New World: Landscape, Gender, and American Fiction* (Athens: University of Georgia Press, 1996).

19. For bibliographical information on Davis, see Jane Atteridge Rose, "A Bibliography of Fiction and Non-Fiction by Rebecca Harding Davis," *American Literary Realism, 1870–1910* 22, no. 3 (spring 1990): 67–86; on her short story innovations, see Jean Pfaelzer, *Parlor Radical: Rebecca Harding Davis and the Origins of American Social Realism* (Pittsburgh: University of Pittsburgh Press, 1996); on realism, see Sharon M. Harris, *Rebecca Harding Davis and American Realism* (Philadelphia: University of Pennsylvania Press, 1991); for biographical information, see Jane Atteridge Rose, *Rebecca Harding Davis* (New York: Twayne, 1993); and, of course, the essay that galvanized modern critical attention to Davis, Tillie Olsen's "A Biographical Interpretation," in *"Life in the Iron Mills" and Other Stories,* by Rebecca Harding Davis, ed. Tillie Olsen, 2d ed. (New York: Feminist Press at City University of New York, 1985), 67–174. Pfaelzer argues for Davis's environmental significance, saying her stories are "shaped by a strong sense of place." Further, she argues, "geography—defined through botany, weather, local history, landscape, and the economics of place—continued to shape character and consciousness" throughout Davis's writing career; Pfaelzer, ed., *A Rebecca Harding Davis Reader* (Pittsburgh: University of Pittsburgh Press, 1995), xiv–xv.

20. Kenneth Noe, "'Deadened Color and Colder Horror': Rebecca Harding Davis and the Myth of Unionist Appalachia," in *Back Talk from Appalachia: Confronting Stereotypes,* ed. Dwight B. Billings, Gurney Norman, and Katherine Ledford (Lexington: University Press of Kentucky, 2000), 79. Davis is listed in neither Farr's nor Shapiro's bibliographies. Collins lists only one children's book by her during this time period, 7. Boger seems unique in considering *Silhouettes of American Life* as part of the literature of southern Appalachia, 21.

21. Davis, "Yares," 239.

22. This story has been much discussed of late; see, for instance, Pfaelzer, "Engendered Nature/Denatured History: The Yares of the Black Mountains," in *Speaking the Other Self: American Women Writers,* ed. Jeanne Campbell Reesman (Athens: University of Georgia Press, 1997), 229–45; also, Pfaelzer, "The Politics of Nature," in *Parlor Radical,* 189–204; Harris, 249–53; and Noe, 67–84.

23. Sears, 6.

24. Pool, 51. On Digger Indians, some sources suggest this derogatory term was generally applied to western Native American tribes (Shoshone, Miwok, etc.) and that it derived from the white, colonialist belief that these tribes dug all of their food out of the ground with sticks: see *Columbia Encyclopedia,* 6th ed., s.v. Digger Indians, accessed 29

July 2001. Available from World Wide Web: <www.bartleby.com/65/>. Notice the startling similarity to a quotation from Campbell during her own tour of the region: "She had a dark full-blooded face. . . . They said they had come over from North Carolina. Mr. W says they are the digger Indian type—the lowest of the mountaineers"; Campbell diary, 5 Feb. 1909, Campbell Papers. That the term appears in stories and diaries about Appalachia suggests how, once exoticized, Appalachians of all ethnicities were fair game for any race-based insult. For a discussion of the article by Will Wallace Harney, see Shapiro, 3.

    25. Carter, 235.

    26. Baker, 10, 40, 71.

    27. Ibid., 72–77.

    28. Pfaelzer, *Rebecca Harding Davis Reader,* xliii.

    29. Davis, "A Wayside Episode," 145–55.

    30. Ibid., 159, 162–63.

    31. Ibid., 163–64.

    32. Shapiro, 65.

CHAPTER 3

    1. On the influx of reformers, see Nancy K. Forderhase, "Eve Returns to the Garden: Women Reformers in Appalachian Kentucky in the Early Twentieth Century," *Register of the Kentucky Historical Society* 85, no. 3 (summer 1987): 237–61; Karen W. Tice, "School-work and Mother-work: The Interplay of Maternalism and Cultural Politics in the Educational Narratives of Kentucky Settlement Workers, 1910–1930," *Journal of Appalachian Studies* 4, no. 2 (fall 1998): 191–224; Sandra Lee Barney, "Maternalism and the Promotion of Scientific Medicine during the Industrial Transformation of Appalachia, 1880–1930," *NWSA Journal* 11, no. 3 (fall 1999): 68–92.

    2. Margaret W. Morley, *The Carolina Mountains* (Boston: Houghton Mifflin, 1913), 158, 160.

    3. Ibid., 160.

    4. Lucy Furman, *The Quare Women: A Story of the Kentucky Mountains* (Boston: Atlantic Monthly Press, 1923), 67.

    5. David E. Whisnant, *All That Is Native and Fine: The Politics of Culture in an American Region* (Chapel Hill: University of North Carolina Press, 1983), 34; Furman, 67.

    6. Information on Gladys Coleman is in Margaret Supplee Smith and Emily Herring Wilson, *North Carolina Women: Making History* (Chapel Hill: University of North Carolina Press, 1999), 175; Rebecca Harding Davis, "The Yares of the Black Mountains," in *Silhouettes of American Life* (New York: Charles Scribner's Sons, 1892), 242; the population figures for Hindman and Hazard come from May Stone and Katherine Pettit, *The Quare Women's Journals: May Stone and Katherine Pettit's Summers in the Kentucky Mountains and the Founding of the Hindman Settlement School,* ed. Jess Stoddart (Ashland, Ky.: Jesse Stuart Foundation, 1997), 88, 60.

    7. Stone and Pettit, 200.

    8. Mary Martin's original letters are not available, but the Presbyterian Church Archives in Montreat has published an edited facsimile copy of them, an "adaptation" (as it says on the frontispiece) by her daughter. See Mary R. Martin, *Mother Pioneered at*

Montreat (Her Letters 1898–1899), adapted by Emilie Miller Vaughan (Montreat, N.C.: Presbyterian Church [U.S.A.] Department of History and Records Management Services, 1996).

9. Martin, 3, 6. I have inserted *[sic]* in the first quote because one usually refers to "Mt. Pisgah and the Rat," when speaking of these particular mountains. However, it is possible that, among her friends, Martin renamed the peak "Mr. Pisgah."

10. Ibid., 12–14.

11. Morley, *Carolina Mountains*, 362. Although all are out of print today, Morley's books went through many editions during her life. Her science books include *A Few Familiar Flowers: How to Love Them at Home or in School* (Boston: Ginn and Co., 1897), and *The Bee People*, 8th ed. (Chicago: A. C. McClurg and Co., 1909). Her sexual education books include *Life and Love*, 8th ed. (Chicago: A. C. McClurg and Co., 1913), and *The Renewal of Life: How and When to Tell the Story to the Young*, 2d ed. (Chicago: A. C. McClurg and Co., 1909).

12. Martin, 6–7.

13. Lila Marz Harper, *Solitary Travelers: Nineteenth-Century Women's Narratives and the Scientific Vocation* (Madison, N.J.: Fairleigh Dickinson University Press, 2001), 153.

14. Martin, 19, 34, 41–42.

15. Daisy Gertrude Dame to Billy [brother], 17 Aug. 1909, Daisy Gertrude Dame Papers, 4331, Southern Historical Collection, Wilson Library, University of North Carolina at Chapel Hill (hereafter cited as Dame Papers).

16. Dame to her family, 29 and 15 Aug. 1909 and 18 Jan. 1910, Dame Papers. On "The Greenhorn Brigade," see Dame photograph album, PA-3800/18, John Charles and Olive Dame Campbell Papers, 3800, Southern Historical Collection, Wilson Library, University of North Carolina at Chapel Hill (hereafter cited as Campbell Papers). On regular saddles, see Dame to family, 22 Aug. 1909, and on the two-day trip, Dame to "My Dear," 24 July 1909, Dame Papers.

17. For description of the river trip, see Dame to "My Dear," 24 July 1909, Dame Papers. The catfish is in Dame photograph album, PA-3800/18, and Campbell photograph album, PA-3800/19, Campbell Papers. On "wooded hill," see Dame to Mother, 1 Aug. 1909, Dame Papers.

18. On the Pinnacle Mountain trip, Campbell diary, 13 Nov. 1908; for a picture of the cornerstone, see Campbell photograph album, PA-3800/16; "to Hindman," Campbell diary, 2 Dec. 1908, Campbell Papers.

19. For examples of women on horseback, see Campbell photograph album, PA-3800/17, Campbell Papers.

20. Stone and Pettit, 174.

21. Ibid., 174.

22. Alison Byerly, "The Uses of Landscape: The Picturesque Aesthetic and the National Park System," in *Ecocriticism Reader: Landmarks in Literary Ecology*, ed. Cheryll Glotfelty and Harold Fromm (Athens: University of Georgia Press, 1996), 55; Stone and Pettit, 166.

23. Martin, 27.

24. Stone and Pettit, 75.

25. Furman, *Quare Women*, 104; Stone and Pettit, 236. Minimizing male presence is analogous to the racism and colonialism involved in the rhetoric of "claiming" an empty West for the United States, never seeing the peoples who had lived there for centuries,

or, earlier, "discovering" America for the first time without seeing that millions of people had already been living there.

26. Lucy Furman, *Mothering on Perilous* (New York: MacMillan, 1913), 14; Martha Berry, "The Evolution of a Sunday School," *Charities and the Commons* 17, no. 5 (3 Nov. 1906): 200; Campbell diary, 5 Dec. 1908, Campbell Papers. The Dame-Lyttle relationship runs throughout Dame's letters. She relates his confession of love, Dame to family, 18 Sept. 1909, Dame Papers.

27. Eleanor Marsh Frost, "Mountain Trip 1914, Kentucky–North Carolina," Eleanor Marsh Frost correspondence, reports, and diary, the papers of William Goodell Frost, Berea College Archives, Hutchins Library, Berea, Kentucky (hereafter cited as Frost Papers).

28. Morley, *Carolina Mountains*, 274.

29. For a discussion of nineteenth-century women's environmental education, see Vera Norwood, *Made from This Earth: American Women and Nature* (Chapel Hill: University of North Carolina Press, 1993); and Peter J. Schmitt, *Back to Nature: The Arcadian Myth in Urban America* (New York: Oxford University Press, 1969).

30. Goodrich, "Extracts from letters," 14 Dec. 1890 and 24 Feb. 1891, vols. 1–2, Frances Louisa Goodrich Papers, Rare Book, Manuscript, and Special Collections Library, Duke University, Durham, North Carolina (hereafter cited as Goodrich Papers).

31. Stone and Pettit, 71; Campbell diary, 9 Oct. 1908, Campbell Papers; Martin, 31. Martin refers to Frances Theodora Smith Dana Parsons, *How to Know the Wild Flowers: A Guide to the Names, Haunts, and Habits of Our Common Wild Flowers, by Mrs. William Starr Dana* (New York: C. Scribner's Sons, 1895).

32. Frost diary, 10 June 1901, Frost Papers; Norwood, 43; Morley, *Carolina Mountains*, 384.

33. Campbell diary, 19 Nov. 1908, Campbell Papers; Frances Louisa Goodrich, *Mountain Homespun* (New Haven: Yale University Press, 1931), 65.

34. Grace MacGowan Cooke, *The Power and the Glory: An Appalachian Novel* (1910; reprinted, with an introduction by Elizabeth S. D. Engelhardt, Boston: Northeastern University Press, 2003), 60–61. Page references are the same for both editions.

35. Mrs. F. L. [Meta] Townsend, *In the Nantahalas* (Nashville: Publishing House M. E. Church, South, 1910), 181, 184. For Thomas Ivey's preface, see 5. See also Schmitt, 78. Unfortunately, most of early records from the Brevard School were lost in a fire, making it hard to know what difference Townsend's book may have made.

36. Goodrich, *Mountain Homespun*, 65.

37. Stone and Pettit, 69; Morley, *Carolina Mountains*, 284.

38. Martin, 31.

39. Goodrich, "Extracts from letters," 13 Jan. 1891, vol. 1, Goodrich Papers; Morley, *Carolina Mountains*, 274; Frost, "Mountain Trip 1914, Kentucky–North Carolina," Frost Papers; Dame to "My Dear," 24 July 1909, Dame Papers.

40. Goodrich, "Extracts from letters," 27 Nov. 1893, vol. 3, Goodrich Papers.

41. Goodrich describes lily root and onion poultices in "Extracts from letters," 15 Feb. 1891; poke root, 10 Mar. 1891; and teas, 10 Apr. 1893, vols. 1–3, Goodrich Papers. Goodrich, *Mountain Homespun*, 84–88.

42. Whisnant, *All That Is Native and Fine*, 60–61.

43. Goodrich, "Extracts from letters," 29 Nov. 1890 and 13 Jan. 1891, vol. 1, Goodrich Papers; Campbell diary, 5 Feb. 1909, Campbell Papers.

44. For "Mission Barrel" picture, see Campbell photograph album, PA-3800/14A; "Betty's Troublesome" picture, PA-3800/19, Campbell Papers. "Betty's Troublesome" is a creek in the region. For the pictures of the boy and girl, I am purposefully not reproducing their names even though the Campbells provide them, because I do not wish to repeat their *ad hominem* comments. For both, see Campbell photograph album, PA-3800/6, Campbell Papers.

45. Campbell photograph album, PA-3800/9, Campbell Papers. For a discussion of scientific racism and mental, medical, and racial language, see Siobhan Somerville, "Scientific Racism and the Emergence of the Homosexual Body," *Journal of the History of Sexuality* 5, no. 2 (October 1994): 243–66. Somerville specifically discusses sexuality, but the workings of power are similar. For a related discussion of "scientific" constructions of black and white bodies in the nineteenth century, see Sander L. Gilman, "Black Bodies, White Bodies: Toward an Iconography of Female Sexuality in Late Nineteenth-Century Art, Medicine, and Literature," *Critical Inquiry* 12, no. 1 (autumn 1985): 204–42.

46. Lucy R. Lippard, introduction to *Partial Recall,* ed. Lucy R. Lippard (New York: New Press, 1992), 13–14.

47. Campbell photograph album, PA-3800/9, Campbell Papers.

48. The photograph has corresponding numbers and an "x" written in ink over specific figures. Campbell photograph album, PA-3800/6, Campbell Papers. Sallie O'Hear Dickson, *The Story of Marthy* (Richmond: Presbyterian Committee of Publication, 1898), 55.

49. The handwriting differs from all of the other albums, "FLW" initials many of the pictures, and there are labels such as "Workers' Cottage, Walker's Valley, built by FLW" and "Last day of my first school—Walker's Valley." See Campbell photograph album, PA-3800/6, Campbell Papers. This is likely the same Mr. Webb who judged some mountaineers to be the "digger Indian" type (Campbell diary, 5 Feb. 1909, Campbell Papers), which further suggests his practice of categorizing people not like him.

50. Campbell diary, 13 Feb. 1909, Campbell Papers.

51. Amelie Rives [Troubetzkoy], *Tanis, the Sang-Digger* (New York: Town Topics, 1893); Davis, "The Yares of the Black Mountains," 239–68; Campbell photograph album, PA-3800/19, Campbell Papers; Goodrich, "Extracts from Letters," 13 Jan. 1891, vol. 1, Goodrich Papers.

52. Lucy Furman, *The Glass Window: A Story of the Quare Women* (Boston: Little, Brown, and Co., 1925), 43.

53. Stone and Pettit, 62, 187.

54. Ibid., 173–79.

55. Ibid., 139.

56. Martin, 40.

57. Frost to Miles [her brother], 2 Oct. 1892, Frost Papers.

58. On buckeye bonnets, see Nickum to Mother, 22 Oct. 1901; for her discussion of places she may go, see Nickum to "Old Folks at Home," 28 Oct. 1901; on her illness, see Nickum to Mother, 23 Jan. 1902, Bertha Daisy Nickum Letters and Photographs, Record Group 8: Students. Berea College Archives, Hutchins Library, Berea, Kentucky (hereafter cited as Nickum Papers).

59. The "before" picture is labeled "Mary Stinnett's family 'B' March 1902. Mrs. Bill Walker in group, and a grandson of Mary Ann Moore. 1. 'Patriarch's' legal wife, 2. Illegal wife." The "after" picture is "Mary Stinnett's family—August 1903." Campbell photograph album, PA-3800/6, Campbell Papers.

60. Dame to "My Dear," 24 July 1909, Dame Papers.

61. Stone and Pettit, 173; Campbell photograph album, PA-3800/6, Campbell Papers.

62. Goodrich, "Extracts from letters," 10 Jan. 1894, vol. 3, Goodrich Papers; Stone and Pettit, 94.

63. Troubetzkoy, 29; Stone and Pettit, 175.

64. Goodrich, "Extracts from letters," 18 Mar. 1891, vol. 1, Goodrich Papers; Dame to "My Dear," 24 July 1909, Dame Papers; Barbara Ellen Smith, "Walk-ons in the Third Act: The Role of Women in Appalachian Historiography," *Journal of Appalachian Studies* 4, no. 1 (spring 1998): 13.

65. For the history of African American women as washerwomen, see Jacqueline Jones, *Labor of Love, Labor of Sorrow: Black Women, Work and the Family, From Slavery to the Present* (New York: Vintage, 1985), 125.

66. Nickum to family, 12 Mar. 1902, and photographs, Nickum Papers.

67. Campbell photograph album, PA-3800/9, Campbell Papers.

68. Stone and Pettit, 177–80, 217–18.

69. However, the number of women they employ in a summer might suggest some resistance by African American Appalachians to Pettit and Stone's approach.

70. Emma Bell Miles, *The Spirit of the Mountains* (1905; reprinted, with a foreword by Roger D. Abrahams and introduction by David E. Whisnant, Knoxville: University of Tennessee Press, 1975), 20, 195.

71. Sarah Barnwell Elliott, *The Durket Sperret* (New York: Henry Holt, 1898), 152–53. Subsequent references appear in parentheses in the text.

CHAPTER 4

1. On Mary Noailles Murfree's contribution to American Literature, see "Minor Notes," *Literary World* 15 (31 May 1884): 179; on "finding speech," see Katherine Lee Bates, *American Literature* (New York: MacMillan, 1898), 135. Both citations come from Reese M. Carleton, "Mary Noailles Murfree (1850–1922): An Annotated Bibliography," *American Literary Realism, 1870–1910* 7, no. 4 (autumn 1974): 303, 335. Murfree [Charles Egbert Craddock, pseud.], "The Star in the Valley" and "Over on T'other Mounting" in *In the Tennessee Mountains* (Boston: Houghton Mifflin, 1884); *The Young Mountaineers* (Boston: Houghton Mifflin, 1898).

2. Murfree was lame from a childhood fever. See Emily Satterwhite, "Such a Thing as 'Literary Material'": Unveiling the "Habitats and Habits of Charles Egbert Craddock," (draft) accessed 3 Feb. 2002. Available from World Wide Web: <http://www.etsu.edu/writing/apptravel/murfree.htm>. For biographical information on Murfree, see Judith Fetterley and Marjorie Pryse, eds. *American Women Regionalists, 1850–1910* (New York: W. W. Norton, 1992), 254–56; also, see Richard Cary, "Mary Noailles Murfree," *American Literary Regionalism 1870–1910* 1 (fall 1967): 79–83.

3. Peter Clay, "To Effie Waller," in Effie Waller Smith, *Songs of the Months* (1904; reprinted in *The Collected Works of Effie Waller Smith,* with an introduction by David Deskins, Schomburg Library of Nineteenth-Century Black Women Writers, New York: Oxford University Press, 1991), xvii. For biographical information on Smith, see Deskins's introduction, 3–26; also see, Deskins, "Effie Waller Smith: An Echo within the Hills," *Kentucky Review* 8, no. 3 (autumn 1988): 26–46.

4. In an introduction to one of Smith's volumes, Mary Elliott Flanery compares Smith with Paul Laurence Dunbar; see *Collected Works of Effie Waller Smith*, xvi.

5. Amelie Rives [Troubetzkoy], *Tanis, the Sang-Digger* (New York: Town Topics, 1893); Olive Dame Campbell photograph album, PA-3800/9, John Charles and Olive Dame Campbell Papers, 3800, Southern Historical Collection, Wilson Library, University of North Carolina at Chapel Hill (hereafter cited as Campbell Papers).

6. Mary Noailles Murfree [pseud. Charles Egbert Craddock], *His Vanished Star* (Boston: Houghton Mifflin, 1894), 1–2. Subsequent parenthetical references are to this edition.

7. Mary Louise Pratt calls this the "monarch-of-all-I-survey" trope when she finds it in early travel literature; see Pratt, *Imperial Eyes: Travel Writing and Transculturation* (London: Routledge, 1992), 201–6. She suggests that such viewing achieves the imperialist aim of conquering new lands. Although Kenniston is an American viewing long-since conquered American space, he is presented as the first white man with the proper class position to look over the great property. While I do not wish to overstate the situation of white people viewing other (in Murfree's world) white people, the colonization of Appalachia (and its subsequent legacy of extractive industry, cycles of poverty, and stereotypes) has long been theorized in Appalachian studies.

8. I am indebted to Marjorie Pryse, who pushed me to think more deeply about Murfree's use of language. She and Judith Fetterley call this Murfree's "'literary' language" in contrast to her mountain dialect; see Fetterley and Pryse, 255. I am modifying their interpretation to argue this constitutes a third voice in this particular novel, one that applies to the place, not to any of the people in the place.

9. Judith Fetterley, "'Not in the Least American': Nineteenth-Century Literary Regionalism as UnAmerican Literature," in *Nineteenth-Century American Women Writers: A Critical Reader*, ed. Karen Kilcup (Oxford: Blackwell, 1998), 21; Marjorie Pryse, "Writing Out of the Gap: Regionalism, Resistance, and Relational Reading," *Textual Studies in Canada* 9 (spring 1997): 24.

10. Leslie Marmon Silko, "Landscape, History, and the Pueblo Imagination," in *Ecocriticism Reader: Landmarks in Literary Ecology,* ed. Cheryll Glotfelty and Harold Fromm (Athens: University of Georgia Press, 1996), 265; Gary Snyder, *The Practice of the Wild* (New York: North Point Press, 1990), 20.

11. Pryse, 25; Greta Gaard and Patrick D. Murphy, introduction to *Ecofeminist Literary Criticism: Theory, Interpretation, Pedagogy,* ed. Greta Gaard and Patrick D. Murphy (Urbana: University of Chicago Press, 1998), 5–6. For the most part, scholars have not found many writers who view nature as composed of subjects and not objects until later in the twentieth century. I agree with Murphy, who calls works "protoecological" when they appear significantly prior to 1970, so that one is not left having to justify everything in an early text against modern ecological ideologies; see his *Literature, Nature, and Other: Ecofeminist Critiques* (Albany: State University of New York Press, 1995), 26; a similar concern is what motivates me to suggest these are the *roots* of Appalachian ecological feminism.

12. I agree with Fetterley and Pryse that, unlike many of her New England contemporaries on whose work theories of literary regionalism largely have been built, Murfree "retains the distance of difference rather than the empathetic fusion of narrator and regional character. Murfree can write about the mountaineers without the condescension of the local colorist, but without, either, claiming to be a mountaineer herself"; see Fetterley and Pryse, 256.

13. Murphy, 35, 152.

14. In fact, following Annette Kolodny's ideas of male colonizers' conception of wilderness as an unspoiled virgin, Kenniston's frustration with the Tems farm—he calls it the "trail of the serpent in this seeming Paradise" (7)—is that the "virgin" has already been despoiled—that is, someone got to her before he did; see Kolodny's *The Lay of the Land: Metaphor as Experience and History in American Life and Letters* (Chapel Hill: University of North Carolina Press, 1975).

15. "Literature," *Critic* 31 [NS 28] (20 Nov. 1897): 301. Cited in Carleton, 334.

16. This is a moment in the text when the moonshining and developer's stories come together. It is a moonshiner, trying to protect the location of his still, who sets the charge under the rock. For Kenniston, it is the last straw; his building is burned, the picturesque scene he thought he owned seems to belong to someone else, and his various blind spots keep him from finding any answers to these problems.

17. Susan Griffin, *Woman and Nature: The Roaring Inside Her* (New York: Harper Colophon, 1978), 207, 1, 150.

18. Durwood Dunn, "Mary Noailles Murfree: A Reappraisal," *Appalachian Journal* 6, no. 3 (spring 1979): 202.

19. Although it is not fully explored, Murfree hints at one of the acceptable paths to progress when she describes the hotel workers who are willing to discuss patiently the new building with the mountaineers (166). This communication with people who are also in disagreement with Kenniston's practices (early in the novel (166) they are forced to move to inconvenient lodgings down the mountain because Kenniston is too cheap to purchase adequate housing for these workers) might lead to considered development in the community, were it allowed to flourish.

20. William H. Turner, "The Demography of Black Appalachia: Past and Present," in *Blacks in Appalachia,* ed. William H. Turner and Edward J. Cabbell (Lexington: University of Kentucky Press, 1985), 238; Lenwood Davis, *The Black Heritage of Western North Carolina* (Asheville: University Graphics, University of North Carolina, Asheville, n.d.), 20, 23; George S. Dickerman, "Ten Years' Changes in East Tennessee," *Southern Workman* 34, no. 5 (May 1905): 267.

21. Emily K. Herron, "Our Cherokee Neighbors," *Southern Workman* 29, no. 8 (August 1900): 467; Churchill memorandum roll, 1906–1909, Frank C. Churchill Papers, Rare Book, Manuscript, and Special Collections Library, Duke University. Churchill divided applicants into categories such as "Indian," various fractions ($\frac{1}{2}$, $\frac{1}{4}$, etc.) of "Indian," "Doubtful," "Mulatto," and "Colored." He relied on personal interviews, family histories, and cross-references to determine each person's status. On other Native Americans in Appalachia, see John Ehle, *Trail of Tears: The Rise and Fall of the Cherokee Nation* (New York: Anchor, 1989), 393. Of course, the mountains had other kinds of diversity as well, such as religious, sexuality, and ethnicity. For instance, Olive Campbell mentions meeting a Jewish "drummer" (a peddler) on a train outside of Chattanooga, Tennessee; see Campbell diary, 3 Nov. 1908, Campbell Papers.

22. Smith, "Answer to Verses Addressed to Me by Peter Clay," *Songs of the Months,* in *Collected Works of Effie Waller Smith,* 167–68. Subsequent parenthetical references are to this edition.

23. Ibid.

24. Smith, "On Receiving a Souvenir Postcard," *Rhymes from the Cumberland,* in

Collected Works of Effie Waller Smith, 45–47. Subsequent parenthetical references are to this edition.

25. Smith, "A Mountain Graveyard," *Rosemary and Pansies,* in *Collected Works of Effie Waller Smith,* 88–89. Subsequent parenthetical references are to this edition.

26. Smith, "A Meadow Brook," *Rhymes From the Cumberland,* in *Collected Works of Effie Waller Smith,* 32–33.

27. "To the Reader," *Songs of the Months,* in *Collected Works of Effie Waller Smith,* iii–v.

28. Ida B. Wells-Barnett, "Lynch Law in America," in *Words of Fire: An Anthology of African-American Feminist Thought,* ed. Beverly Guy-Sheftall (New York: New Press, 1995), 74.

29. "Girls in the Open Air," *Chattanooga Justice,* 24 Dec. 1887.

30. Deskins, introduction, *Collected Works of Effie Waller Smith,* 8.

31. Smith, "The Hills," *Songs of the Months,* in *Collected Works of Effie Waller Smith,* 48. Subsequent parenthetical references are to this edition.

32. For articles on natural sites, birds, and trees, see "Blowing Rock: The Gem of the Blue Ridge Mountains of North Carolina," *Raleigh Gazette,* 24 Apr. 1897; "Falls Church, Virginia," *Martinsburg (Va.) Pioneer Press,* 28 Aug. 1915; "Charlottesville, Its Situation, Population, The Colored People," *Richmond Virginia Star,* 8 Sept. 1877; "From Sevierville," *Knoxville Negro World,* 26 Nov. 1887; "English Sparrows' Exclusiv . . ." [sic, title cut off], *Chattanooga Justice,* 24 Dec. 1887; "Appeal for the Birds," *Richmond Planet,* 27 June 1903; Mabel Earlie, "A Mountain Meadowlark," *Richmond Planet,* 27 June 1903; "Some Ancient Trees," *Boydton (Va.) Midland Express,* 25 Feb. 1893. On nature study in school, see "Suggestions for Spring Lessons," *Southern Workman* 29, no. 4 (Apr. 1900), 235–37.

33. Smith, "Apple Sauce and Chicken Fried," *Songs of the Months,* in *Collected Works of Effie Waller Smith,* 129–30.

34. Smith, "The 'Bachelor Girl,'" *Rhymes from the Cumberland,* in *Collected Works of Effie Waller Smith,* 49–51.

35. Beverly Guy-Sheftall, *Words of Fire: An Anthology of African-American Feminist Thought* (New York: New Press, 1995), xiv; Deborah Gray White, "Mining the Forgotten: Manuscript Sources for Black Women's History," *Journal of American History* 74, no. 1 (June 1987), 238.

36. Edward J. Cabbell, "Black Invisibility and Racism in Appalachia: An Informal Survey," in *Blacks in Appalachia,* ed. William H. Turner and Edward J. Cabbell (Lexington: University Press of Kentucky, 1985), 3–10; Grace Funk Myers, *"Them Missionary Women": or, Work in the Southern Mountains* (Hillsdale, Mich.: by the author, 1911), 105.

37. "Young Men's Institute Building, Nomination Form for National Register of Historic Places." 77.10.3.8, Black Highlander Collection, Ramsey Library, University of North Carolina–Asheville.

38. Wanda Stanard, "Rosscraggon Wood Perpetuates Memory of Miss Rose," *Asheville Citizen-Times,* 26 Jan. 1969. For biographical information, see Rosanna Frances Chapman Papers, Pack Library Buncombe County, Asheville, North Carolina.

CHAPTER 5

1. Emma Bell Miles, *The Spirit of the Mountains* (1905; reprinted, with a foreword by Roger D. Abrahams and introduction by David E. Whisnant, Knoxville: University of Tennessee Press, 1975); Grace MacGowan Cooke, *The Power and the Glory: An Appalachian*

Novel (1910; reprinted, with an introduction by Elizabeth S. D. Engelhardt, Boston: Northeastern University Press, 2003). All subsequent parenthetical references in the text are to these editions.

2. For biographical information on Cooke, see Kay Baker Gaston, "The MacGowan Girls," *California History: The Magazine of the California Historical Society* 59, no. 2 (summer 1980): 116–25. Miles's comment about Cooke appears in Miles to Anna Ricketson, 9 Mar. 1907, Emma Bell Miles Papers, Hist. C. acc. 43, Chattanooga-Hamilton County Bicentennial Library, Chattanooga, Tennessee (hereafter cited as Miles Papers).

3. Miles to Ricketson, 5 Apr. 1907, Miles Papers. For biographical information on Miles, see David Whisnant, introduction to *The Spirit of the Mountains* (1905; reprinted, Knoxville: University of Tennessee Press, 1975), xv–xxxiii; Grace Toney Edwards, "Emma Bell Miles: Appalachian Author, Artist, and Interpreter of Folk Culture" (Ph.D. diss., University of Virginia, 1981); Roger D. Abrahams, foreword to *The Spirit of the Mountains,* v–xii. There are, however, minor disagreements among these sources about Miles's life. For other analyses of Miles's literature, see Danny L. Miller, *Wingless Flights: Appalachian Women in Fiction* (Bowling Green, Oh.: Bowling Green State University Popular Press, 1996), 78–88; also see Shannon Brooks, "Coming Home: Finding My Appalachian Mothers through Emma Bell Miles," *NWSA Journal* 11, no. 3 (fall 1999): 157–71.

4. On leaves as plates, see Miles diary, 8 May 1915, Miles Papers; as a lover of outdoors, Miles to Ricketson, 9 Mar. 1907, Miles Papers.

5. For her apologies about corresponding in pencil, see Miles to Ricketson, 20 Feb. and 5 Apr. 1907, Miles Papers; for a discussion of her lectures, see Edwards, 28; for Miles's own description of lecturing, see Miles to Ricketson, 19 Feb. 1908, Miles Papers.

6. For Miles's newspaper columns, see Kay Baker Gaston, "Emma Bell Miles and the 'Fountain Square' Conversations," *Tennessee Historical Quarterly* 37, no. 4 (winter 1978): 416–29; for socialism, see Miles diary, 28 Apr. 1915, Miles Papers; for solar cooker, see Miles to Ricketson, 6 July 1907, Miles Papers. Cooke's automobile novels include *The Power and the Glory,* as well as *Wild Apples: A California Story* (New York: George H. Doran Co., 1918).

7. Miles, *Spirit of the Mountains,* 17–18.

8. Mary Noailles Murfree [pseud. Charles Egbert Craddock], *His Vanished Star* (Boston: Houghton Mifflin, 1894), 1.

9. Whisnant, introduction to Miles, *Spirit of the Mountains,* xvi, xxi–xxii. Other scholars joining Whisnant are Carole Ganim (who refers to Miles's "dual perspective"), "Herself: Woman and Place in Appalachian Literature," *Appalachian Journal* 13, no. 3 (spring 1986): 261; Edwards (who discusses Miles's "life-long bicultural exposure"), dissertation abstract, n.p.; and Miller (who describes Miles's "ambivalence in her personal and professional life"), 81.

10. The distinction between author and narrator is particularly fuzzy in Miles's case. Although Whisnant believes she taught in a school on Walden's Ridge, Edwards disagrees. Whisnant cautions readers about the untrustworthiness of some earlier biographical work on Miles. Abrahams, in the foreword to the 1975 edition, writes: "I assumed she had come to the community as an outsider, a school teacher bringing enlightenment to the 'simple' folk" (xi). Such disagreements have brought a particular aura of confusion about the genre of the text. Whatever the biographical "facts" in this semiautobiographical work, the space between Miles and her narrator is contested terrain.

11. Patrick D. Murphy, *Literature, Nature, and Other: Ecofeminist Critiques* (Albany: State University of New York Press, 1995), 50.

12. Miles to Ricketson, 9 Mar. 1907, Miles Papers.

13. Rebecca Harding Davis, "A Wayside Episode," in *Silhouettes of American Life* (New York: Charles Scribner's Sons, 1892), 145–71.

14. Whisnant, introduction to Miles, *Spirit of the Mountains*, xv.

15. Whisnant (ibid., xxvii) interprets the passage to say that Miles is commenting on the culture of her students. According to him, Miles suggests here that the students "are nevertheless veritable mines of ancient and valuable lore, legends, and tales." Whisnant, however, includes ellipses in two places in his rendering of Miles's quote. He leaves out the phrases: "with the scampering and flitting of little brothers of tree-top and burrow" and "at such times," so that his version of the quote reads: "If the young minds wander afield . . . what matter? Perhaps they learn . . . something not to be found between the covers of Webster." I am arguing that those two phrases are the crux of Miles's point.

16. Arlie Hochschild, *The Second Shift: Working Parents and the Revolution at Home* (New York: Viking, 1989).

17. Miles diary, 28 Apr. 1915, Miles Papers.

18. Murfree, 1–2; Effie Waller Smith, "The 'Bachelor Girl,'" in *Rhymes From the Cumberland* (1909; reprinted in *The Collected Works of Effie Waller Smith,* with an introduction by David Deskins, Schomburg Library of Nineteenth-Century Black Women Writers, New York: Oxford University Press, 1991), 49–51.

19. Cooke, *Power and Glory*, 36, 113–14.

20. In the end, Lydia Sessions resorts to lying and participating in the kidnapping scheme that is the dramatic conclusion of the novel. Ibid., 275.

21. Gaston suggests that Cooke often took on what she calls "adventurous" subjects—such as a "series of stories for *Everybody's Magazine* exploring the racial question in the South" and the "ethnic material" for Cooke's "Hopi novel"; see Gaston, "MacGowan Girls," 124.

22. In contrast, Lydia Sessions discusses "negresses—they're much better servants, you know" (234), expects obedience to every command (212), and behaves toward Johnnie and her servants with "a judicious mixture of patronage and mild reproof" (213). Unlike others in the story, Lydia seems unaware that slavery has ended.

23. Carolyn Merchant, *Earthcare: Women and the Environment* (New York: Routledge, 1995), 217.

AFTERWORD

1. Mary Noailles Murfree [Charles Egbert Craddock, pseud.], *His Vanished Star* (Boston: Houghton Mifflin, 1894), 392.

2. David Deskins, introduction to *The Collected Works of Effie Waller Smith* (Schomburg Library of Nineteenth-Century Black Women Writers, New York: Oxford University Press, 1991), 22–23.

3. Emma Bell Miles, *The Spirit of the Mountains* (1905; reprinted, with a foreword by Roger D. Abrahams and an introduction by David E. Whisnant, Knoxville: University

of Tennessee Press, 1975); Emma Bell Miles, *Our Southern Birds* (1919; reprinted, Chatta-nooga: National Book Co., 1983).

4. Grace MacGowan Cooke, *The Power and the Glory* (1910; reprinted with an intro-duction by Elizabeth S. D. Engelhardt, Boston: Northeastern University Press, 2003), 369–73.

5. Wilma Dykeman, *The French Broad,* Rivers of America Series (New York: Rine-hart, 1955), 290–91.

6. Ibid., 346.

Bibliography

Abrahams, Roger D. Foreword to *The Spirit of the Mountains,* by Emma Bell Miles. 1905. Reprint, Knoxville: University of Tennessee Press, 1975.

Alaimo, Stacy. *Undomesticated Ground: Recasting Nature as Feminist Space.* Ithaca: Cornell University Press, 2000.

American Council of Learned Societies, Committee on Negro Studies. *Microfilm Series Negro Newspaper: Microform.* Washington, D.C.: Library of Congress, 1947. Microform.

Appalachian Regional Commission. "The Appalachian Region." Accessed 6 May 2002. Available from World Wide Web: <http://www.arc.gov/aboutarc/region/abtapreg.htm>.

Baker, Louise R. *Cis Martin, Or, The Furriners in the Tennessee Mountains.* New York: Eaton and Mains, 1898.

Barnes, Annie Maria. *The Ferry Maid of the Chattahoochee: A Story for Girls.* Philadelphia: Pennsylvania Publishing Co., 1899.

Barney, Sandra Lee. "Maternalism and the Promotion of Scientific Medicine during the Industrial Transformation of Appalachia, 1880–1930." *NWSA Journal* 11, no. 3 (fall 1999): 68–92.

Bates, Katherine Lee. *American Literature.* New York: MacMillan, 1898.

Berry, Martha. "The Evolution of a Sunday School." *Charities and the Commons* 17, no. 5 (3 Nov. 1906): 195–200.

Bickley, Ancella R., and Lynda Ann Ewen, eds. *Memphis Tennessee Garrison: The Remarkable Story of a Black Appalachian Woman.* Athens: Ohio University Press, 2001.

Billings, Dwight, Gurney Norman, and Katherine Ledford, eds. *Back Talk from Appalachia: Confronting Stereotypes.* Lexington: University Press of Kentucky, 2000.

Blackwell, Deborah L. "Eleanor Marsh Frost and the Gender Dimensions of Appalachian Reform Efforts." *Register of the Kentucky Historical Society* 94, no. 3 (summer 1996): 225–46.

Boger, Lorise C. *The Southern Mountaineer in Literature: An Annotated Bibliography.* Morgantown: West Virginia University Library, 1964.

Bonta, Marcia, ed., *American Women Afield: Writings by Pioneering Women Naturalists.* College Station: Texas A & M University Press, 1995.

Brooks, Shannon. "Coming Home: Finding My Appalachian Mothers through Emma Bell Miles." *NWSA Journal* 11, no. 3 (fall 1999): 157–71.

Byerly, Alison. "The Uses of Landscape: The Picturesque Aesthetic and the National Park System." In *Ecocriticism Reader: Landmarks in Literary Ecology*, edited by Cheryll Glotfelty and Harold Fromm. Athens: University of Georgia Press, 1996.

Cabbell, Edward J. "Black Invisibility and Racism in Appalachia: An Informal Survey." In *Blacks in Appalachia*, edited by William H. Turner and Edward J. Cabbell. Lexington: University Press of Kentucky, 1985.

Campbell, Carlos C. *Birth of a National Park in the Great Smoky Mountains*. 2d ed. Knoxville: University of Tennessee Press, 1969.

Campbell, John Charles, and Olive Dame Campbell. Papers. Letters, diary, and photograph albums. 3800, Southern Historical Collection, Wilson Library, University of North Carolina at Chapel Hill. Chapel Hill, North Carolina.

Campbell, Olive Dame. Preface to *The Southern Highlander and His Homeland*, by John C. Campbell. New York: Russell Sage Foundation, 1921.

Carleton, Reese M. "Mary Noailles Murfree (1850–1922): An Annotated Bibliography." *American Literary Realism, 1870–1910* 7, no. 4 (autumn 1974): 293–378.

Carson, Rachel. *Silent Spring*. Greenwich, Conn.: Fawcett, 1962.

Carter, Mary Nelson. *North Carolina Sketches: Phases of Life Where the Galax Grows*. Chicago: A. C. McClurg, 1900.

Cary, Richard. "Mary Noailles Murfree." *American Literary Realism, 1870–1910* 1 (fall 1967): 79–83.

Chapman, Rosanna Frances. Papers. Pack Library, Buncombe County. Asheville, North Carolina.

Churchill, Frank C. Papers. Rare Book, Manuscript, and Special Collections Library, Duke University. Durham, North Carolina.

City Directory, Colored Section, Asheville, North Carolina, 1900–1901. Pack Library, Archives. Buncombe County. Asheville, North Carolina.

Collins, Carvel. "The Literary Tradition of the Southern Mountaineer, 1824–1900." Reprinted from *The Bulletin of Bibliography* 17, nos. 9–10 (September–December 1942; January–April 1943). North Carolina Collection, Wilson Library, University of North Carolina at Chapel Hill. Chapel Hill, North Carolina.

Cooke, Grace MacGowan. "The Capture of Andy Proudfoot." In *Southern Lights and Shadows*, edited by William Dean Howells and Henry Mills Alden. New York: Harper and Brothers, 1907.

———. *The Power and the Glory: An Appalachian Novel*. 1910. Reprint, with an introduction by Elizabeth S. D. Engelhardt. Boston: Northeastern University Press, 2003.

———. *Wild Apples: A California Story*. New York: George H. Doran Co., 1918.

Cowdrey, Albert E. *This Land, This South: An Environmental History*. Lexington: University Press of Kentucky, 1983.

Crim, [Miss] Matt. "The Strike at Mr. Mobley's." *Century* 50 (July 1895): 378–84.

Cuomo, Chris J. *Feminism and Ecological Communities: An Ethic of Flourishing.* London: Routledge, 1998.

Dame, Daisy Gertrude. Papers. Letters. 4331, Southern Historical Collection, Wilson Library, University of North Carolina at Chapel Hill. Chapel Hill, North Carolina.

Danky, James. *African-American Newspapers and Periodicals: A National Bibliography.* Cambridge: Harvard University Press, 1998.

Davis, Lenwood. *The Black Heritage of Western North Carolina.* Asheville, N.C.: University Graphics, University of North Carolina, Asheville, n.d.

Davis, Rebecca Harding. *Silhouettes of American Life.* New York: Charles Scribner's Sons, 1892.

Deskins, David. "Effie Waller Smith: An Echo within the Hills." *Kentucky Review* 8, no. 3 (autumn 1988): 26–46.

———. Introduction to *The Collected Works of Effie Waller Smith.* Schomburg Library of Nineteenth-Century Black Women Writers. New York: Oxford University Press, 1991.

Di Chiro, Giovanna. "Nature as Community: The Convergence of Environment and Social Justice." In *Uncommon Ground: Rethinking the Human Place in Nature,* edited by William Cronon. New York: W. W. Norton, 1996.

Dickerman, George S. "Ten Years' Changes in East Tennessee." *Southern Workman* 34, no. 5 (May 1905): 266–70.

Dickson, Sallie O'Hear. *The Story of Marthy.* Richmond, Va.: Presbyterian Committee of Publication, 1898.

Dunn, Durwood. "Mary Noailles Murfree: A Reappraisal." *Appalachian Journal* 6, no. 3 (spring 1979): 197–204.

Dykeman, Wilma. *The French Broad.* Rivers of America Series. New York: Rinehart, 1955.

Edwards, Grace Toney. "Emma Bell Miles: Appalachian Author, Artist, and Interpreter of Folk Culture." Ph.D. diss., University of Virginia, 1981.

Ehle, John. *Trail of Tears: The Rise and Fall of the Cherokee Nation.* New York: Anchor, 1989.

Elliott, Sarah Barnwell. *The Durket Sperret.* New York: Henry Holt, 1898.

Farr, Sydney Saylor. *Appalachian Women: An Annotated Bibliography.* Lexington: University Press of Kentucky, 1981.

Fetterley, Judith. "'Not in the Least American': Nineteenth-Century Literary Regionalism as UnAmerican Literature." In *Nineteenth-Century American Women Writers: A Critical Reader,* edited by Karen Kilcup. Oxford: Blackwell, 1998.

Fetterley, Judith, and Marjorie Pryse, eds. *American Women Regionalists, 1850–1910.* New York: W. W. Norton, 1992.

Fisher, Stephen L., ed. *Fighting Back in Appalachia: Traditions of Resistance and Change.* Philadelphia: Temple University Press, 1993.

Forderhase, Nancy K. "Eve Returns to the Garden: Women Reformers in Appalachian

Kentucky in the Early Twentieth Century." *Register of the Kentucky Historical Society* 85, no. 3 (summer 1987): 237–61.

Frome, Michael. *Strangers in High Places: The Story of the Great Smoky Mountains.* Knoxville: University of Tennessee Press, 1994.

Frost, Eleanor Marsh. Correspondence, reports, and diary. The papers of William Goodall Frost. Berea College Archives. Hutchins Library, Berea, Kentucky.

Furman, Lucy. *The Glass Window: A Story of the Quare Women.* Boston: Little, Brown, and Co., 1925.

———. "Katherine Pettit: A Pioneer Mountain Worker." *Mountain Life and Work* 12 (October 1936): 16–20.

———. *Mothering on Perilous.* New York: MacMillan, 1913.

———. *The Quare Women: A Story of the Kentucky Mountains.* Boston: Atlantic Monthly Press, 1923.

Gaard, Greta, and Patrick D. Murphy. Introduction to *Ecofeminist Literary Criticism: Theory, Interpretation, Pedagogy,* edited by Greta Gaard and Patrick D. Murphy. Urbana: University of Chicago Press, 1998.

Ganim, Carole. "Herself: Woman and Place in Appalachian Literature." *Appalachian Journal* 13, no. 3 (spring 1986): 258–74.

Gaskill, Gayle. "Sarah Barnwell Elliott." In *American Women Writers: A Critical Reference Guide from Colonial Times to the Present.* Vol. 1. Edited by Lina Mainiero. New York: Frederick Ungar, 1979.

Gaston, Kay Baker. "Emma Bell Miles and the 'Fountain Square' Conversations." *Tennessee Historical Quarterly* 37, no. 4 (winter 1978): 416–29.

———. "The MacGowan Girls." *California History: The Magazine of the California Historical Society* 59, no. 2 (summer 1980): 116–25.

Georgi-Findlay, Brigitte. *The Frontiers of Women's Writing: Women's Narratives and the Rhetoric of Westward Expansion.* Tucson: University of Arizona Press, 1996.

Gielow, Martha S. *Old Andy, the Moonshiner.* Washington, D.C.: W. F. Roberts, 1909.

Gilman, Sander L. "Black Bodies, White Bodies: Toward an Iconography of Female Sexuality in Late Nineteenth-Century Art, Medicine, and Literature." *Critical Inquiry* 12, no. 1 (autumn 1985): 204–42.

Glotfelty, Cheryll. "Introduction: Literary Studies in an Age of Environmental Crisis." In *Ecocriticism Reader: Landmarks in Literary Ecology,* edited by Cheryll Glotfelty and Harold Fromm. Athens: University of Georgia Press, 1996.

Goodrich, Frances Louisa. *Mountain Homespun.* New Haven: Yale University Press, 1931.

———. Papers. Rare Book, Manuscript, and Special Collections Library, Duke University. Durham, North Carolina.

Griffin, Susan. *Woman and Nature: The Roaring Inside Her.* New York: Harper Colophon, 1978.

Grout, Laura Maria Miller. Papers. Rare Book, Manuscript, and Special Collections Library, Duke University. Durham, North Carolina.

Guy-Sheftall, Beverly, ed. *Words of Fire: An Anthology of African-American Feminist Thought*. New York: New Press, 1995.

Hall, Jacquelyn Dowd. "Disorderly Women: Gender and Labor Militancy in the Appalachian South." *Journal of American History* 73, no. 2 (September 1986): 354–82.

Harper, Lila Marz. *Solitary Travelers: Nineteenth-Century Women's Narratives and the Scientific Vocation*. Madison, N.J.: Fairleigh Dickinson University Press, 2001.

Harris, Sharon M. *Rebecca Harding Davis and American Realism*. Philadelphia: University of Pennsylvania Press, 1991.

Herron, Emily K. "Our Cherokee Neighbors." *Southern Workman* 29, no. 8 (August 1900): 465–69.

Hochschild, Arlie. *The Second Shift: Working Parents and the Revolution at Home*. New York: Viking, 1989.

Hsiung, David C. *Two Worlds in the Tennessee Mountains: Exploring the Origins of Appalachian Stereotypes*. Lexington: University Press of Kentucky, 1997.

Jones, Jacqueline. *Labor of Love, Labor of Sorrow: Black Women, Work, and the Family, From Slavery to the Present*. New York: Vintage, 1985.

Kaufman, Polly Welts. *National Parks and the Woman's Voice: A History*. Albuquerque: University of New Mexico Press, 1996.

Kolodny, Annette. *The Land Before Her: Fantasy and Experience of the American Frontiers, 1630–1860*. Chapel Hill: University of North Carolina Press, 1984.

———. *The Lay of the Land: Metaphor as Experience and History in American Life and Letters*. Chapel Hill: University of North Carolina Press, 1975.

Lippard, Lucy R. Introduction to *Partial Recall*, edited by Lucy R. Lippard. New York: New Press, 1992.

"Literature." *Critic* 31 [NS 28] (20 Nov. 1897): 301.

MacGowan, Alice. *Judith of the Cumberlands*. New York: Putnam, 1908.

———. "The Home-coming of Byrd Forebush: A Love Story of Little Turkey Track." *Munsey's Magazine* 30, no. 3 (December 1903): 397–404.

MacKenzie, Clara Childs. *Sarah Barnwell Elliott*. Boston: Twayne, 1980.

Marshall, Ian. *Story Line: Exploring the Literature of the Appalachian Trail*. Charlottesville: University Press of Virginia, 1998.

Martin, Mary R. *Mother Pioneered at Montreat (Her Letters 1898–1899)*, adapted by Emilie Miller Vaughan. Montreat, N.C.: Presbyterian Church [U.S.A.] Department of History and Records Management Services, 1996.

McBain, Anna D. "What It Means to Be a Teacher." *Berea Quarterly* (May 1901): 19–21.

McMurry, Linda O. *To Keep the Waters Troubled: The Life of Ida B. Wells*. New York: Oxford University Press, 1998.

Merchant, Carolyn. *Earthcare: Women and the Environment*. New York: Routledge, 1995.

Miles, Emma Bell. Papers. Letters and diary. Hist. C. acc. 43. Chattanooga-Hamilton County Bicentennial Library. Chattanooga, Tennessee.

———. *Our Southern Birds.* 1919. Reprint, Chattanooga: National Book Co., 1983.

———. *The Spirit of the Mountains.* 1905. Reprint, with a foreword by Roger D. Abrahams and an introduction by David E. Whisnant. Knoxville: University of Tennessee Press, 1975.

Miller, Danny L. *Wingless Flights: Appalachian Women in Fiction.* Bowling Green, Oh.: Bowling Green State University Popular Press, 1996.

"Minor Notes." *Literary World* 15 (31 May 1884): 179.

Molin, Paulette Fairbanks. "'Training the Hand, the Head, and the Heart': Indian Education at Hampton Institute." *Minnesota History* 51, no. 3 (fall 1988): 82–98.

Montague, Mary P. "Little Kaintuck." *Atlantic Monthly* 105, no. 5 (May 1910): 609–16.

Morley, Margaret W. *The Bee People.* 8th ed. Chicago: A. C. McClurg and Co., 1909.

———. *The Carolina Mountains.* Boston: Houghton Mifflin, 1913.

———. *A Few Familiar Flowers: How to Love Them at Home or in School.* Boston: Ginn and Co., 1897.

———. *Life and Love.* 8th ed. Chicago: A. C. McClurg and Co., 1913.

———. *The Renewal of Life: How and When to Tell the Story to the Young.* 2d ed. Chicago: A. C. McClurg and Co., 1909.

Murfree, Mary Noailles [Charles Egbert Craddock, pseud.]. *His Vanished Star.* Boston: Houghton Mifflin, 1894.

———. *In the Tennessee Mountains.* Boston: Houghton Mifflin, 1884.

———. *The Young Mountaineers.* Boston: Houghton Mifflin, 1898.

Murphy, Patrick D. *Literature, Nature, and Other: Ecofeminist Critiques.* Albany: State University of New York Press, 1995.

Myers, Grace Funk. *"Them Missionary Women": or, Work in the Southern Mountains.* Hillsdale, Mich.: by the author, 1911.

Nickum, Bertha Daisy. Letters and photographs. Record group 8: Students. Berea College Archives. Hutchins Library, Berea, Kentucky.

Noe, Kenneth. "'Deadened Color and Colder Horror': Rebecca Harding Davis and the Myth of Unionist Appalachia." In *Back Talk from Appalachia: Confronting Stereotypes,* edited by Dwight B. Billings, Gurney Norman, and Katherine Ledford. Lexington: University Press of Kentucky, 2000.

Norwood, Vera. *Made from This Earth: American Women and Nature.* Chapel Hill: University of North Carolina Press, 1993.

Olsen, Tillie. "A Biographical Interpretation." In *"Life in the Iron Mills" and Other Stories,* by Rebecca Harding Davis. 2d ed. Edited by Tillie Olsen. New York: Feminist Press at City University of New York, 1985.

Orleck, Annelise. *Common Sense and a Little Fire: Women and Working-Class Politics in the United States, 1900–1965.* Chapel Hill: University of North Carolina Press, 1995.

Parsons, Frances Theodora Smith Dana. *How to Know the Wild Flowers: A Guide to the Names, Haunts, and Habits of Our Common Wild Flowers,* by Mrs. William Starr Dana. New York: C. Scribner's Sons, 1895.

Peck, Elizabeth S. "Katherine Pettit." In *Notable American Women, 1607–1950: A Biographical Dictionary,* edited by Edward T. James. Vol. 3. Cambridge: Belknap of Harvard University Press, 1971.

Penn, I. Garland. *Afro-American Press and Its Editors.* 1891. Reprint. New York: Arno Press, 1969.

Pettit, Katherine. "Come One, Come All." Flier. Katherine Pettit Papers. Southern Appalachian Archives. Hutchins Library, Berea College, Berea, Kentucky.

Pfaelzer, Jean. "Engendered Nature/Denatured History: 'The Yares of Black Mountain' by Rebecca Harding Davis." In *Speaking the Other Self: American Women Writers,* edited by Jeanne Campbell Reesman. Athens: University of Georgia Press, 1997.

———. *Parlor Radical: Rebecca Harding Davis and the Origins of American Social Realism.* Pittsburgh: University of Pittsburgh Press, 1996.

———., ed. *A Rebecca Harding Davis Reader.* Pittsburgh: University of Pittsburgh Press, 1995.

Pool, Maria Louise. *In Buncombe County.* Chicago: Herbert S. Stone, 1896.

Pratt, Mary Louise. *Imperial Eyes: Travel Writing and Transculturation.* London: Routledge, 1992.

Price, Jennifer. *Flight Maps: Adventures with Nature in Modern America.* New York: Basic Books, 1999.

Pryse, Marjorie. "Writing Out of the Gap: Regionalism, Resistance, and Relational Reading." *Textual Studies in Canada* 9 (spring 1997): 19–34.

Rose, Jane Atteridge. "A Bibliography of Fiction and Non-Fiction by Rebecca Harding Davis." *American Literary Realism, 1870–1910* 22, no. 3 (spring 1990): 67–86.

———. *Rebecca Harding Davis.* New York: Twayne, 1993.

Satterwhite, Emily. "Such a Thing as 'Literary Material'": Unveiling the "Habitats and Habits of Charles Egbert Craddock." Draft, accessed 3 Feb. 2002. Available from World Wide Web: <http://www.etsu.edu/writing/apptravel/murfree.htm>.

Schmitt, Peter J. *Back to Nature: The Arcadian Myth in Urban America.* New York: Oxford University Press, 1969.

Scott, Anne Firor. *Making the Invisible Woman Visible.* Urbana: University of Illinois Press, 1984.

Scott, Anne Firor, and Andrew MacKay Scott. *One Half the People: The Fight for Woman Suffrage.* Urbana: University of Illinois Press, 1982.

Sears, John F. *Sacred Places: American Tourist Attractions in the Nineteenth Century.* New York: Oxford University Press, 1989.

Shapiro, Henry D. *Appalachia on Our Mind: The Southern Mountains and Mountaineers in the American Consciousness, 1870–1920.* Chapel Hill: University of North Carolina Press, 1978.

Silko, Leslie Marmon. "Landscape, History, and the Pueblo Imagination." In *Ecocriticism Reader: Landmarks in Literary Ecology,* edited by Cheryll Glotfelty and Harold Fromm. Athens: University of Georgia Press, 1996.

Smith, Barbara Ellen. "'Beyond the Mountains': The Paradox of Women's Place in Appalachian History." *NWSA Journal* 11, no. 3 (fall 1999): 1–17.

———. "Walk-ons in the Third Act: The Role of Women in Appalachian Historiography." *Journal of Appalachian Studies* 4, no. 1 (spring 1998): 5–23.

Smith, Effie Waller. *The Collected Works of Effie Waller Smith,* with an introduction by David Deskins. Schomburg Library of Nineteenth-Century Black Women Writers. New York: Oxford University Press, 1991.

Smith, Margaret Supplee, and Emily Herring Wilson. *North Carolina Women: Making History.* Chapel Hill: University of North Carolina Press, 1999.

Smith-Rosenberg, Carroll. *Disorderly Conduct: Visions of Gender in Victorian America.* New York: Alfred A. Knopf, 1985.

Snyder, Gary. *The Practice of the Wild.* New York: North Point Press, 1990.

Somerville, Siobhan. "Scientific Racism and the Emergence of the Homosexual Body." *Journal of the History of Sexuality* 5, no. 2 (October 1994): 243–66.

Spears, Ellen Griffith. *The Newtown Story: One Community's Fight for Environmental Justice.* Atlanta: Center for Democratic Renewal and Newtown Florist Club, 1998.

Stoddart, Jess. Introduction to *The Quare Women's Journals: May Stone and Katherine Pettit's Summers in the Kentucky Mountains and the Founding of the Hindman Settlement School,* by May Stone and Katherine Pettit, edited by Jess Stoddart. Ashland, Ky.: Jesse Stuart Foundation, 1997.

Stone, May, and Katherine Pettit. *The Quare Women's Journals: May Stone and Katherine Pettit's Summers in the Kentucky Mountains and the Founding of the Hindman Settlement School,* edited by Jess Stoddart. Ashland, Ky.: Jesse Stuart Foundation, 1997.

"Suggestions for Spring Lessons." *Southern Workman* 29, no. 4 (April 1900): 235–37.

Taylor, A. Elizabeth. *The Woman Suffrage Movement in Tennessee.* New York: Bookman, 1957.

Taylor, Lloyd C., Jr. "Amelie Louise Rives." In *Notable American Women, 1607–1950: A Biographical Dictionary,* edited by Edward T. James. Vol. 3. Cambridge: Belknap of Harvard University Press, 1971.

Taylor, Welford Dunaway. *Amelie Rives (Princess Troubetzkoy).* New York: Twayne, 1973.

Tice, Karen W. "School-work and Mother-work: The Interplay of Maternalism and Cultural Politics in the Educational Narratives of Kentucky Settlement Workers, 1910–1930." *Journal of Appalachian Studies* 4, no. 2 (fall 1998): 191–224.

Toren, Beth Jane, and Alisha Myers. "Storer College: A Photographic Exhibit of the First African American College in West Virginia." Accessed 12 May 2002. Available from World Wide Web: <http://www.libraries.wvu.edu/storer/>.

Townsend, Mrs. F. L. [Meta]. *In the Nantahalas.* Nashville: Publishing House M. E. Church, South, 1910.

[Troubetzkoy], Amelie Rives. *Tanis, the Sang-Digger.* New York: Town Topics, 1893.

Turner, William H. "The Demography of Black Appalachia: Past and Present." In *Blacks in Appalachia,* edited by William H. Turner and Edward J. Cabbell. Lexington: University of Kentucky Press, 1985.

Van Vorst, Marie. *Amanda of the Mill.* New York: Dodd, Mead and Co., 1905.

Wagner, Melinda Bollar, et al. "Appalachia: A Tourist Attraction?" In *The Impact of Institutions in Appalachia: Proceedings of the Eighth Annual Appalachian Studies Conference,* edited by Jim Lloyd and Anne G. Campbell. Boone, N.C.: Appalachian Consortium Press, 1986.

Warren, Karen J. *Ecofeminist Philosophy: A Western Perspective on What It Is and Why It Matters.* Lanham, Md.: Rowman and Littlefield, 2000.

Weiner, Deborah. "Jewish Women in the Central Appalachian Coal Fields, 1880–1960: From Breadwinners to Community Builders." *American Jewish Archives Journal* 52, nos. 1–2 (2000). Accessed 12 May 2002. Available from World Wide Web: <http://huc.edu/aja/00–1.htm>.

Wells-Barnett, Ida. "Lynch Law in America." In *Words of Fire: An Anthology of African-American Feminist Thought,* edited by Beverly Guy-Sheftall. New York: New Press, 1995.

Westling, Louise H. *The Green Breast of the New World: Landscape, Gender, and American Fiction.* Athens: University of Georgia Press, 1996.

Whisnant, David E. *All That Is Native and Fine: The Politics of Culture in an American Region.* Chapel Hill: University of North Carolina Press, 1983.

———. Introduction to *The Spirit of the Mountains,* by Emma Bell Miles. 1905. Reprint, Knoxville: University of Tennessee Press, 1975.

———. "Second-level Appalachian History: Another Look at Some Fotched-On Women." *Appalachian Journal* 9, nos. 2–3 (winter–spring 1982): 115–23.

White, Deborah Gray. "Mining the Forgotten: Manuscript Sources for Black Women's History." *Journal of American History* 74, no. 1 (June 1987): 237–42.

Woodward, C. Vann. *Origins of the New South, 1877–1913,* with a critical essay on recent works by Charles B. Dew. Baton Rouge: Louisiana State University Press, 1971.

"Young Men's Institute Building, Nomination Form for National Register of Historic Places." 77.10.3.8. Black Highlander Collection, Ramsey Library, University of North Carolina–Asheville. Asheville, North Carolina.

Index

Page numbers in italics indicate photographs.